1968
8 G

$6.00

University of St. Francis
GEN   821.77 B271
Barrell
Shelley and the thought of his

SO-AFU-546

Shelley and the Thought of His Time

A Study in The History of Ideas

BY

JOSEPH BARRELL

ARCHON BOOKS
1967

LIBRARY
College of St. Francis
JOLIET, ILL.

Copyright, 1947, by Yale University Press

Reprinted 1967 with permission
in an unaltered and unabridged edition

[*Yale Studies in English, Vol. 106*]

Library of Congress Catalog Card Number: 67-19511
Printed in the United States of America

821.77
B271

To

PROFESSOR FREDERICK A. POTTLE,

*in whose class this study was conceived, and
who has read the whole of it in manuscript.*

45087

PREFACE

THE ensuing study is primarily a study in the history of ideas. But almost as essentially, it is a study in the history of English literature. In fact, its true locus is in that mid-region where the forms of literature step out to incorporate the ideas of philosophy —where the ideas of philosophy leave philosophy to take on a literary dress. Hence in this study the more purely literary chapters alternate with the more purely philosophical, until, in the last chapter, the two kinds of chapter finally fuse.

Chapter I is an introduction to the philosophical side of this essay. Similarly, Chapter II is an introduction to the literary side. Here the philological problem is discussed, and the initial hypothesis is made: that the two chief intellectual influences in Shelley's life and writings were the doctrines of Godwin and the French philosophers, the doctrines of Plato and the Greeks.

Chapter III then presents a brief sketch of the ideas of the French intellectualists, of Rousseau, and of Godwin. Shelley is barely mentioned, since the purpose of this chapter is to provide an objective base for the Shelleyan study of the next. The following chapter, Chapter IV, takes up Shelley's use of the above ideas and, in particular, attempts toward the end to segregate the personal element in Shelley's thought. The chapter is entitled "Shelley and the Thought of the Eighteenth Century."

In the manner of the chapter on French thought, Chapter V presents a brief history of the Greek Revival. Once again an objective basis is sought and the matter looked upon apart from Shelley. Chapter VI then takes up "Shelley and the Thought of the Greeks." Toward the end of this chapter (as toward the end of the chapter on "Shelley and the Thought of the Eighteenth Century"), the discussion is concerned less with Shelley's debt to the Greeks than with Shelley's departure from the Greeks, and it becomes the contention of this study that the development of the personal element in Shelley's thought parallels the development of the dominant philosophy of Shelley's time, that of the German idealists. No direct, literary influence is assumed or maintained. Rather, it is the contention of this study that the thought of an age springs from currents so deep that they are irrespective of language or literary influence.

The last chapter, Chapter VII, repeats the title of the study itself. In it, what has long been shadowed forth is now definitely asserted: that Shelley was at one with the thought of his time; indeed, that he was closer to it than many of his more characteristically English contemporaries.

This study was presented in partial fulfillment of the requirements for the degree of Doctor of Philosophy in Yale University. It is, in fact, a record of the writer's years in the Yale Graduate School. For, at the beginning of these, the late Professor Karl Young not only encouraged his interest in the history of ideas but in a course in the Age of Chaucer introduced him to Maurice de Wulf and wrote out for him long bibliographies in the philosophy of the Middle Ages. In a later course in the Age of Spenser, Professor John Milton Berdan gladly accepted a year's paper on the relationship between the poetry and the philosophy of the Renaissance. It was finally Professor Pottle who encouraged the writer to undertake a full-length study in the history of ideas, and who, when the writer expressed his fears that such a study might be too speculative, characteristically replied, "So much the better."

To these men, and to his other professors in the Yale Graduate School, the writer owes a large debt. They made his graduate years more memorable than his undergraduate.

J. B.

Pomfret, Connecticut
March 25, 1946

CONTENTS

SHELLEY AND THE THOUGHT OF HIS TIME

The History of Ideas

THE twentieth century has seen the full growth of two types of literary research, the bibliographical and the biographical. The bibliographical approach to literature makes use largely of the printed, though occasionally of the spoken, word. The bibliographers have combed the world for the missing manuscript, the missing volume. They have searched for the forgotten notebook, for the neglected portfolio. They have traced out the influence of every writer on every other writer, not stopping at the barrier of language, nor failing to employ, in their desire to explain the extraordinary scope of literary influence, the twentieth-century concept of the unconscious mind.

The biographical approach to the history of literature has to do rather with the individual's life than with his thoughts. It is interested in personal influence rather than in literary. The biographers have dug into parish registers and municipal archives, examined the files of yellowing periodicals, and, above all, sought out the personal letter. No detail of the individual's life has been too small to escape their attention.

Originating in the Romantic Movement itself, in a concern for sources as well as for opinions, the attempt to construct a real history rather than a fabled one has in these two branches produced fruit of astonishing maturity.

The student of literature today can only be grateful for the success that has attended these two branches of scholarship. Surely the end of all scholarship is the evocation of that whole which experience presents to us as life at any moment, and which our intuitions tell us has always been the condition of life. The evocation of this whole, in greater detail even than that of the present, is just what the bibliographers and biographers of the past two centuries have accomplished.

Take the Romantic Movement, where the chief interest of this study is going to fall. Biographically, we know more about the lives of the major and minor poets who flourished at the end of the eighteenth and beginning of the nineteenth centuries than we do about our intimate friends today. Secrets known scarce to anyone then are clear to all now.[1] We are familiar with their meetings with one another, with what they thought and felt about one another, with the literary and cultural influences on each of their lives. We perceive Wordsworth and Sir George Beaumont baiting Crabbe with the snuffing of a candle to see whether he had any imagination;[2] we read (except for the unprintable words) Byron's private opinion of the one dispassionate review Keats received in his lifetime;[3] we note the remarkable manner in which the latter's ship, on its way to Italy, and Brown's packet, just in from Scotland, lay next to each other at anchor in the Thames without either of the friends being aware of it.[4] We are given the astonishing range of Coleridge's reading, not from a mere list of the books in his library (which he may or may not have read), but from the indubitable traces of his reading evident in his poetry.[5]

There is little question, though, that both the biographical and bibliographical reconstructions of the past are in a fair way to completion. There is still much to be done, perhaps, but surely it is in the way of landscaping a house that has already been built. As Professor Lovejoy suspects,[6] the period of diminishing returns has been reached in these two fields of specialization. To employ his reversion to Hegelian terminology,[7] the antithesis, now fully developed, is demanding its synthesis. Such a synthesis, and an approach to the literary past that has hardly been ventured upon, may be described by the new phrase, "the history of ideas."

On second thought, it is questionable if "new" really describes the phrase, history of ideas. After the William James lectures for 1933 when Professor Lovejoy followed three basic notions of philosophy and literature from their appearance among the Greeks to modern times, and after the founding in 1940 of a learned journal expressly devoted to the subject, the concept can hardly be described as new. But there is no question, either, that in comparison with its

1. Cf. Émile Legouis, *William Wordsworth and Annette Vallon* (London, Toronto, and New York, 1922).

2. Excerpted by Lockhart from Scott's Journal under date of January 1, 1827 (*Memoirs of the Life of Sir Walter Scott* [Edinburgh, 1837–38], VII, 4–5).

3. Cf. Moore's *Life* (London, 1830), letters 396, 398, and 399; Prothero's *Letters and Journals* (London and New York, 1898–1901), letters 843, 845, and 846. Prothero supplies "dirty blackguard" for one of Moore's deletions. But for the most part, as Colvin says (*John Keats* [London, 1917]), the reader perceives the fury of Byron's attack by the cloud of asterisks.

4. Discovered after the event by Brown and set down in his manuscript "Life," where it was noted by Milnes in 1848. The *Life of John Keats* by Charles Armitage Brown was finally published in 1937 (London, Toronto, and New York).

5. Cf. J. L. Lowes, *The Road to Xanadu* (Boston and New York, 1927).

6. A. O. Lovejoy, "The Historiography of Ideas," *Proceedings of the American Philosophical Society*, 78, 4 (March, 1938), 535.

7. *Idem*, pp. 535–536.

elderly brothers and sisters, this branch of humanistic study is at least "adolescent"—to make use of Professor Lovejoy's own phrase.[8]

In the hope, then, of the increasing returns to be got from relatively untilled fields of scholarship, this study turns to the ideological approach to literature.

But the student of literature seeking to examine his subject from the point of view of the history of ideas is surely called upon to set down with some care the aims of his approach. Professor Lovejoy is professionally a student of philosophy, and his *Great Chain of Being*,[9] while enriched with generous quotations from literature, is primarily a philosophical study. The student of literature, on the contrary, has spent his life reading the poets rather than the philosophers. He knows better than the philosophers how thoroughly his field has already been examined, and is the more called upon carefully to demarcate his new approach from those he knows immediately to be adjoining. The literary historian of ideas must say what he is attempting to do, what methods he will use, and what his ulterior motives may be.

In the first place, then, as a historian of ideas he will be concerned with what a writer is generally conceived by his readers to have meant, rather than with what he may actually have intended to mean. The latter problem belongs to the biographers, who, by the way, are not always agreed about it. Take the case of Kant, and of the remarkable influence he exerted both directly and indirectly on English and American literature in the first half of the nineteenth century. To many students of literature, as well as of philosophy, it seems entirely unwarrantable that Kant's successors should have passed over the *Critique of Pure Reason* to seize upon the volitional doctrine of the *Critique of Practical Reason*.[10] And this is not the entirety of the problem. For Kant, like many another gentleman before and after him, issued a second edition of his first (and we feel greater) *Critique*, in which he changed his mind on divers points. The result has been a biographical controversy as to what Kant really meant: whether his transcendental unity was of a universal consciousness (like the later idealists), or merely of the individual consciousness (like the eighteenth-century empiricists).[11]

Now this type of controversy the historian of ideas seeks to avoid. Whatever Kant himself may have meant, there is no doubt he was the father of the volitional philosophy formulated by his German succes-

8. *Idem*, p. 539.

9. A. O. Lovejoy, *The Great Chain of Being* (Cambridge, Mass., 1936).

10. So Josiah Royce, *The Spirit of Modern Philosophy* (Boston and New York, 1892), p. 155. So H. N. Fairchild, *The Romantic Quest* (New York, 1931), chap. XVII.

11. Cf. Royce, *op. cit.*, Appendix B.

sors and passed on by them to the romantic generations of the English-speaking world.[12]

Similarly, the historian of ideas will devote himself, if not to the major works of a writer, at least to those works that have been deemed either characteristic or important by the reading public. The biographers have been remarkably successful in explaining obscure passages in both great and little poems. But the reading public never picks upon a poem where the meaning (at least the essential meaning) has to be explained by biographical or any other kind of research. The poems that are significant to the reading public are those poems that answer some public need, and in this first stratum of literature as far as the historian of ideas is concerned, it will generally be found that the basic meaning is intuitively clear. Take "Tintern Abbey," that most perennial of Wordsworth's poems. In it one finds perhaps the clearest statement ever made of pantheistic belief. No matter that the lines express but a stage in Wordsworth's individual development. In their very clarity of expression they tell us something about the nineteenth century which so eagerly read them. Or take *Prometheus Unbound*, admittedly a difficult poem, but nevertheless one placed very high by the nineteenth century when belatedly it came to regard Shelley as one of its chief poets. Our present-day understanding of the poem has been increased by Professor Grabo's bibliographical researches into the scientific background of the poem.[13] Yet few would maintain that these researches have clarified the essential meaning of the poem, or explained its appeal to the literary young, who read it as eagerly today as they read it fifty or seventy-five years ago.

In much the same vein, the historian of ideas will liberally avail himself of secondary and even tertiary sources. Here if anywhere he is likely to bring down upon his head the wrath of the bibliographers and biographers (in whose schools he has undoubtedly been trained), and here if anywhere he must make his apology plain. For it is not that he undervalues primary sources. Naturally, if the end in view is the accurate reconstruction of a writer's life or cultural development, it is of the highest importance not to accept latter-day opinion but to go to firsthand and documentary evidence. But the historian of ideas would be able to accomplish nothing were he to become a specialist in each of the many fields he must survey. On the whole, it takes a sizable portion of a man's lifetime to become a specialist, and the historian of ideas would need many lifetimes to reach his goal of

12. Lovejoy makes the same assertion as regards the responsibility of the historical Plato for "Platonism." Cf. *The Great Chain of Being*, p. 35.

13. Carl Grabo, *A Newton among Poets* (Chapel Hill, 1930), and *Prometheus Unbound* (Chapel Hill, 1935).

the whole sweep, the entire view. He must make use of the specialist's findings, and go on to his own. Indeed, in many cases, the specialists are themselves too specialized, and he must go to specialists of specialists.

Take Plato, for example. Whether the historian of ideas agrees or disagrees with Professor Whitehead's much-quoted remark that the history of Western thought might be described as a series of footnotes to Plato,[14] he must familiarize himself with Plato's works. Yet what we have said about the lack of time and energy is clearly apparent here. Plato's writings are as extensive as Scripture. It would take an age to read all the dialogues, dissociate the Platonic from the Socratic elements, work out the growth of Plato's thought, and arrive at his final metaphysical position. Indeed, were the student to attain this goal, he would then be an authority on Plato and not a historian of ideas.

Hence he turns to the authorities on Plato, resolved to let them be authorities and himself be a historian of ideas.

But what does he find here? He finds that the specialists even of his own time are hopelessly divided into schools. There is the German school of Maier and Ritter, and the Scotch school of Burnet and Taylor. There are nominalists and realists—as if one were back in the Middle Ages. In desperation the historian of ideas turns to men like Jaeger and Lovejoy, who mediate between the schools. And though, in a sense, nothing could be more inappropriate than to label these great scholars as tertiary sources, yet, in another sense (at least to the historian of ideas), that is just what they are.

Nor is it entirely a question of the war between the specialists. Again and again, these latter simply do not contain what the historian of ideas is looking for. Regretting the lack of truly general treatises, Professor Lovejoy refers to the legendary anatomical student set to describe the skeleton of a fish.[15] This the student did, faithfully and well, only neglecting to mention the fish's most obvious characteristic, its bilateral symmetry. Now, if one is going to pack a number of fish in a box, the fact of a fish's bilateral symmetry is of the highest consequence. Indeed, it is this search for the bilaterally symmetrical aspect of things that sends the historian of ideas to encyclopedias and handbooks. There, where the limitations of space force the specialist to be obvious about his specialty—there alone, many times, can the historian of ideas discover what he wants. And if he has the courage of his convictions, his references will include many an encyclopedia and handbook in their number.

To introduce a bit of summary, then, the historian of ideas will take

14. A. N. Whitehead, *Process and Reality* (New York, 1929), p. 63.
15. *Proceedings of the American Philosophical Society*, 78, 4 (March, 1938), 536.

a man's thought as it is construed by those who use it, he will take those writings that were or are in vogue, and when the matter becomes technical or controversial, he will go to those authorities who are the least specialized, the most general, in their point of view.

This brings us to still another peculiarity of the historian of ideas. He is relatively unconcerned with the transmission of ideas. His day is made when he recognizes an old friend in modern costume. The late Mr. Justice Holmes's remark over the radio on the occasion of his ninetieth birthday that "to live is to function" surely evoked many a memory of the Greeks. But whether the Justice had been reading Aristotle,[16] or knew he was paraphrasing the *Republic*,[17] belongs rather to the biographer's realm of interest than to that of the historian of ideas. In fact, the biographer or bibliographer cannot but be struck by the indifference to such matters evinced by Professor Lovejoy's distinguished work of scholarship, *The Great Chain of Being*. As probably the nearest source for the theodicial arguments of King and Leibniz, the reader is referred to St. Thomas,[18] as though a dozen generations did not separate the seventeenth from the thirteenth century.

Now there is more than one reason for this apparent and real indifference to the actual transmission of ideas. In the first place, the fact of an idea's reëmergence is always more important to the student of the history of thought than the circumstances of the idea's transmission. In the second place, the historian of ideas is more acutely aware than the biographer or bibliographer of how manifold are the sources of ideas. There is the bibliographical source, to be sure. The individual reads a book and thereafter is equipped with a new idea. Of this the examples are literally too numerous to mention. There is also the oral transmission of ideas. To consider only the period we are particularly interested in, there can be no doubt that the ideas of German transcendentalism were transmitted to the English-speaking world as much by word of mouth as by word of print. Just

16. As a matter of fact, the remark was a favorite one with Holmes, and appears throughout his life. When he told the members of the Suffolk Bar in 1900 that "life is action, the use of one's powers," William James complained that he was a man of one speech (cf. Biddle, *Mr. Justice Holmes* [New York, 1942], p. 99). Hence the historian of ideas is very loath to credit the remark to any specific reading on Holmes's part, although we know that he wrote a prize essay on Plato while an undergraduate (cf. C. D. Bowen, *Yankee from Olympus* [Boston, 1944], pp. 127–132), and that much of August, 1914, was taken up with Aristotle's *Ethics* (cf. M. DeW. Howe, ed., *Holmes-Pollock Letters* [Cambridge, Mass., 1941], I, 219). Undoubtedly the conception, though again and again phrased in Greek form, was simply the formulization of an independent conviction about life.

17. This thought becomes the theme of discussion at the close of Book I of the *Republic*. It recurs in the *Nichomachean Ethics* in the seventh and sixth sections of the first and second books respectively, and is indeed a typically Greek thought.

18. *The Great Chain of Being*, p. 76.

to take the case of their most conspicuous transmission, it can be mentioned that Coleridge, always the lecturer and conversationalist, spread the doctrine as much by talk as by print, and that his disciple Carlyle, and the latter's disciple Emerson, appeared as frequently on the lecture platform as in the press.

Finally, the brute fact remains that ideas do not have to be transmitted at all. It is demonstrable that the same circumstances produce the same ideas, all over the world, in different ages and climes. There is the Darwin–Wallace theory of natural selection, which was conceived independently in England and the Moluccas. There is the James–Lange theory of the emotions, which was worked out separately in Massachusetts and Denmark.

But one of the best examples to be had, and one much nearer our field of central interest, is that of the German philosopher Leibniz and the Scotch philosopher Thomas Reid. Quite independently of each other, and a generation apart, the two reacted in entirely the same way to the assumptions and conclusions of the Lockian school. With Leibniz, the reaction followed his reading of Locke's famous *Essay*. In 1696 he jotted down his objections to the *Essay*, worked them out in 1703 and 1704, but withheld them from publication in the latter year on account of Locke's death. His *New Essays* were first published in 1765 by Raspe,[19] and are of unusual interest to the student of the history of thought. They are, in fact, an abstract of Kant's position that the mind coöperates with sensation in the production of knowledge, and in so doing furnishes the "necessity" of necessary truths. As a matter of fact, it is with Leibniz, and not with Kant, that the concept of "apperception" originates. But our concern is with the fact that in 1739, a generation before the publication of the *New Essays*, Thomas Reid, upon his reading of Hume's anonymous *Treatise*, had quite the same reaction to the *tabula rasa* school of philosophy. It seemed to him wholly unjustified to assume that the mind can know only its own disconnected sensations. The intellect's contribution to knowledge he called the "principles of common sense" instead of "apperception," but his notion that knowledge is judgment rather than passive sensation is quite the same as that of Leibniz. Yet Reid, though much the junior of the two philosophers, could not have got his idea either by oral or by bibliographical transmission. As a matter of fact, we know that his reaction came almost at the moment of his reading Hume's *Treatise*.

No, quite as much as ideas are transmitted, they are begotten— begotten by the universal working of the force of human reaction.

Thus the historian of ideas is very reluctant to investigate in detail the dissemination of ideas. As the late Émile Legouis declared,

19. The acquaintance of Horace Walpole and the creator of Baron Munchausen.

"Men's ideas are their least individual possessions,"[20] or as Professor Beach has more recently said, "The thought of any given period is something in the air."[21] Indeed, the historian of ideas would as soon trace out the passage of prairie-grass seed in the windy fall air. He conceives that his function is not to trace, but to sift.

The historian of ideas makes only one claim. He asserts only one goal. He hopes to be able to sift the ingredients of a writer's thought more accurately than others may have done. Surely the attempts of the bibliographers and biographers in this field have been very unsatisfactory. One gains the distinct impression that the literary scholar is brushing up his Bruno for the sake of his Spenser, his Leibniz for the sake of his Pope, his Plato for the sake of his Shelley. And in so doing he nearly always misses the wood for the trees. There is no branch of learning where the part is so dependent upon the whole as in the history of philosophy. One cannot understand Leibniz without being acquainted with St. Thomas, without being acquainted with Aristotle, without being acquainted with Plato, without being acquainted with Philolaus, and so on, and so on, like mirrors within mirrors, until one comes to the beginning of Western philosophy in Thales, its traditional founder.

This is not to say that the ultracrepidarian literary scholar had better stick to his last. If that were the case the present writer had better give up now, on the eighth page. It is only to say that before taking up the philosophical aspects of literature, and laying claim to being a historian of ideas, the literary scholar must be conversant with the history of philosophy, and be not without experience in the use of philosophical concepts and in the recognition of their various implications.

For, as Professor Lovejoy says, the history of philosophy is the "common seed-plot" of the history of ideas.[22] The fundamental notions as to what is real, what is knowledge, what is of most value, and what is the nature of the universe appear in philosophy before they appear in literature.

Yet, if the history of philosophy is the common seed-plot of the history of ideas, the history of literature is its fertile garden. It is in literature that the basic thoughts of men increase and multiply, and in their fructification show how different, in reality, the seeds were from one another. It is in literature, as Professor Lovejoy has remarked in another article, that the thoughts of men find their most

20. Article on "William Wordsworth," *Cambridge History of English Literature* (New York, 1914), XI, 103.

21. Joseph Warren Beach, *The Concept of Nature in 19th-Century English Poetry* (New York, 1936), p. 11.

22. *Proceedings of the American Philosophical Society*, 78, 4 (March, 1938), 537.

extensive, and often their most adequate, expression.[23] Or as Professor Whitehead has more succinctly put it, it is in literature that the outlook of humanity receives its concrete expression.[24] Hence, whether he is of literary or philosophic lineage, the historian of ideas will turn toward literature as toward a field where there is an abundant harvest.

There is a final *caveat* to be entered, however, before completing this chapter and going on to the next. The just-concluded statement of aims and principles is in no sense a manifesto. It is without the slightest revolutionary intent. All scholars, no matter what their field or especial interest, must take a common pride in the accomplishments of modern bibliographical and biographical research. This study will go to these accomplishments as to a rich treasure house. It will endeavor to avail itself of the latest and most detailed findings both in bibliography and in biography. In fact, as regards material, it will limit itself in no way whatsoever. It only will not seek to add to biographical or bibliographical knowledge, but rather will content itself with a more accurate sifting of a writer's thought.

23. A. O. Lovejoy, "Reflections on the History of Ideas," *Journal of the History of Ideas*, I, 1 (1940), 9.

24. A. N. Whitehead, *Science and the Modern World* (Cambridge, 1926), p. 106.

II

The Problem

1. Introduction

THE history of thought, like the history of a family, is often best visualized as a never-ending genealogical tree. Like a family tree, the thought of an age divides and redivides, some of its branches proving ephemeral and unreproductive, others central and continuous. And, as in the early years of a generation of a family it is impossible to tell who will die without issue, so at the time one cannot perceive which thoughts of an age are dead or dying, and which thoughts will develop into new conceptions, and these into still others. On looking back, however, from the vantage point of a succeeding age, nothing can be clearer.

One could cite Carlyle and Michelet and Froude as instances of this.[1] These men go back to the primitive notion of the individual as the determiner of history, to a conception of history one might describe as the "Plutarchian." Today it is clear that they were out of the main stream of historical development. The main stream passed through Hegel and finally, of course, through Marx. Its watchword was development, development through struggle, which we perceive to be at the bottom of modern works so different as *The Rise of American Civilization* by Charles and Mary Beard[2] and the *Paideia* of Werner Jaeger.[3] We perceive today that, historically speaking, the romantic concept of development, which goes back to Herder[4] and Lessing,[5] was the living conception, and not the romantic concept of individualism, with its roots in Rousseau.[6] But in the year of Carlyle's *Heroes and Hero-Worship* it was by no means clear.

Thus one is led to think of Shelley's much-quoted remark in the preface to *Prometheus Unbound:* "For my part I had rather be damned with Plato and Lord Bacon, than go to Heaven with Paley and Malthus." The former pair, we are given to understand, had, like Shelley, "a passion for reforming the world"; the latter pair were without this passion.

1. Cf. E. R. Trattner, *Architects of Ideas* (New York, 1938), p. 253.
2. Charles and Mary Beard, *The Rise of American Civilization* (2 vols. New York, 1927).
3. Werner Jaeger, *Paideia: the Ideals of Greek Culture* (3 vols. New York, 1939–44). Translated by Gilbert Highet.
4. Cf. Herder's *Ideen zur Philosophie der Geschichte der Menschheit* (1784–91).
5. Cf. Lessing's *Die Erziehung des Menschengeschlechts* (1780).
6. Cf. Rousseau's *Émile* (1762), etc.

But what do we perceive today? From the vantage point of the twentieth century it is clear that Malthus was the progenitor of two distinct movements for reform. The first is the movement for birth control, which derives from Malthus through Francis Place and Richard Carlile. From England it passed to America, to Robert Dale Owen and Charles Knowlton. But then it returned to England under the tutelage of Charles Bradlaugh and Annie Besant, receiving prominence in the famous trial of 1876. The other movement attributable to Malthus is that of eugenics, which derives from him through Darwin and Sir Francis Galton.[7]

Yet who in Malthus' day would have classed him with the reformers? Though he was a man without political bias, and in his original essay was interested solely in pointing out the fallacies in the optimistic thinking of Godwin, Condorcet, and his father, yet his ideas were taken up by the Tories, and his very talk of the benefits of misery and vice could serve only to dampen the perfectibilitarian ardor that was the mainspring of the reform movement. Shelley could not have thought otherwise than he did, especially since Place's *Illustrations and Proofs* did not appear until the year of Shelley's death. As for Darwin's development of the implications latent in Malthus' thinking, this did not occur until the 1830's and was not given to the world until 1859, when Percy Florence Shelley had been the third baronet for fifteen years and was in his fortieth year.

7. For whole paragraph, cf. Trattner, *op. cit.*, chap. vii.

2. The Evidence of Shelley's Writings

IT IS no accident that a line of thinking such as we have been pursuing should lead to a mention of the poet Shelley. Shelley was a "social" poet, much in our modern sense—a poet alive to the struggle and conflict of his time, and imbued with a presentiment of issue. In that same preface to *Prometheus Unbound* he writes: "The great writers of our own age are, we have reason to suppose, the companions and forerunners of some unimagined change in our social condition or the opinions which cement it. The cloud of mind is discharging its collected lightning, and the equilibrium between institutions and opinions is now restoring, or is about to be restored." Shelley, like other writers since his time, was aware of a "wave of the future," conscious of the flux of contemporary opinions and values, and sure that this latter was pregnant with some new construction of thought or society. Yet as we have seen in our own day, it is easy to be mistaken as to which of the many waves on the horizon is the particular wave of the future. Only the event can tell, the event which may come in one's own day but more often does not, especially if one dies young, as Shelley did.

Shelley did not live to see the partial fulfillment of his dreams and hopes in the Reform Bill of 1832, let alone such a sweeping fulfillment of all he stood for as the proposed Beveridge Plan.[8] But there can be no more appropriate problem than to take his thought, sift out its principal ingredients, and measure them against the waves of his time which led, or did not lead, to those future waves that have now lapped upon our shore. The problem is appropriate not only because Shelley was a philosophical poet, conscious to an unusual degree of the intellectual currents of his age, but because he regarded himself as a thinker rather than as the "master singer"[9] which, since Swinburne's day, it has been a fashion to regard him. Indeed the upholders of the latter theory would do well to remember that Shelley's most celebrated "song" is an impassioned plea for the dissemination of his ideas.[10] Thus it is as a thinker rather than as a singer that this study will regard Shelley. It will be concerned with the substance rather than with the form of Shelley's poetry.

8. For an amusing parallel between Shelley's *Philosophical View of Reform* and the Beveridge Report, as well as for an ironic comment on the fact that Sir William Beveridge is Master of University College, Oxford, consult Professor Evans' letter to *Time*, December 18, 1944, p. 4.

9. The phrase is Swinburne's. See conclusion to his "Notes on the Text of Shelley," *Fortnightly Review*, May, 1869, p. 561.

10. Alluding to the *Ode to the West Wind*.

The thinking of Shelley's poetry presents a most interesting problem. For it is clear that Shelley's thinking was colored by two principal enthusiasms—by his passion for reform and by his zeal for
idealism. Furthermore it is clear that these two principal biases to
Shelley's thought stand in a major-minor relationship to each other,
that there is no period of his life when Shelley can be said to have
abandoned either the one or the other. Nevertheless, in the first half
of Shelley's literary career, say from 1812 to 1817, his interest in
reform is clearly dominant (though his latent idealism is just as
clearly present); while in the second half of his career, from 1817 to
1822, Shelley's idealism is no less clearly triumphant, though he never
lost his interest in reform.

A quick survey of the main body of Shelley's poetry bears out the
preceding rough analysis. Shelley's career begins with *Queen Mab*,
his first important poem, which, as everybody knows, became a sort
of testament to the Owenites in the second quarter of the nineteenth
century. It is Shelley's most radical poem, and under their auspices
went through at least fourteen pirated editions in the period alluded
to.[11] As Professor White observes,[12] none of the poet's later poems
had half its effect upon the actual behavior of men. Yet radical as
the poem is—radical, and even deterministic—there is nevertheless
a distinct idealistic minor to it, as the following lines (quoted by
Professor Gingerich to the same effect)[13] clearly show:

> Throughout this varied and eternal world
> Soul is the only element: the block
> That for uncounted ages has remained
> The moveless pillar of a mountain's weight
> Is active, living spirit.
> *Queen Mab*, IV, 139–143[14]

The events of the two or three years that intervened between the
composition of *Queen Mab* and *Alastor*, Shelley's next important
poem, are too well known to need more than a passing mention. Undoubtedly the chief thing to be noticed about them is the simple
running down of the clock, the self-exhaustion and abatement that
attends all movements and enthusiasms unless freshened from the

11. Cf. N. I. White, *Shelley* (New York, 1940), I, 294.
12. *Ibid.*
13. S. F. Gingerich, *Essays in the Romantic Poets* (New York, 1924), p. 204.
14. Though perhaps the most striking instance of Shelley's 1812 idealism, the cited
passage is but one of many. One could quote from the sixth canto as readily:

> Throughout these infinite orbs of mingling light,
> Of which yon earth is one, is wide diffused
> A Spirit of activity and life,
> That knows no term, cessation, or decay.
> *Queen Mab*, VI, 146–149

outside. No such freshening came to Shelley's schemes and projects.
The land-reclamation venture ended[15] in frustration and in an attack upon Shelley's life,[16] while the second Irish expedition was
less successful than the first. The disillusion that had overtaken
Miss Hitchener extended to Eliza and Harriet. Godwin proved far
from the lofty sage envisioned, and after his return from his second
elopement Shelley found himself, save for Peacock, ostracized from
the few friends he had made since his marriage with Harriet.

As a result, *Alastor* is a poem of groping, a poem that, like *Julian
and Maddalo* and *The Cenci*, seems to be out of the main stream of
Shelley's poetry. The fact is (as Shelley's father recognized from the
first)[17] that *Alastor* is starkly autobiographical, perhaps the most
autobiographical poem that Shelley ever wrote. Apparently its purpose is to tell the poet, and after the poet us, that the ideal and the
real are not to be combined, that one must be either an out-and-out
reformer or an out-and-out idealist. The poem is interesting in its
Greek title suggested by Peacock,[18] an indication of that compensat-
ing Hellenism about which we shall have much to say later on—a
Hellenism that must have stemmed chiefly from Peacock.

Thus, after the groping of *Alastor,* and after the idealistic experiments of the *Hymn to Intellectual Beauty* and *Mont Blanc*, it is something of a surprise to find that Shelley has returned in his next major
poem, *The Revolt of Islam*, to his revolutionary enthusiasm. To be
sure, the ardor is somewhat cooled. Nevertheless Laon is a radical,
as is Lionel, the hero of *Rosalind and Helen*, the poem which immediately followed *The Revolt of Islam*.

Though apparently few of Shelley's biographers have dwelt upon
this particular aspect of Shelley's last period in England, it is clear
that between 1816 (the year of the idealistic hymns) and 1817 (the
year of *The Revolt of Islam* and the greater part of *Rosalind and
Helen*), Shelley must have effected some kind of reconstruction of
his early and passionate interest in reform. Shelley was not a poet
of caprice. He could write occasional verse "upon occasion," and
tangential poems of various descriptions dot his works. But his major

15. On February 19, 1813, a couple of weeks before his departure from Tanyrallt,
Shelley wrote Hookham that *Queen Mab* was "finished and transcribed" (Julian *Works*,
IX, 47). Hence the collapse of the Tremadoc enthusiasm really belongs to the period
between *Queen Mab* and *Alastor*.

16. It is true that Hogg and Peacock, and later Dowden, were skeptical as to the
reality of the attack, and that Professor White was finally able to prove that the assailant
of Miss Crofts's article was, in 1813, three years old. Nevertheless there can be no
question that to Shelley the attack was real enough.

17. Cf. Sir Timothy's letter of February 27, 1816, to William Whitton, his counsel:
"P. B. has published a poem with some fragments, somewhat in his usual style, not
altogether free from former sentiments, and wants to find out one person on earth the
Prototype of himself." (R. Ingpen, *Shelley in England* [London, 1917], II, 463.)

18. Cf. Peacock, *Memoirs of Shelley* (London, Wolfe, 1933), II, 341.

poems without exception show the essential, indeed the dominant, drift of his thinking. Undoubtedly, the two chief poems of 1817 show a return to the reformer's fold.

The explanation is not far to seek. Coinciding almost to the day with Shelley's twenty-one-year lease of Albion House in Marlow,[19] and with his consequent plans for really settling down this time,[20] came Shelley's new friendship with Hunt and with the circle to which friendship with Hunt was an introduction. For the first time in two years Shelley had a group of friends to replace those he had lost, and its central personality, if not a radical, was at least a liberal who had done penance in prison for the strength of his convictions.[21] In spite of Harriet's death and the impending lawsuit over the children, 1817 opened with a greater stability of house and companionship than the Shelleys had been used to. No wonder that in March, Mary could write to Hunt, "Ought we not be happy? And so indeed we are, in spite of the Lord Chancellor and the Suspension Act."[22]

Thus it is not surprising that about this time Shelley should have commenced work on *The Revolt of Islam*. He worked on it steadily all summer, and when it was finished in September, it was by far the longest poem he had ever written or, for that matter, ever would write.[23]

Yet he completed the poem as if it were the communication of a dying man. The phrase is Shelley's own, taken from the letter to Godwin quoted by Mrs. Shelley in her note to the poem. Now such revolutions of feeling, such reversals of good and ill health, even in six short months, were by no means rare in Shelley's life. But this time the consequences were so extensive that we must once again offer a résumé of the attendant circumstances—although, as before, they are so well known as to need but the barest mention.

When we come to examine the circumstances, we note that Mary's letter to Hunt was written at the beginning of March, while the Shelleys were staying with Peacock, and before they had actually moved into their new house. It reflected the mood of their anticipation. Lord Eldon had as yet given no judgment on the children, and Shelley's pamphlet, *A Proposal for Putting Reform to the Vote throughout the Kingdom*, was about to appear. The Shelleys' hopes, though soon to be impaired, were as yet without abatement.

The Shelleys moved into Albion House on the eighteenth, and at about the same time the pamphlet appeared. The latter, though

19. Cf. White, *op. cit.*, I, 478 *et seq.*   20. Cf. Peacock, *op. cit.*, II, 344.
21. From February, 1813, to February, 1815. Hunt and his brother could have had the imprisonment and the fine remitted had they agreed to abstain from attacking the Regent.
22. Cf. H. H. Harper, *Letters of Mary Shelley* (Boston, 1918), p. 32.
23. For the facts of this paragraph cf. White, *op. cit.*, I, 527.

Shelley had gone to particular trouble and expense to bring it to the public's attention, received comment only from Hunt, while the new house, almost from the start, proved cold and miserable. Then, on the twenty-seventh, Lord Eldon gave judgment, depriving Shelley of the custody of his elder children.[24]

Lord Eldon's judgment was the most dramatic event of 1817, and Shelley himself,[25] and many of Shelley's biographers,[26] have made much of it.

Yet the fact that Shelley persevered in so vast an undertaking as *The Revolt of Islam,* and also in the course of the year largely completed *Rosalind and Helen,* makes it clear that we should not give too much prominence to the Chancery trial in accounting for Shelley's revulsion of feeling in 1817. The forces drawing Shelley away from England and from his revolutionary enthusiasm, this time for good, were far more subtle than any single act of "oppression."

Not the least of these subtle and corroding forces must have been the failure of Shelley's political pamphlet. Then, as White makes clear,[27] the old struggle with the bailiffs returned, culminating in Shelley's arrest in October at the instance of his uncle and former champion, Captain Pilfold. Lastly, it became apparent that life in England was tolerable only if one followed the beaten path of conventional existence. No adoptions, or quasi-adoptions, were possible—no *ménages à trois ou à quatre.* A female disciple, even if chaperoned day and night, would inescapably be set down as a concubine; and when it came to the combination of discipleship and adoption exhibited in Claire and Allegra, the matter was simply out of the question. Shelley's and Mary's letters on the necessity of getting the little Alba to Italy and to her father grow more and more urgent, until finally it is decided that they shall go with her themselves.[28] Needless to say, all this stress and strain had its effect upon Shelley's susceptible health;[29] nor is it surprising, after the issue of *Laon and Cythna* (as the poem was first called) had been suppressed, that Shelley should write to his father-in-law as if the whole poem had been the bequest of a dying man to posterity.[30]

24. For the facts of this paragraph cf. *idem,* I, 495–515, 730–733.
25. In *To the Lord Chancellor* and *To William Shelley,* composed after the event, in 1817, but not published until the *Poetical Works* of 1839.
26. So Mrs. Shelley, Medwin, and Hunt (in his *Autobiography*).
27. *Op. cit.,* I, 540–542.   28. Cf. *idem,* I, 539–540.
29. For a sensible, realistic discussion of Shelley's health at this time, see *idem,* I, 736–737. In I, 543, White observes as elsewhere that Shelley's ill health usually coincided with psychic strain, and that on this occasion, as soon as Italy had been decided upon, and the money to go there made certain (c. December 15), Shelley's health improved and remained excellent until he left England.
30. It is interesting to note that Shelley's letter to Godwin was written on the same day (December 11, 1817) as his eloquent appeal to the Olliers to "assume the high and secure ground of courage" (Julian *Works,* IX, 262–267).

Thus the forces of disillusion, in spite of the auspicious beginning of 1817, returned with the lesson of 1815—the lesson that one could not be a poet and a reformer too, a radical and an idealist in the same breath. The lesson of 1815 came back, now with a kind of ultimate significance, and Shelley chose poetry, as Mrs. Shelley points out in her note to *The Revolt of Islam.*[31]

Hence the fragments of *Prince Athanase,* written toward the end of 1817, are of the greatest interest to the student of Shelley's intellectual and emotional development. Their similarity to *Alastor* is striking, as Mrs. Shelley remarked when she published them in the *Posthumous Poems* of 1824. Athanase is suffering from the same *Weltschmerz* as the poet in *Alastor,* and we observe that the groping of the earlier poem has returned.

Yet in *Prince Athanase* there are indications of solution that *Alastor* is without. In the first place, the Hellenic coloring (which in *Alastor* had been limited to a Greek title selected by somebody else, and in *The Revolt of Islam* had scarcely gone further than the nationality of the principal characters)—the Hellenic coloring now extends to the poem's content as well: Zonoras, the prince's aged and beloved counselor, instructs his young charge in the lore of the great Academician, particularly in the lore of Agathon and Diotima. In the second place, the poem includes a beautiful apostrophe to Love (the best thing in it), and suggests that a philosophy of love under the auspices of Plato may offer the poet a way out.

Except for one or two short trifles such as the sonnet written in competition with Keats and Hunt, and the twelve-line fragment on the "Passage of the Apennines," Shelley attempted no new poetic composition until September, 1818, when he began *Prometheus Unbound.* The summer at the Baths of Lucca is memorable chiefly for Shelley's continued preoccupation with Plato—for his translation of the *Symposium,* that dialogue in which Agathon and Diotima (through the medium of Socrates) deliver the principal speeches on love.

Thus we are not unprepared to find that *Prometheus Unbound,* Shelley's new poem, is thoroughly Greek in character, in form being patterned after Æschylus (whose plays Shelley had been reading since 1815), and in content being colored by Plato. Indeed, we observe that from now on all the major works of Shelley are clearly in the Greek Revival—in fact, that they constitute one of the chief reasons for our being able to speak of a Greek Revival in English literature.

True, between the composition of the first and second acts of

31. To be sure, Mrs. Shelley draws the issue as between metaphysics and poetry rather than as between radicalism and poetry, as we conceive it.

Prometheus there is the period of Shelley's estrangement from Mary, so brilliantly analyzed by White,[32] commencing with Shelley's resumption of *Julian and Maddalo* and terminating, perhaps, with the *Stanzas Written in Dejection near Naples*. And there is *The Cenci*, Shelley's contribution to the current Elizabethan Revival.

But Shelley's main works, the poems that gave him his reputation when it came to him and that maintain it today—these are Greek in name, Greek in enthusiasm, and Greek in intellectual coloring. Whether one considers *Prometheus Unbound* or *Epipsychidion* or *Adonais* or *Hellas*, one perceives that the idealism long struggling to become dominant in Shelley, in becoming dominant, acquired a definitely Hellenic cast.

The delineation and criticism of this idealism, together with a consideration of Shelley's revolutionary thinking, is to constitute the principal concern of this study. Thus at the present moment we shall observe only in passing that the testimony of Shelley's own writings points to the year 1817 as the last of the transitional years. With its close, the exchange of Shelley's major and minor interests had been completed, nor did they ever reverse themselves again. Idealism and radicalism had jockeyed back and forth for the last couple of years. But the victory was with idealism, and with the victory came the best of Shelley's poetry.

32. *Op. cit.*, II, 40–56, 68–71.

3. The Evidence of Shelley's Reading

THE testimony of Shelley's writings, however, is not all that we possess. Shelley was perhaps the most assiduous reader who ever lived. Hogg tells us that he would read for sixteen out of the twenty-four hours,[33] and Trelawny remarks that with Shelley reading accompanied nearly every other activity of the day or night.[34] Thus a study of Shelley's reading should offer an additional clue to the development of Shelley's mind.

A generation ago, in her valuable because initiating essay on "Platonism in Shelley," Miss Winstanley observed that Shelley "found his sustenance mainly in two types of authors: in the Materialist writers who prepared the way for the French Revolution . . . and in the Greek Tragedians and Plato."[35] To us, this remark seems one of the most suggestive yet made on the subject of Shelley's reading. If in addition it appears that Shelley's reading of the philosophers of the Enlightenment coincided with the dominance of his radicalism, his reading of the Greeks, with the ascendancy of his idealism, then our problem is coarse-sifted before we take it up, and the main departments of our inquiry determined in advance. Let us make, then, a brief survey of Shelley's reading.

For a brief survey, Droop[36] is helpful, and we find that the conclusions to be drawn from his pages do indeed support the conjectures of the preceding paragraph. The general confinement of the writers of the Enlightenment to the first part of Shelley's career is as marked as the preponderance of Greek authors in the second; the tapering off of Shelley's interest in the literature of the eighteenth century, as clear as his gathering enthusiasm for the literature of the Greeks. Yet we observe that Shelley never entirely gave up his reading of the former writers, any more than he can ever be said to have been without an interest in Plato and the Greeks.

To begin our survey with Voltaire, it would appear from Droop that Shelley read him most extensively in the years leading up to *Queen Mab*, taking, as everyone knows, Voltaire's famous saying *"Écrasez l'infâme!"* as a motto of his poem. By 1814 this reading had declined to a perusal of the two novels, *Zadig* and *Candide,* and in 1815 was limited to the reading of *Charles XII* and the *Essay on Nations.* After this, we hear chiefly of the obstruction caused by Vol-

33. Hogg, *Life of Shelley* (London, Wolfe, 1933), I, 85.
34. Trelawny, *Recollections of the Last Days of Shelley and Byron* (London, Wolfe, 1933), II, 203.
35. *Essays and Studies by Members of the English Association* (Oxford, 1913), IV, 72.
36. Adolf Droop, *Die Belesenheit Percy Bysshe Shelley's* (Weimar, 1906).

taire to the Shelleys' smooth crossing of the Savoyard frontier in 1818, and observe the mention of Shelley's having read the *Memoirs* in 1820. As for D'Alembert, Helvétius, and Cabanis, these writers do not seem to have survived the year 1812, and though D'Holbach's *Système de la nature* is referred to in the *Refutation of Deism* (which is dated 1814), Droop finds no evidence that Shelley read him after 1812. Condorcet lasted longer than the rest. But as if to support our hypothesis, it is to be observed that it is not one of his philosophical writings, but his *Life of Voltaire,* that figures in Shelley's reading for the first half-year in Pisa.

The English philosophers of the Enlightenment showed a greater power of survival than the French. Yet Locke, whom Shelley synopsized at Oxford, and sent to Harriet Grove and Miss Hitchener— Locke does not really survive beyond 1816. Shelley and Mary read him at Bath upon their return from Switzerland, but after that, there is only the mention in the reading list for 1820. Berkeley was not read beyond 1817. Hume lasted until the next summer; but we note that it is the *History of England* that is being read then. Godwin stayed with Shelley the longest. The inheritor, as Locke had been the progenitor, of the *philosophes,* Godwin was the nearest to Shelley of all the eighteenth-century writers. Hence it is not surprising that *Political Justice* should be on the reading list for 1820 (as it had been on those for 1814, 1816, and 1817), and that as late as 1821 Shelley should be reading Godwin's *Answer to Malthus.* But these late readings only support our point that Shelley's interest in these writers never ceased.

The beginnings of Shelley's Hellenism are as indeterminate as the endings of his radicalism. According to Medwin,[37] Shelley began the study of Greek before he went to Sion House, and we must remember that the early Greek mottoes and allusions in his writings could have been—and probably were—taken from school or commonplace books. As for the Greek classics ordered in 1812, the fact remains that they formed but part of very much larger book orders[38] and that Shelley specified they "should have Latin or English versions printed opposite."[39] The whole matter is one to be discussed at greater length in the sixth chapter of this study. Nevertheless we may express the opinion now that Shelley's interest in Greek literature *per se* does not begin before his trip to Edinburgh in 1813 with Harriet and Peacock, and that this interest does not become serious until 1815 when he is settled at Bishopsgate, and once again in close association with Peacock.

According to Droop, the first dated mention of Shelley's reading of Homer comes from the Edinburgh visit, in a letter to Hogg,[40] who

37. Medwin, *Revised Life of Shelley* (London, 1913), p. 14.
38. Cf. White, *op. cit.,* I, 243, 637–638.
39. Julian *Works,* IX, 33.   40. *Idem,* IX, 80.

says of the 1813–14 period that Shelley's delight was to read Homer, that he possessed a copy of the two-volume Grenville *Homer,* one volume of which was never away from his hand.[41] In 1815 Shelley read Homer again, and so in nearly all the subsequent years up to and including 1822, when he translated Homer, along with Calderon and Goethe, for the *Liberal.*[42]

As for the Greek dramatists, it would appear that Æschylus as a serious interest dates from 1815. After 1815, there is scarcely a year without the reading of one or more of his plays. As late as the autumn of 1821, Shelley is again reading over the Greek dramatists and again using Æschylus as a model, this time the *Persae,* for his *Hellas.* The reading of Sophocles begins at the same time, and goes through to the end, as we recall from the copy recovered from Shelley's body. We recollect also that the motto of *Hellas* is composed of those favorite words from *Œdipus Coloneus,* "I am a prophet of brave struggles," which the preceding spring Shelley had had engraved on a seal for Mavrocordato.[43] The reading of Euripides also begins in 1815,[44] reaches its height in 1819 with the translation of the *Cyclops,* and continues until 1820 or 1821. Finally, we observe that Shelley read Aristophanes in 1818, the latter's Chorus of the Frogs suggesting two years later *Swellfoot the Tyrant,* as Shelley was interrupted in his declamation of the *Ode to Liberty* by a herd of pigs outside his window in San Giuliano.

But Plato was Shelley's great favorite, the Greek of Greeks, the prophet who came to take, in the later half of Shelley's career, the place that Godwin had held in the earlier half. Like Godwin, Plato can be said to have accompanied the whole of Shelley's career, for Hogg tells us that he and Shelley, while still in college, read Plato in an English version of Dacier's French translation.[45] Plato was also among the many books ordered from Hookham and Rickman in 1812. There is a lag, though, in Shelley's reading of Plato after this, and it is not until the Marlow days of 1817 that Shelley returned to the great Greek philosopher. But from then on, Plato became one of Shelley's mainstays, there being no subsequent year of Shelley's life when he did not read one or more of the dialogues.

41. Hogg, *op. cit.,* II, 59–60. Dowden observes (*The Life of Percy Bysshe Shelley* [London, 1886], I, 397n.) that this was undoubtedly the small Clarendon Press edition of 1808, which reprinted the Grenville text.
42. Cf. White, *op. cit.,* II, 374; *Shelley Memorials* (London, 1859), p. 176.
43. Droop gives Dowden, *op. cit.,* II, 444; Helene Richter, *P. B. Shelley* (Weimar, 1898), p. 572.
44. The authority for the reading of Æschylus, Sophocles, and Euripides in 1815 is a single reference in the Journal under date of February, 1815 (Lady Jane Shelley, comp., *Shelley and Mary* [London, 1882], I, 65), Æschylus and Sophocles being omitted from the reading list for that year. It is not until 1817 and 1818 that the Journal shows a systematic reading of the Greek dramatists.
45. Hogg, *op. cit.,* I, 121.

4. The Problem

THE preceding sketch of Shelley's reading has been based largely upon Droop, who still remains the handiest guide to the subject. To be sure, Droop did his work some forty years ago, and his findings must be revised (as in this study they have been revised) in the light of recent scholarship.[46] There is, furthermore, a margin of possible error in the fact that at the beginning and the end of Shelley's literary career the record of his reading is not so detailed as in the middle. Yet it is highly unlikely that the main outlines to be perceived from Droop's work will be disturbed. Nor is it likely that modern criticism will overset the general purport of Miss Winstanley's remark. Shelley's total reading was, as we know, enormous; and perhaps, title for title, his reading of the Greeks and of the writers of the Enlightenment amounts to but a fraction of the whole. But when it comes to what he took from his reading, when it comes to color and point of view and ideas, then it would seem incontrovertible that Shelley did indeed find his "sustenance" in one or the other of the above two sources. At least that is to be one of the assumptions of this study, as is the other assumption, that these two sources generally stand in a major and minor relationship to each other, reversing themselves around the middle of Shelley's poetical career.

Yet, much as it is to be hoped that these assumptions may be progressively verified in the course of this study, they hardly constitute its major interest. They still belong to the provinces of biography and bibliography, whereas the history of ideas begins where these provinces leave off. The history of ideas is interested in the "what" of a writer's sustenance, rather than in the "whence" and the "how." What is the nature of Shelley's Greek thought? the historian of ideas asks. And what is the nature of his radicalism, so largely colored by his reading of the French and English writers of the Enlightenment? How closely does Shelley follow the sources of his ideas? How much is his, and how much theirs?

For it goes without saying that one is incapable, humanly speaking, of sheer reproduction. There is a subjective element not to be disallowed. No matter how ardent a disciple one may be of his master, he gives a new twist to the master's doctrine, and we have a series of Kants being enraged with Fichte, of Fichtes being enraged with Schelling, and of Schellings being enraged with Hegel. As for Hegel, is it not on record that he affirmed that not one of his followers under-

---

46. Droop's findings have been checked with his sources, with Professor White's *Shelley*, and with the Journal as printed in *Shelley and Mary*.

stood his doctrine, only he himself? It must be thus with Shelley and the writers of the Enlightenment. No matter how extreme his enthusiasm for their ideas (and it was extreme), it is impossible that he should have reproduced a pure Voltairianism, or a pure Godwinism. There must be something of Shelley and not of his masters in his espousal of their doctrines. This subjective element the historian of ideas would very much like to sift out. And when he has it sifted out, he would like to ascertain whither it points. He would like to know what is its meaning. Is it a backwater in the stream of thought? Or is it in the swim of things toward new and distant horizons?

No less does it go without saying that no "revival" truly revives. There is no contrivance of man that can restore the past to the present. One of the most valuable lessons to be learned from the late Professor Beers's *History of English Romanticism in the Nineteenth Century*[47] is that each of the many medieval revivals that dotted the nineteenth century revived but one aspect of the Middle Ages. Scott caught their outward and public character—the tourney, the banquet hall, and the comings and goings of the knights errant and crusaders.[48] The Tractarians reflected the religiousness of the Middle Ages, the Pre-Raphaelites their decorative arts and sense of design.[49] No one of these separate revivals could catch more than an element of the original Middle Ages, and there were aspects (the less pleasant ones) that nobody revived at all. We in New England have seen Gothic chapels and Doric temples alike manufactured out of our native white pine and fitted with sliding sashes, cord, and window weights. Surely it may be accepted as an axiom that a revival only in part revives.

Hence the historian of ideas asks, How then does Shelley stand in comparison with the Greeks? What does he omit from Plato's thought? And what does he add? What do the omissions and additions tell us of Shelley, and of the times? To employ again our figure of the tree of thought, the historian of ideas asks, Is Shelley a leaf on a withering branch, or is Shelley a shoot on a growing stem?

As a matter of fact, the disallowance of the personal element is the chief error into which the bibliographers fall when they become too highly specialized, when their preoccupation with source analysis blinds them to the other avenues to knowledge. With Shelley, the error becomes particularly noticeable. For with Shelley, as with few poets, we have an exact, day-by-day account of his reading for four or five years, and for all years an account that, when put to-

47. Henry A. Beers, *A History of English Romanticism in the Nineteenth Century* (New York, 1901).
48. *Idem*, pp. 39–40.
49. *Idem*, pp. 290–293.

gether, is only slightly less reliable. Now the account is conspicuous for its lack of Neoplatonic literature.[50] Hence to go ransacking Plotinus and Proclus for possible sources, as Professor Grabo has done in *The Meaning of "The Witch of Atlas,"*[51] is certainly wearing the bibliographical spectacles when they ought to be taken off. When one has sifted out the known from the unknown, and when there remains (as there always will remain) an *x* quantity, then it is wiser to look for analogical parallels between the central figure and others of his day.[52]

But, as is not surprising, those who travel too blindly down the bibliographical road are best set aright by their fellows. In four pages of the most careful and balanced criticism, Professor White has removed Professor Grabo's learned treatise from the realm of serious consideration.[53] Professor White remarks, "Parallels mean nothing unless a bridge can be made to connect them, either by strong verbal links, or by definite proof of a connection between the author and his putative source."[54]

Indeed, the search for the subjective element makes clear to the historian of ideas the necessity for a bridge of connection. It is all very well in a general account to deal with the broad correspondences of history, and in the third and fifth chapters of this study we shall attempt in a comprehensive way to survey (as they affected Shelley) "The Thought of the Eighteenth Century" and "The Greek Revival." But the problem is different when it comes to the individual writer. With the individual writer the subjective appears, and the only way to segregate it is to eliminate the objective. Here possible and probable parallels are of no value. The objective can be based only on the real and the known. Though the historian of ideas works with ideas rather than with phrases or biographical data, yet when it comes to the individual writer he must cross the bridge of biographical and bibliographical facts. This bridge we have faithfully set out upon in the preceding sections. We hope to complete the journey in the first sections of our chapters on "Shelley and the Thought of the Eighteenth Century" and "Shelley and the Thought of the Greeks."

Presumably in the last-mentioned chapters we shall have disengaged the subjective from the objective, the Shelleyan from the God-

50. Thus Professor Notopoulos observes in *PMLA*, LVIII, 583, that "Plotinus and the other Neo-Platonists do not appear in Shelley's reading," and Professor White remarks even of their translator that "Shelley read . . . Thomas Taylor, but not his neo-Platonic writings" (*op. cit.*, II, 597).

51. Carl Grabo, *The Meaning of "The Witch of Atlas"* (Chapel Hill, 1935).

52. This thought is scarcely original. In the latter half of the remark quoted in Chapter I (p. 8), Professor Beach observes, "frequently a mere analogue may be as illuminating as an authentic source."

53. White, *op. cit.*, II, 596–599.

54. *Idem*, II, 597.

winian and the Platonic. That leaves the significance of the Shelleyan to be determined, and prescribes the final chapter of this study. In our last chapter on "Shelley and the Thought of His Time," we shall look at Shelley not as regards his forbears but as regards his contemporaries. In individuals like the philosopher and poet Schelling, like the poet and budding scientist Novalis, like the poet and traveler Nerval, we shall find, unless we are much mistaken, analogical parallels which will make clear that Shelley expressed a certain strain of the broader Romantic Movement not conspicuous in the other British poets of his day.

48687   L I B R A R Y
College of St. Francis
JOLIET, ILL.

III

The Thought of the Eighteenth Century [1]

1. The Main Currents

RATIONALISM

IT is a commonplace that one of the chief inheritances of the eighteenth century from the seventeenth century was a rationalistic way of thinking. The rationalism that the eighteenth century received from the seventeenth century is described in every textbook on the history of philosophy, and does not need to be explained again.

Yet any serious study must define the terms it intends to use, and we must make clear, as briefly as possible, what we take to be the rationalistic way of thought. In this we shall follow Professor Mornet's suggestion that it is essentially the mathematical way of thinking.[2] One postulates an abstraction, like the $\sqrt{-1}$, for instance, and then sees what can be done with it. We take the $\sqrt{-1}$ as an example because, although algebraically illogical when first conceived, the abstraction was later found to have a geometrical meaning, and ended by proving of great value to the Maxwell equations, upon which the modern advance in wireless communication has been achieved. Clearly the rationalistic way of thought is one of the basic ways of human thinking, and must be given a high place in the story of man's development.

Thus, although Locke is known chiefly for his banishment of the assumption of innate ideas, his own unverified assumptions form an impressive list. Let alone such general assumptions as knowledge of the self's existence, or as knowledge of real, exterior objects, we find in Locke such specific suppositions as of a social pact and the natural rights of man. The assumption by Leibniz of an essential

1. The following chapter should be regarded as an application of the principles set forth in Chapter I. It seeks only to fill in the background necessary for an appreciation of Shelley's radicalism, and eschews alike both the specialized and the controversial. When it comes to Rousseau, for instance, it will be found that the discussion entirely avoids the modern controversy, and is dependent solely upon the writings of Rousseau and upon those of his critics who write from a general point of view rather than as specialists. The following chapter is simply a sketch of the history of ideas in the eighteenth century.

2. Daniel Mornet, *French Thought in the 18th Century* (New York, 1929), pp. 57–60. Translated by Lawrence M. Levin.

monad, endowed with thought and feeling, is another such rationalistic, or mathematical, postulation.

Similar postulations dot the thought of the entire eighteenth century. One recalls the assumption of a moral sense by Shaftesbury, the assumption of a universal mind by Helvétius, and last, but not least, the assumption by Rousseau of the native goodness of man. It is clear that no appraisal of eighteenth-century thought can be complete without a recognition of this element in it. In spite of the decline in rationalism that is usually taken to mark the century's course, rationalism remained an ever-present factor, and probably must be premised as the basic factor.

EMPIRICISM

It is also a commonplace that the intellectual tide which had been running strongly in a rationalistic direction throughout the seventeenth century was turned by Locke. In his celebrated *Essay concerning Human Understanding*, published in 1690, Locke attacked and successfully undermined the favorite postulation of the seventeenth century, that of innate or eternal ideas. To Locke the assumption was gratuitous and false, not because it was an assumption, but because it ended in contradiction rather than in affirmation. In his Epistle to the Reader, Locke describes the impasse that occurred in his chambers, and offers it as the reason for his investigation of the sources of knowledge. Locke's investigation, as everybody knows, led him to regard experience as a more trustworthy source of information than postulation. In particular, it led him to conceive of sensation as the basis of human knowledge.

But Locke did more than afford a healthful check to the extravagances of rationalistic thinking. He did more than call attention to experience as an essential factor in human knowledge. By investigating the human mind itself, and by provocatively declaring the basis of knowledge to be sensation, Locke turned the tide of human thought from the outer world to the inner. In so doing, as Royce makes clear,[3] he initiated the philosophical development that was to lead to Kant and the German idealists, gave rise (by way of contrast) to the classical school of English moralists, and became the sponsor not only of the Enlightenment in France but even of the modern novel and Rousseau.

The shift from a pure rationalism to a rational empiricism, and the further shift to an emotional point of view that occurred in the latter part of the eighteenth century, are to constitute the subject matter of this chapter, and need not detain us now. What does demand a word of recognition at this moment is the development of science

3. *The Spirit of Modern Philosophy*, pp. 80–81.

that went along at the same time, not fluctuating from innate ideas to sensations to feelings, but steadily, without interruptions marking its course.

Beginning with Galileo, the exact contemporary of Shakespeare, modern science came into being. In one of the most illuminating passages of his *Spirit of Modern Philosophy*,[4] Royce explains Galileo's method, and makes clear the intoxicating effect it had upon the seventeenth century. Galileo's method of coping with a problem that experience had presented to him was to formulate a hypothesis (applying mathematics if he could), and then to test the hypothesis by experiment. If the experimental answer accorded with the theoretical supposition, the hypothesis was regarded as truth, and became knowledge. As Royce points out, the method is only an extension of the method of geometry. But, applied to science, it produced brilliant results and became the scientific method of the century.

The aspect of the matter, however, that is of especial interest to us is that from the point of view of the nineteenth century it hardly seems to be science at all, but rather mathematics, or philosophy. To us, who have been brought up in the shadow of the nineteenth century, and who can scarcely glance at an advertisement for canned soup without perceiving in the background a vista of alembics and U-tubes—to us Lavoisier, or perhaps even Faraday, seems to be the first scientist truly worthy of the name, the first scientist to depend upon apparatus rather than upon assumption. Galileo seems to have speculated more than he experimented. More essentially than inductive, he seems to have used deductive thinking, which the age of the laboratory has taught us to distrust. In fact, with his hypotheses, Newton no less than Galileo seems to be a rationalist with the rest of his age, and it is difficult for us to understand that the Enlightenment turned to him as well as to Locke for empirical encouragement and precedent.

Yet Voltaire's *Lettres philosophiques*[5] (to name an early popularizing work) gives four letters to Newton and but one to Locke, while Sir William Drummond's *Academical Questions*[6] (to take a late popularizing work, and one that meant a great deal to Shelley) devotes an entire chapter to Newton and only random reflections to Locke.

The truth of the matter is that "modern" science, whether it refers to Galileo or to Faraday, means empirical science, and that although within itself it may have swung from rational to empirical poles, it has always remained within the bounds of sober fact. The eighteenth century was right in regarding Newton as an exponent not of rationalist thought but of empirical thought. For his problems originated

4. *Idem*, pp. 38–41.   5. Rouen, 1734.   6. London, 1805.

in experience, and his hypotheses sought to explain experience. His corpuscular theory of light may have had to yield to the wave theory of Huyghens; but, as events have proved, it was anything but a wild guess, and had no other purpose than to account for the phenomena of light.

Throughout the seventeenth century there was a steady accumulation of factual, empirical knowledge. Naturally, the theoretical sciences came first. The appalling lack of scientific equipment and of technological skill dictated that in the development of science astronomy should precede physics, and physics, chemistry. Yet astronomy, no less than chemistry, is an empirical science, as far removed from astrology as chemistry is from alchemy. In fact, by the end of the eighteenth century, when Laplace wrote his popular *Système du monde* (which Shelley read, and refers to in his notes to *Queen Mab*), the body of astronomical knowledge had become truly impressive. One perceives, if only from the notes to *Queen Mab,* that the astronomical world by Shelley's time had taken on essentially the aspect that it wears today.[7]

In other words, during the eighteenth century the influence of science is ever present, and in our study of Shelley's debt to the eighteenth century it must ever be borne in mind. By Shelley's time, science had been demonstrating for two centuries the advantages of reason. For two centuries it had also been pointing in a single direction —away from the world of abstract speculation toward the world of facts and things. Indeed, it is not too much to say that Locke himself, by profession a physician, was turned toward the world of experience as much by the scientific tendency of his age as by the "standstill" he describes in his chambers. Nor did this tendency alter as the eighteenth century supervened.

Yet the dual advance of science, toward the world of experience on the one hand and by means of the intellect on the other, posed a problem for the emotionalists of the eighteenth century. To be sure, the emotionalist reaction was away from the city toward the country, and as such was away from the world of talk and ideas toward the scientists' world of facts and things. Thus in his walks through the woods and fields, Rousseau's inseparable companion is the *Systema naturae* of Linnaeus. We also observe that Saussure, the popularizer of the high Alps as Rousseau had been of the country around the Lake of Geneva—we observe that Saussure never made a trip to the Alps without a cargo of scientific instruments—barometers, hygrometers, thermometers, anemometers, and the like. Yet in a deeper sense the reaction of the emotionalists was away from the means of

7. The rise of non-Euclidean conceptions has scarcely altered the *aspect* of the astronomical world.

science, away from the intellect itself. Hence, a generation later, we find Wordsworth crying out against the botany that Rousseau loved,[8] and going to the Alps,[9] not like Saussure for the gathering of scientific data, but simply for the sake of the emotions they aroused.

The emotionalist reaction, however, was so wide and deep a thing that it must be taken up by itself.

EMOTIONALISM

Indeed, important as was the swing toward empiricism in the seventeenth and eighteenth centuries, important as was the influence of Locke and Newton, an even greater shift occurred in the latter half of the eighteenth century, and an individual influence arose as strong as, if not stronger than, that of Locke or Newton. If the year 1750 is memorable for the issuance of the Prospectus to the great *Encyclopedia*, that work which was to embody everything that Locke and Newton stood for, the year is no less remarkable for the publication of Rousseau's *Discours sur les arts et les sciences*. This essay, for the very novelty of its point of view, brought Rousseau instant fame, and indeed marks the beginning of a divergence in thought, not merely from the Enlightenment, but from the preceding century and a half. The breach with the past was widened in 1754 with the appearance of Rousseau's second Dijon discourse, this time on "Inequality," and was rendered irreparable in 1758 by the publication of his *Lettre à d'Alembert contre les spectacles*.

By the time of the letter to D'Alembert the issue had, of course, become embroiled with Rousseau's personality, and it is not too much to say that the dispute rocked intellectual Paris. The late Viscount Morley, whose studies of the eighteenth century must always command our admiration for their perception of the intellectual tendencies involved, does not belittle the breach between Rousseau and the philosophers. In his *Diderot and the Encyclopaedists* he writes, "This was no mere quarrel of rival authors. It marked a fundamental divergence in thought, and proclaimed the beginning of a disastrous reaction in the very heart of the school of Illumination . . . The crisis of 1758–59 . . . is a date of the highest importance."[10]

But the full significance of the split in the ranks of the philosophers can best be seen by going back for a moment to Locke. Locke's *Thoughts Concerning Education* have frequently been taken as a ground for *Émile*, and there is no denying that Locke, like a wise physician, knew the value of the assistance of nature. Hence many

8. In *A Poet's Epitaph* (composed 1799; published 1800).
9. In the summer of 1790.
10. John Viscount Morley, *Diderot and the Encyclopaedists* (2 vols. London, 1923), I, 154.

of his admonishments have to do with letting nature take its course, and in this he certainly anticipates Rousseau. But let us look at the end toward which Locke would direct his pupil's education. Far from the highly developed emotive sensibility that would seem to have been the goal of Émile's education, Locke's training, we observe, was to produce a well-rounded human being with wide knowledge and good judgment. From the beginning, Locke would have the tutor reason with his charges (81),[11] he would have their curiosities encouraged (118), he would "accustom them to truth and sincerity; to a submission to reason; and as much as may be, to reflection on their own actions" (140). Finally, in a well-known passage, Locke says, "The great business of all is virtue and wisdom . . . Teach him to get mastery over his inclinations, and *submit his appetite to reason*" (200).

In other words, for all the empiricism of *Thoughts Concerning Education* (and Locke wrote nothing more empirical), Locke's point of view remains strictly intellectualistic. To Locke, quite as much as to his predecessors in the seventeenth century, the intellect is chief of the human faculties, its exercise the principal activity of human life. The shift from hypotheses to facts and things has not altered the basic conviction of rationalism. This basic conviction colors the entire course of the Enlightenment, informs all seventeen volumes of the *Encyclopedia*, and receives its final tribute in the enthronement of Reason in Notre Dame in November, 1793.

That is why, when referring to the shift in thought which Locke initiated, we prefer to speak of a rational empiricism, or of an empirical rationalism. The schism of the Enlightenment seems to us no more than a family quarrel. The rationalists of the seventeenth century had gone too far, and within their own ranks there arose individuals to say that a corrective should be applied. The word "system" fell into disrepute,[12] and rationalists were admonished by their fellows to look to the bases of their assertions. There was no change, however, in fundamental point of view. As a matter of fact, the demand arose that even the institutions of society should be shaped in accordance with the teachings of reason. Reason remained, as always, man's chief counselor and guide, and now became the basis of the social ideal.

Yet all this while—indeed, long before Rousseau—there is to be found an opposite way of looking at things. Mornet finds the germs of an emotionalist point of view as early as the beginning of the seventeenth century. He points to St. Francis de Sales, who at the beginning of the century sought to lead men along the path of love

11. The numbers in the parentheses refer to the paragraphs of Locke's essay.
12. Cf. Condillac's *Traité des systèmes* (1749).

and ecstasy rather than along the path of wisdom and reflection.[13] Indeed, the influence of St. Francis' *Introduction to a Devout Life,* published in 1609, is felt all through the century. Then comes quietism, with its insistence on the language of the heart. Mme. Guyon carries the cult to the French court and counts Fénelon, tutor to the king's grandson, as her disciple. In 1697 the latter's *Maximes* sum up the movement, giving voice to a religion of pure love. Like the Savoyard vicar, one believes in God for no other reason except that one loves Him. We note, though, that in the resultant controversy with the intellectualist Bossuet, Fénelon was decisively defeated. The tendency he represented did not express the point of view of the majority, and the controversy ended in his banishment from Versailles and in his censure by the Pope.

This was in 1699. In the century that followed, intellectualism, as we have observed, seemed to grow stronger, and it is not surprising that emotionalism should have been forced to seek refuge in the novel. The novel, as Mornet points out,[14] was the one literary form for which there was no classical—and intellectualist—model. Thus in the first half of the eighteenth century it is the Abbé Prévost who keeps alive the spark of St. Francis de Sales and Fénelon, not only in his own novels, but in the translations of Richardson which he renders in the 1740's and 1750's.

In other words, the *Discours sur les arts et les sciences* did not originate the tendency which it represents. Rather, it simply called attention to the emergence of a man of genius in the emotionalist ranks. Hitherto the men of genius had all belonged to the other side. Now a writer of the first order took up the case for the emotionalist point of view. The *Discours sur les arts et les sciences* is, in fact, one long indictment of intellectualism. The range of history from ancient Egypt to medieval China is summoned to show that the cultivation of the mind is the prelude to degeneracy and conquest.

In his 1754 *Discours,* Rousseau returned to the theme. It is the wretched comparative faculty that has destroyed the equality of nature.

Men began to examine into the difference of objects, and to make comparisons; they acquired imperceptibly the ideas of beauty and merit, which soon gave rise to sentiments of preference and distinction . . . This was the first step toward inequality, and at the same time toward vice. From these first distinctions arose on one side vanity and contempt; and on the other shame and envy: the fermentation caused by which new leavens produced at length combinations the most fatal to innocence and happiness.[15]

13. Mornet, *op. cit.,* p. 190.
14. *Idem,* p. 17.
15. *The Miscellaneous Works of Mr. J. J. Rousseau* (5 vols. London, 1767), I, 221–222.

In fact, in the most-quoted statement from the 1754 *Discours,* Rousseau conjectures "that a state of reflection is a state contrary to nature, and that a thinking man is a depraved animal."[16]

After such extreme statements, there would appear to be little left that one might urge against intellectualism and the cultivation of the mind, and in truth much of the rest of Rousseau is less stricture of the present sorry plight of man than evocation of a substitute to serve for the lost state of nature. Hence the idealized portrait of Geneva to be found in the *Lettre à d'Alembert.* Geneva, Rousseau would have us believe, was, if not quite the state of nature, at least next best to it.

Indeed, recollecting Voltaire's remarks to Rousseau, Morley writes of this portrait of Geneva:

The reader who was not moved to turn brute and walk on all fours by the pictures of the state of nature in the Discourses, may find it more difficult to resist the charm of the brotherly festivities and simple pastimes which in the Letter to D'Alembert the patriot holds up to the admiration of his countryman and the envy of foreigners . . . And the interest of these pictures is much more than literary . . . They were the original version of those great gatherings in the Champ de Mars and strange suppers of fraternity during the progress of the Revolution in Paris . . . The fine gentlemen whom Rousseau did so well to despise had then all fled, and the common people under Rousseauite leaders were doing the best they could to realize on the banks of the Seine the imaginary joymaking and simple fellowship which had been first dreamed of for the banks of Lake Leman.[17]

In fact, as Höffding suggests in his *History of Modern Philosophy,*[18] it is with Rousseau that the problem of worth takes on its modern significance. In daring to question, in their own language, the intellectualism that the philosophers had for so long been agreed upon, he made them conscious of the problem of its validity. Hitherto the exponents of emotionalism had been for the most part religious mystics, scarcely meriting the philosophers' attention. But, as Höffding points out in his special essay upon Rousseau,[19] Jean Jacques made mysticism secular.

SUMMARY

To conclude this outline of the chief intellectual tendencies of the eighteenth century, we shall call attention to the three moralities which they subtended, and which are to be found at some time or

16. *Idem,* I, 174.
17. John Viscount Morley, *Rousseau and His Era* (2 vols. London, 1923), I, 323–324.
18. Harald Höffding, *A History of Modern Philosophy* (2 vols. London and New York, 1900), I, pp. 457–458. Translated from the German edition by B. E. Meyer.
19. Harald Höffding, *Jean Jacques Rousseau and His Philosophy* (New Haven, 1930), p. 77. Translated from the second Danish edition by Richards and Saidla.

other throughout the period. The classic, rational morality sprang up in England with Shaftesbury's postulation of a moral sense, and had a distinguished career as its various aspects were discussed by Hutcheson and Butler, by Hume and Adam Smith. It entered France under the aegis of Diderot but attracted no general attention. The morality of general acceptance in France among the philosophers was the empirical morality of utilitarianism. This saw in societal experience, and in the obvious advantages of the common good, the ground for good and bad, right and wrong. Finally, there arose in the latter half of the century the morality of sentiment. Its prophet was Rousseau, and its Bible was *La nouvelle Héloïse*. The arbiter of actions was now the feelings, no longer the intellect. In making her decision to renounce Saint-Preux, Julie consults her heart, not her head, and thus unconsciously bows to what conditions her heart—to the influences and training of childhood and early youth. The morality of sentiment resolves into the morality of respectability, and we perceive the beginnings of that ethical incubus which was to plague the whole of the nineteenth century.

2. Voltaire and the French Intellectualists

WHEN we speak of "Voltaire and the French Intellectualists," it should be clear that we take Voltaire not as the originator of his school but as its leader and most typical representative. The French Enlightenment has its origins in the seventeenth rather than in the eighteenth century, and if we must have a pioneer in Voltaire's own century, Montesquieu rather than Voltaire would seem to deserve the title. His *Lettres persanes* precede the *Lettres philosophiques* by a good dozen of years, and it is questionable if any work of Voltaire's so affected the course of history as the *Esprit des lois,* which introduced Locke's political thinking to the Continent. Yet Montesquieu died shortly after the publication of his great work, in 1755, while Voltaire, from that very year (the year of his purchase of Les Délices), became more and more the inspirer of the younger writers and thinkers who were using reason as a guide. He was in constant correspondence with Turgot and Helvétius. A visit on D'Alembert's part preceded the famous article on "Geneva" in the *Encyclopedia,* and when D'Alembert returned to Geneva he brought Condorcet with him. Grimm and Mme. d'Épinay but followed the beaten track in paying their respects to the sage of Ferney. Not only does Voltaire in his life and writings betray the chief traits of the French Enlightenment, but he was regarded by its members as their leader.

Now one of the characteristics of the Enlightenment in France was that practical as well as theoretical "philosophers" made it up. Individuals like Voltaire and Turgot were first of all men of affairs. Whatever one may think of Turgot's subsequent career as comptroller-general of France, his thirteen-year intendancy of Limousin was a triumph of administration. Again, no politician ever conducted a three-year campaign to gain a certain end with more consummate skill than Voltaire managed the Calas affair. As Brailsford points out,[20] until the test case was won, Voltaire would allow no exaggeration, no general argument for tolerance—even buying up a rash book by a Protestant pastor lest it weaken his side. This is not to imply, though, that individuals like Voltaire and Turgot left abstract questions alone. The former's *Philosophical Dictionary* and the latter's *Reflections on the Distribution of Wealth* would by themselves assure us of the contrary. It simply means that to Turgot the thousand and one irrationalities of an outworn economic system claimed his first attention; that to Voltaire everything else was dwarfed before the infamous collusion between church and state. As Brailsford points

20. Henry Noel Brailsford, *Voltaire* (London and New York, 1935), p. 197.

out,[21] the issue raised by Voltaire received its final settlement only with the Dreyfus Case in the twentieth century. Clearly one of the chief characteristics of the French Enlightenment was its warfare against real, concrete abuses.

Thus Shelley is correct in seizing upon Voltaire's slogan of "*Écrasez l'infâme!*" as representative of the man's life and philosophy. Voltaire's anticlericalism was the chief thing about him. Speculatively, he remained a moderate—so as to concentrate, one almost suspects, upon what he thought the most monstrous abuse of the day. Indeed, he joined with Frederick of Prussia in the hue and cry against the pseudonymous *Système de la nature,* and at first expressed his disapproval even of *De l'esprit,* the work of his disciple Helvétius. The two works represented the logical extremes of the speculative side of the French Enlightenment, and it is not surprising that Voltaire found himself without sympathy for them. Most interesting of all is Turgot's specific censure of *De l'esprit* for its weakening of the good cause by the violence of its theoretical opinions.[22]

But there were many traits that all the philosophers of the Enlightenment in France shared in common, whether men of affairs or theoreticians. Unless we are much mistaken, these traits are inherent in the intellectualist position.

The first of these is optimism. Here we see the Enlightenment in its role as a corrective to the pure rationalism of the preceding age. The optimism of Leibniz and of Shaftesbury had been static, a glorification of the existing order of things. The new optimism is an optimism that looks ahead. It is based not upon the present, where facts controvert a too sanguine point of view, but upon the future, where it is possible that men may approach the perfection implied by their present progress. Thus *Candide,* though its purpose be to prick the Leibnizian bubble, is still an optimistic tale. As Mornet expresses it, "Candide, after having sounded the depths of human despair, still has the courage to 'cultivate his garden.' That is because, in spite of everything, he has faith in the future."[23]

Optimism in some degree characterizes the whole movement of the French Enlightenment, reaching its culmination in Condorcet's *Historical Sketch.* Probably, as we have suggested, it is inherent in the intellectualist position. Newton so palpably demonstrates an advance over Galileo, Galileo over Archimedes, that it must be difficult for the person who believes in the intellect not to become hopeful when he thinks of the future. The doctrine of perfectibility has, in fact, an Aristotelian ring. It suggests a progressive fulfillment of

21. *Idem,* p. 211.
22. Turgot to Condorcet, *Oeuvres* (Paris, 1844), ii, 795–799; quoted by Morley, *Diderot and the Encyclopaedists,* ii, 130–132.
23. *Op. cit.,* p. 56.

what was all along latent, and images perfection as the τέλος of the process. The concept of perfectibility is thus contrary to the notion of evolution which superseded it in the nineteenth century. Stemming from the emotionalists, the latter idea sees no end to the process of development. Indeed, it finds the notion of perfection as a human limit unintelligible.

A second general characteristic to be observed among the French intellectualists of the eighteenth century is that the rational, or "good," life consists in some kind of constructive activity. This is to be observed whether one looks at their writings or their lives. Voltaire's life at Ferney exemplifies the philosophy expressed in *Candide*. Montesquieu at La Brède, Helvétius at Voré, D'Holbach at Grandval, take a similar, active interest in the cultivation of their gardens. In literature, the doctrine of function finds its expression in the great *Encyclopedia*. As Morley so well expresses it,

The Encyclopaedia seems inspired by . . . earnest enthusiasm for all the purposes, interests, and details of productive industry . . . The illustrative plates to which Diderot gave the most laborious attention for a period of almost thirty years . . . strike us . . . by the semi-poetic feeling that transforms the mere representation of a process into an animated scene of human life, stirring the sympathy and touching the imagination of the onlooker as by something dramatic.[24]

Indeed, the notion of leisure as an end of life is curiously alien to the conceptions of the intellectualist school, and belongs not to them but to the emotionalists. As we need not point out, the intellect is an active function, needing truth to discover and problems to work out, and the ideal of leisure *per se* presupposes some other faculty of the mind as chief in the individual's estimation.

A last general characteristic of the Enlightenment which we should like to point out is the absence of personal bias. We have today become so Marxianized that we cannot look upon social or political reform except in terms of class struggle. It seems incredible that the great seminal minds of this period of radical incubation should have had no axes to grind, that they belonged to the privileged rather than to the depressed orders. Montesquieu, Voltaire, Helvétius, and D'Holbach were, in fact, men of wealth. Diderot, the son of a cutler, seems never to have thought twice about his humble origins. The group seems to have cared little whether they got credit for their ideas or not, and many of them, like Turgot, specified that their contributions to the *Encyclopedia* should go unsigned.

The truth of the matter is that the great radical force of the Enlightenment was the great radical force of reason. The "infamous thing" was infamous because it was irrational. The *gabelle*, the

24. *Diderot and the Encyclopaedists*, I, 183–184.

corvée, the *lettre de cachet,* the exemption from taxation of those most able to pay—these abuses were intolerable because they too were irrational. In spite of Marx, the French Revolution as it stemmed from the Enlightenment was the product of intellectualism rather than of the class struggle.

But in an inquiry that is to lead to Shelley, the practical philosophers must give place to the theoretical. We must consider the chief speculative tendencies of the age. These tendencies, perhaps from the very hardihood of the opinions they advanced, seem to have affected Godwin more strongly than the rest of the Enlightenment, and through Godwin, Shelley.

The first tendency stems directly from Locke and is chiefly psychologic. Locke had derived knowledge from sensation and reflection, and Condillac followed him in rejecting an innate element in knowledge. In fact, Condillac's greater hostility to the rationalism of the previous age led him finally, in his third treatise—the celebrated *Traité des sensations*—to derive knowledge from sensation alone. As an epistemologist, Condillac advances to the empirical extreme. For, in deriving knowledge in part from reflection, Locke had still allowed the soul an active role in the acquisition of knowledge. But with Condillac the soul—if it can be called a soul—becomes the sport of its sensations, the soil of their automatic growth, the passive register of whatever the world sees fit to inscribe.

Three or four years later, in 1758, Helvétius drew the ultimate conclusions in his *De l'esprit.* If we play but a passive role in the creation of our world of knowledge, then our souls must be composed of a uniform substance, and we must be entirely the product of our surroundings. Thus Helvétius advances to the extreme environmentalist position, the implication of Condillac's epistemological point of view. Helvétius' doctrine of environmentalism is, in fact, the most significant thing about his book, and in the years that followed had an ever-increasing influence. It led, in the French Revolution, to an attempt to eradicate mental deficiency by a program of special education, and, as everybody knows, colors much of the thinking of Godwin's *Political Justice.* Indeed, a strong environmentalism has characterized the apostles of social reform ever since.

But there is another aspect of Helvétius' great work, almost, if not quite, as important as its environmentalism. *De l'esprit* is systematically utilitarian, and perhaps suggested the doctrine to Priestley, Bentham, and Godwin, who were the English forerunners of the two Mills.

Once again the tendency stems from Locke and Condillac. For Locke had said that "good and evil . . . are nothing but pleasure or pain, or that which occasions or procures pleasure or pain,"[25] and Condillac had followed him in allowing pleasure and pain as the master principle of the soul, the passive sensitivity upon which the external world builds. Locke had also based his political thinking upon the concept of the common good, so that it was but a step explicitly to combine the two, to find the common good in the common pleasure. Helvétius takes the step and, indeed, devotes the second discourse of his treatise to it. In fact, to his contemporaries, the most striking thing about the book was the paradox of his finding pleasure, or self-interest, to be at the bottom even of beneficence.

There was, finally, a last conclusion to be drawn from the thinking of Locke and Condillac. That Condillac himself was aware of it is shown by his dissertation on the freedom of the will appended to the *Traité des sensations*. For if man's reactivity is limited to the involuntary emotions of pain and pleasure, if sensations and ideas multiply within his soul without benefit of the guiding hand of thought, man becomes the victim as well as the product of his environment. Thus Helvétius, in pointing out that men's actions proceed from their characters, which are the product of their circumstances, pleads for a greater understanding of evildoers and becomes, in fact, the spiritual father of Beccaria's great treatise *On Crimes and Punishments*.

Yet the chief concern of *De l'esprit* is with the effect of external forces and circumstances, with the influence of government and education, and its determinism is not stressed.

The idea of determinism is stressed, however, in the *Système de la nature*, which, after D'Holbach's death in 1789, became known as the product of his pen. The idea of determinism is stressed, and the work becomes in this and in its materialism the crowning piece of radicalism of the French Enlightenment. It must be noted, though, that D'Holbach arrives at his determinism not through psychology and the influence of environment, but through physical science and a denial of the soul.

Strictly speaking, modern materialism begins with Hobbes. But, as far as the French Enlightenment goes, its progenitor is the physician Lamettrie—even as its last important representative is the physician Cabanis, famous for having declared that thought is a secretion of the brain. Lamettrie was much impressed by the influence of the body upon the mind, particularly in fever. He was also impressed by the disclosures of comparative anatomy as to the similarity between man and the animals. Following the principle of economy, he could see no reason for assuming a spiritual substance at the top of the scale that is denied at the bottom. Rather did it seem sen-

25. *Essay concerning Human Understanding* (London, 1690), II, 27, 5 (p. 157).

sible to him to extend the attributes of spirit to matter, to conceive, with Leibniz, of matter as endowed with thought and feeling, even if unconsciously so. Thus Lamettrie explains sensation as inherent in the nature of matter. At death, the special organization of matter we call consciousness is dispersed, soon to be followed by the dispersal of the body itself. As for God, the supersoul, need we say that Lamettrie denied this also? He ends with a philosophy as consistent as it is simple, a philosophy that seemed to the extremists of the French Enlightenment to be the only rational one. Lamettrie's collected works were published in London, Berlin, and Amsterdam within a few years of his death in 1751, and thus were early disseminated through the philosophic world.

It was Diderot, undoubtedly, who carried the torch to D'Holbach. In the opinion of Höffding, Diderot's two materialistic dialogues, the *Entretien entre d'Alembert et Diderot* and the *Rêve d'Alembert*, both in form and in content, rank among the classics of philosophy.[26] But Diderot's materialism and atheism were confined largely to his own circle (the above dialogues were published only in 1830), and we pass on to the *Système de la nature*, whence the French materialistic philosophy was transmitted to Godwin and to Shelley.

In endowing matter with the attributes of spirit, Lamettrie and Diderot had, for all their atheism, approached an idealistic point of view. But D'Holbach had the intellectual courage, or logical consistency, to proceed to the materialistic extreme. D'Holbach does not regard sensation as an original endowment of matter, but holds that it arises from a combination of elements, none of which individually possesses the capacity. To D'Holbach thought, or consciousness, is simply an effect of the same molecular motion that underlies all the processes of life. The soul as a separate substance is merely a figment of the imagination, and its freedom, the figment of a figment. D'Holbach writes of consciousness, "It is the result of a disposition or combination peculiar to living beings, in virtue of which a lifeless and insentient matter ceases to be lifeless and obtains the capacity of feeling by being taken up into the living being. This is what happens to milk, bread, and wine, when these are taken up into the human system."[27]

In other words, ethics, along with psychology, becomes a department of physical science, and duty and virtue become natural relationships. As with Helvétius, the individual is conceived as seeking his own happiness. That he seeks the happiness of others is simply because reason, or "physical science applied to the behavior of men

26. *A History of Modern Philosophy*, I, 478.
27. Our discussion of D'Holbach is based upon the unusually able summary in Höffding (1, 481–484), and our quotations from the *Système de la nature* are taken therefrom.

in society," teaches him that the happiness of the individual is bound up with the happiness of the group. Thus D'Holbach establishes a thoroughgoing materialism, free from all traces of idealism or sentiment.

Indeed, not content with reducing spirit to matter, D'Holbach turns upon the whole dualistic conception of spirit and matter as the source of all our woes. Here D'Holbach joins hands with the "fools-and-knaves" theory of Voltaire. For D'Holbach holds that the idea of a spiritual substance arose through the ignorance and naïveté of primitive men and was perpetuated by the tribe of priests, who, quick to seize upon the opportunity offered for their profit and aggrandizement, invented a whole world of invisible and suppositious rewards and punishments. In fact, so thoroughgoing are D'Holbach's materialism and anticlericalism, that he would abolish natural along with revealed religion. Any toying with the fiction of a spiritual substance can lead only to further knavery on the part of the unscrupulous, and the whole notion must be abandoned, not only as fallacious, but as injurious to the human race.

One does not see how the radical speculations of the French Enlightenment could have been carried any farther.

3. Rousseau

No DOUBT, for the sake of symmetry, this section should be entitled "Rousseau and the French Emotionalists." Like Voltaire, Rousseau was the leader of his school, and remains to us its chief representative. But Rousseau's influence came late in life. His great works did not appear until the 1760's, and his followers did not start up until the 1770's. As a matter of fact, Bernardin de Saint-Pierre's famous *Studies of Nature* did not come out until the 1780's, when their author was in his turn nearly fifty. The result is that, as far as Shelley is concerned, the French emotionalists who followed Rousseau present a problem of literary analogy rather than one of literary influence. There is no evidence that Shelley ever read Saint-Pierre or Chateaubriand or Benjamin Constant or Sénancourt.[28] With Rousseau himself, however, the case is different. Godwin names him, along with Helvétius and D'Holbach, as one of the writers to whom he is most indebted. Thus Rousseau falls in the line of Shelley's intellectual inheritance through Godwin. Furthermore, in the notes to *Queen Mab*, Shelley refers to Rousseau directly. Hence we must devote to Rousseau alone the attention we gave to Voltaire and the entire group of French intellectualists.

We have touched upon the violent quarrel between Rousseau and the Encyclopedists that rocked the Paris of the salons in 1757 and 1758. It is not surprising that it happened. In fact, we should be at a loss to explain Rousseau's ever having taken up with the philosophers did we not have the story of his youthful conversion to Catholicism. In *Émile*, speaking as the tutor, Rousseau tells us quite frankly that this conversion was for bread, and we might add that in the Paris of the 1740's and 1750's there was nothing for a young man of letters to do save join the philosophic coterie. Thus we find Jean Jacques contributing to the great *Encyclopedia* itself.

How alien all this was to Rousseau's real nature, the *Discourses* and *Letters* of the 1750's abundantly prove. Rousseau finally elaborated his point of view in his three major works, *La nouvelle Héloïse, Du contrat social,* and *Émile,* which appeared almost within a year of one another, early in the 1760's. The first of these deals with the woods and fields, passionate love, and the domestic affections; the second with politics; and the third with education. The works were composed more or less at the same time, while Rousseau was sojourning in or

28. Of the French followers of Rousseau, Mme. de Staël is apparently the only one with whom Shelley was acquainted. In 1815 he read her *De la Littérature considérée dans ses rapports avec les institutions sociales,* and during the winter in Naples, *Corinne.*

near the forest of Montmorency, and present, for all their differences, a unitary point of view.

In these three works Rousseau finally returned to the Rousseau of Chambéry and Les Charmettes, his removal to the Hermitage, in point of fact, furnishing an outward symbol of his abandonment of the city and the philosophic point of view. As Mornet points out, the *Discourses* had still employed the method of the philosophers. Rousseau had still reasoned like one of them, "basing his argumentation upon logic, historical facts, natural history, travels."[29] But by the 1760's Rousseau had abandoned demonstration for simple description, and was endeavoring not to prove but to portray his philosophy. This philosophy is everywhere, we observe, a philosophy of the emotional needs of the individual.

In this respect, our increased knowledge of the length and nature of Rousseau's stay with Mme. de Warens is helpful. It is clear that Rousseau was already *de trop* when he came back from Montpellier in January, 1738, and found M. Winzenried in his place. Yet the curious *ménage à trois* that ensued apparently lasted, in spite of lapses and a steady deterioration, until the spring of 1742, and testifies that Rousseau at that period asked nothing from life except the enjoyment of his emotions—not even self-respect. As for the rugged independence of Rousseau's later years, the obsession of supporting himself by music copying at no matter what the cost—this, we recall, comes after the *Discourses,* in which Rousseau had set himself up to the public as the philosopher of antique frugality and self-sufficiency. In spite of this later role, the Rousseau who lived with Mme. de Warens as an idler until he was nearly thirty would appear to be the essential Jean Jacques Rousseau. We find a note of solipsistic individualism to be present throughout the major works.

In the *Social Contract,* one of the leading doctrines is that of the parity of all members of the body politic—that body politic which was founded in the first place not for the group but for the individual. Morley points out that the cult of *fraternité* in the French Revolution, and even the significance of the term *citoyen,* stem from this aspect of the *Social Contract.*[30] Similarly, in *Émile,* the child's individuality is absolutely sacred and is to be controverted by no outer authority or will.

More interesting is the end to which the freedom of the individual is applied. This is hardly the province of the *Social Contract,* but is very much the concern of *La nouvelle Héloïse* and *Émile.* Clearly in these latter works the freedom of the individual is to be used simply for the cultivation of the emotions. Saint-Preux does not join the expedition of Admiral Anson to further the cause of science but to as-

29. Mornet, *op. cit.,* p. 196.   30. *Rousseau and His Era,* II, 207.

suage himself of one emotion, and perhaps to gain another. Julie deplores the atheism of her husband, not because he will be damned in Hell, but because he misses the emotions of faith in God and belief in the immortality of the soul. She gives alms to mendicants for the pleasure it affords her, and in her spare moments reads Fénelon. As for Émile, we can do no better than quote Morley, who writes, "The ideal of Emilius was an ideal of quietism: to possess his own soul in patience, with a suppressed intelligence, a suppressed sociality, without a single spark of generous emulation in the courses of strong-fibred virtue, or a single thrill of heroical pursuit after so much as one great forlorn cause."[31] The objective world has been abandoned for the subjective, and we find the retrogressive social ideal in place of the progressive.

It is in the social ideal, as a matter of fact, that the cleft between Rousseau and the Encyclopedists becomes most marked. The Encyclopedists, as we have noted, stood for the arts and sciences, glorying in the achievements that had been made thus far, and looking forward to the future, in which still greater accomplishments, and a richer and more complex civilization, would ensue. Rousseau set his face in the opposite direction. Turning from the objective world of facts and things that intellectualism needs to think about, Rousseau looked inward upon the world of the emotions, which, as everyone knows, is far less dependent upon the outer world. To be sure, the emotionalist needs the outer world to arouse his feelings, but once his feelings have been aroused they are more important than the world. Thus he prefers the world of nature to the world of man. The world of man requires thought that its contrivances may be understood; but the world of nature requires nothing in return. The emotionalist will accordingly seek to rid himself of the encumbrances of civilization, that nothing may impede the use of his favored function. He turns his face in the direction of the tub of Diogenes, though Rousseau looked no farther than a Swiss chalet. Mandeville, who clearly saw what the divergence in point of view implied, describes it in his *Fable of the Bees* as the choice between a wretched hollow tree and a comfortable, well-ordered hive. To Voltaire it was the choice between being a man and walking on all fours.[32]

Thus Wolmar, though his wealth and social position prevent him from receding to any of these extremes, nevertheless returns to primitive barter to effect the marketing of his surplus produce. He feels that the way to be prosperous is to have as little as possible to do with money. And, though his estate is but a few miles from the watch-makers of Geneva and Ferney, it might as well have been in the marshes of Poland for all it bears witness to the progress of industry

31. *Idem*, II, 281.   32. Voltaire to Rousseau, August 30, 1755.

and science. Again, Émile, like Locke's young gentleman, must learn a trade. But do we think it is for the sake of the recreation which Locke points out, and which can come only from pursuit of the trade in its own right? Not at all. We read, "Learning a trade matters less than overcoming . . . prejudices . . . Work for honor, not for need: stoop to the position of a working man, to rise above your own."[33] In fact, since one learns a trade for sentimental reasons, Rousseau rejects trades that are menial and dirty. He writes of his imaginary charge, "I do not want to see him a Cyclops at the forge. Neither would I have him a mason, still less a shoemaker . . . Cleanliness should be taken into account; this is not a matter of class prejudice, our senses are our guides."[34] Truly, one wonders if Rousseau would have had his pupil learn a trade at all if Locke had not preceded him and made it almost *de rigueur*. We are far indeed from the glorification of the trades and industry that greets us on every hand in the pages of the *Encyclopedia*.

The retrogressive social ideal, with its everlasting exaltation of Sparta at the expense of Athens, runs all through the writings of Rousseau, and received in fact an unexpected corroboration in the French Revolution when the sentimentalists under Robespierre and Saint-Just came to power in 1794. The intellectualists, with their atheism and enthronements of Reason, were beheaded, and the way lay open for a return to nature. The impious deification of Reason was expunged on the eighth of June by the festival of the Supreme Being, and we give a sample of the regulations by which Saint-Just hoped to regenerate his country. No servants were to be allowed, and no gold or silver vessels. No child under sixteen was to eat meat, nor any adult on three days of the decade. Finally, we observe, boys at the age of seven were to be handed over to the school of the nation, where they were to be brought up to speak little, to endure hardships, and to train for war.[35]

Lack of space prevents an adequate treatment of the many aspects of this single divergence in point of view. We are particularly interested in Rousseau's approach to religion through emotional need. As Höffding puts it, "At its height this need attains a superabundance for which there is no room in the finite world. An infinite urge is astir; one seems to be about to smother in the world: 'J'étouffe dans l'univers!' All distinctions and barriers disappear. One feels his unity with all of nature in all that lives." [36] We are also interested in Rousseau's pronounced belief in the freedom of the will, this being the

33. J. J. Rousseau, *Emile or Education* (London and New York, 1911) (Everyman's Library), p. 159. Translated by Barbara Foxley.
34. *Idem*, p. 163.
35. Taken largely from Morley, *Rousseau and His Era*, II, 183–184.
36. *Rousseau and His Philosophy*, p. 120.

third article of the Savoyard vicar's creed. Whatever the theoretical reasons that Rousseau and the Savoyard vicar may give for their voluntarism, to us it is clearly a concomitant of the emotionalist position. In proclaiming the affective faculty chief among the functions of the mind, the emotionalist asserts his independence of that material world about which the intellectualist thinks, and it is but a step further to the doctrine of the freedom of the will. Interesting as these aspects are, we can only touch upon them here.

We must end this section by pointing out a last result of Rousseau's repudiation of the philosophic party. In turning from the world of the object to the world of the subject, in shifting from the intellectualist to an emotionalist point of view, Rousseau unconsciously leagued himself not only with the old rationalism but with the old régime itself. This is evident on every hand. Rousseau's state of nature is a tissue of assumptions and hypotheses that might well have made the hardiest of Cartesians wince. As a moralist, we find him veering away from the utilitarians, with their strictly selfish theory of human conduct, toward the more purely rational conceptions of Shaftesbury and his school. In his letter to Voltaire on the latter's poem concerning the Lisbon earthquake, we find him specifically championing the extreme optimism of Pope and Leibniz. In his letter to D'Alembert on the subject of stage plays, we find him joining those same ecclesiastics who had shoveled Adrienne Lecouvreur into a riverbank, and would not let actors or actresses marry without forswearing their profession. One could cite dozens of instances to show that Rousseau was in many respects linking himself with the very thing that was the chief object of attack of the Encyclopedists. In sober truth, the *Génie du christianisme* was but a step around the corner. The real force of Rousseau was felt not in the French Revolution but in the Romantic Movement that followed the French Rovolution.

Probably Rousseau, who was not a thinker of the first rank and found it easier to employ a hundred devices of rhetoric than to follow out the implications of one of his thoughts—probably Rousseau was unaware of the ultimate bearing of his position. But the philosophers were not unaware of it, and the fact helps explain the bitterness with which they greeted his apostasy. "What," cried Voltaire, "has Jean Jacques turned a father of the church?"[37]

37. Voltaire to Thierot, September 17, 1758.

4. Godwin

Godwin's *Enquiry concerning Political Justice* appeared in 1793, and thus is the last, or very nearly the last,[38] of those radical writings that dot the literature of the eighteenth century. After the *Rights of Man*, the *System of Nature*, the *Social Contract*, Helvétius' essay *On the Mind*, and the rest, one would think there was little left to say. Yet Godwin's work, in England, achieved a fame equal to that of any of its predecessors. This it did by reason of its extreme intellectualism. Then, as now, it was the most striking doctrine in the book and overnight attained celebrity.

After two centuries of intellectualistic thinking, it remained for Godwin, as Sir Leslie Stephen suggests,[39] to reduce intellectualism to the absurd. Godwin's intellectualism is, in fact, absolute, and passes beyond the positive bounds of problems to be solved, and schemes to be thought out, into the negative regions of philosophic anarchism.

To begin with, Godwin accepts the extreme empiricism of Condillac and his followers. Except for the brute reactivity of pleasure and pain, all mind is but an extension of sensation. Thus the "characters of men originate in their perceptions" (the title of Godwin's third chapter), and the formation of character is controlled by environment.

This belief that the formation of character depends upon external circumstances, Brailsford very aptly picks out as the first essential dogma of Godwinian perfectibility. The second, he observes, is that the actions of men originate in their opinions.[40] Thus in Godwin wrong actions spring from wrong opinions, and vice is explained as error.[41]

Now there is nothing new about this intellectualistic theory of evil. It was Plato's theory. But Plato recognized that in whole classes of men the intellectual faculty is weaker than either the appetites or the emotions, and it would never have occurred to him to propose the discourses of his Academy as a panacea for evil. Godwin, though, will admit of no basic difference in the minds of men. Following Helvétius, he exclaims,

Examine the new born son of a peer and a mechanic. Has nature designated in different lineaments their future fortune? Is one of them born with

38. The *Rapports du physique et du moral de l'homme* of Cabanis, read before the Institut in 1796 and 1797, appeared in 1802.

39. "Hours in a Library, No. xx, Godwin and Shelley," *Cornhill Magazine*, xxxix, 286.

40. Henry Noel Brailsford, *Shelley, Godwin, and Their Circle* (London, 1913), p. 102.

41. Cf. William Godwin, *An Enquiry concerning Political Justice* (2 vols. London, 1793), I, 31; II, 563.

callous hands and an ungainly form? Can you trace in the other the early promise of genius and understanding, of virtue and honor? . . . What are the sensations that the lord experiences in his mother's womb, by which his mind is made different from that of the peasant?[42]

Indeed, not only does Godwin suppose that all men are equally capable of reason, but he assumes that intellectuality constitutes the bulk of mental activity. He does not agree with Plato that the appetites and the emotions are faculties in their own right, needing to be harnessed and to be guided, but nevertheless partners in the whole of the personality.

The consequences of Godwin's assumptions are not far to seek. If men are universally rational and if their reasons determine their actions, then all that is needed to achieve the millennium is to persuade men of the true nature of things. The fault in the past was that coercion, not persuasion, was the means employed. In the new age, private judgment will take the place of laws and institutions, and society will be reduced to its individual members, each exercising his right as a thinking being to decide, without prejudice or prescript, whatever issues may arise. Anything less is beneath the dignity of human nature.

The ripples consequent upon the original stone-throw now widen perceptibly. We find that anything at all that derogates from the absolute intellectual liberty of the individual is bad and to be done away with. The dead hand of custom and tradition is of course to be cast aside. Even a man's own past must be insulated from his present. He must make no promises, and contract no marriages, that will impair his future freedom of volition. Indeed, "every thing that is usually understood by the term cooperation, is in some degree an evil."[43] "Why should we have common meals?" Godwin writes. "Am I obliged to be hungry at the same time that you are? Ought I to come at a certain hour, from the museum where I am working, the recess where I meditate, or the observatory where I remark the phenomena of nature, to a certain hall appropriated to the office of eating; instead of eating, as reason bids me, at the time and place most suited to my avocations?"[44] Even "concerts of music" and "theatrical exhibitions" are banned from Godwin's ideal society.[45] By a slight shift in emphasis, Godwin has advanced from the doctrines of Condillac and Helvétius, not toward social reform, but toward philosophic anarchism.

If this were all there were to *Political Justice* and Godwinism, the matter would be very simple and one would be content with observing the ludicrous extreme to which the doctrines and errors of the French philosophers have been carried.

42. *Idem*, ii, 461–462.   43. *Idem*, ii, 844.   44. *Idem*, ii, 842.
45. *Idem*, ii, 846.

However, this is not all there is to *Political Justice,* and in the Preface the reader is warned of the forthcoming complexity by Godwin's avowal of indebtedness to D'Holbach, Rousseau, and Helvétius. Now as between D'Holbach and Helvétius, there is no remarkable divergence in point of view. True, when one thinks of D'Holbach it is apt to be the doctrine of necessity that first comes to mind; when one thinks of Helvétius it is apt to be the doctrine of environmentalism. Yet the two theories are clearly harmonious, if indeed not related; and that Godwin should be both an environmentalist and a necessitarian, a disciple both of Helvétius and of D'Holbach, seems not at all strange.

But between D'Holbach and Helvétius on the one hand, and Rousseau on the other, there is a gulf that is not to be bridged. We have been at pains to describe this gulf and have noted its working among the leaders of the French Revolution. Hence it seems needless to observe that any philosophy composed of such mutually irreconcilable elements will betray a deep contradiction.

The trouble with Godwin, in fact, lies deeper than the usual objection that is leveled against him, namely, that if all human actions spring from necessity it is inconsistent to cry out against kings and priests. This is the sort of objection that the critics of *Queen Mab* directed against that poem when it first appeared.[46] But after all, as Morley points out,[47] D'Holbach answered this objection years before. It is the necessity of all men to work for their betterment and pleasure. The malefactor is simply one whose circumstances have prevented him from seeing that his own good is connected with that of the many. Society punishes the malefactor through necessity, and the moralist follows necessity when he too condemns the evildoer. He must only take pains that no element of vindictiveness or retaliation enters his concept or administration of justice. Shelley, it is true, stepped out of the philosophic role to inveigh passionately against the enemies of society. But Godwin, no less than Helvétius and D'Holbach, practiced the philosophic calm that he preached.

No, the trouble with Godwin lies in a deeper stratum than mere charges of inconsistency between his necessity and his morality. One must penetrate to the fundamental convictions upon which his system rests.

For instance, we observe that, following the Encyclopedists, Godwin is a utilitarian—in fact, because of the temper of his personality, an extreme one. To Godwin, the common good lays an imperative upon the individual as remorseless as the logic of mathematics. In its requirements there is no place for gratitude, friendship, or the family

46. Cf. N. I. White, *The Unextinguished Hearth* (Durham, N. C., 1938), pp. 84–85.
47. *Diderot and the Encyclopaedists,* II, 178–180.

ties. "What magic is there in the pronoun 'my,'" Godwin cries, "to overturn the decisions of everlasting truth?"[48] With Godwin morality becomes a calculation of the benefits to accrue to humanity from each individual act, and in his celebrated figure of Fénelon and the chambermaid in the burning archiepiscopal palace, the rescuer will choose Fénelon with his yet-to-be-written *Télémaque*, though the chambermaid be his mother or his wife.

Thus in his ethical thinking Godwin seems to be at one with the eighteenth-century utilitarians. Fénelon is to be saved rather than the chambermaid because it is he rather than she who will contribute the more to the common good. Yet Godwin strenuously denies the "selfish theory" of human conduct upon which the eighteenth-century utilitarians base their case. He maintains that man's interest in the greatest happiness of the greatest number proceeds, not from knowledge that his own happiness is bound up with that of others, but from pure disinterestedness of heart. Thus Godwin's fundamental position turns out to be not that of the French Encyclopedists, nor that of their lineal descendants, the English Utilitarians, but that of the emotionalist Rousseau. In fact, Godwin out-Rousseaus Rousseau.

For Rousseau, who was born in 1712, clung to the empirical belief of his century in man's essential self-interest; though, to be sure, he took pains to harmonize this belief with his own conception of the natural goodness of man, drawing the distinction between "good" self-love, or *amour de soi* (from which the social virtues and even the love of God proceed), and "bad" self-love, or *amour propre* (which is egoistic and miserable).

But Godwin, who was born in 1756 and lived until 1836, completes the circle back to Shaftesbury and proclaims the innate benevolence of man.

The reader of Godwin, though, may well ask how this can be. He remembers the opening chapters of *Political Justice* with their relegation of man's emotive nature to the pleasure or pain accompanying one's sensations. He recalls Godwin's intellectualistic definition of pity as the remembrance of one's own pain at the sight of pain in others. He recollects Godwin's saying that "fear itself is a species of foresight," and that "by the love of self we understand the approbation of pleasure, and dislike of pain," and that "this is only the faculty of perception under another name."[49]

Thus the reader finds it rather strange that benevolence (which the world has always regarded as an emotion) should take on greater and greater importance as Godwin's treatise progresses, until finally it is the quality upon which the hope of the world depends. That Godwin was himself partly aware of the contradiction involved is apparent

48. *Op. cit.*, I, 83.   49. *Idem*, I, 15–16.

from the labor with which he tries to reconcile benevolence with his general intellectualism. He would have us believe that the "selfish theory" reduces human conduct to the brute, subrational plane, that benevolence is nothing more than the rational play of motive according to the logic of things.[50] Thus benevolence becomes not an emotion, not a subjective power, but an exterior command, the imperative of an external rationality upon a mind that has suppressed all personal predilection.

That this was not the real bearing of Godwin's thought is suggested by the loving complacency with which he returns to the notion of benevolence. We find him writing, "There is no doctrine in which the generous and elevated mind rests with more satisfaction."[51] Some ten pages farther on he writes, "He whose virtues flow from philanthropy alone, whose heart expands with benevolence and good will, and who has no desire to make his superiority felt, will at all times have many friends and few enemies."[52] Finally, at the end of the work, he declares, "Mind without benevolence is a barren and a cold existence. It is in seeking the good of others, in embracing a great and expansive sphere of action, in forgetting our own individual interests, that we find our true element."[53] Surely this is strange language with which to describe the individual who is supposed (according to Godwin's intellectualism) not to "seek" or "embrace" philanthropy, but passively to wait for the reason of things to speak.[54]

Hence it is not surprising that the real implication of Godwin's thinking should come out in his social ideal. As is so often the case, the real import of Godwin's thought does not emerge until the learned argument is all over, and the consequences are being depicted of those principles that have been outlined and substantiated. In the eighth and last book of *Political Justice*, Godwin describes the communistic utopia his principles will bring about, and in so doing lets his pen flow on, unhampered by the restrictions of the logical debate. The eighth book, "Of Property," is lyrical, not disquisitious, and is the part of *Political Justice*, we may well suppose, that led to its adoption by the enthusiastic, and to the ardent dreams of colonies on the banks of the Susquehanna. Curiously enough, it stands in the same relation to the earlier part of the book as Rousseau's *Letter to D'Alembert* stands to the preceding *Discourses*. That letter, too, had

50. *Idem*, I, 344–346. 51. *Idem*, I, 358.
52. *Idem*, I, 369. 53. *Idem*, II, 855–856.
54. In this study we are confining our attention to the first edition of *Political Justice*, which was the edition of the young Bristol Pantisocrats and the edition that Shelley preferred (cf. letter to Miss Hitchener, December 26, 1811). In the second and third editions (1796 and 1798), the sentimental import of Godwin's benevolence becomes unmistakable.

been written *con amore* (as Rousseau tells us), and in it the Rousseauistic ideal issues forth, summing up the *Discourses* and anticipating the *Social Contract*. The only difference between Rousseau and Godwin is that Rousseau's ideal is tinged with nostalgia for the past, whereas Godwin's entertains a wistfulness for the future.

Let us look, then, at the social ideal as envisioned in Godwin's final pages.[55] We are not surprised to find that it is the retrogressive ideal that greets us on every hand, even if this ideal is hoped for in the future rather than sighed for in the past. In Godwin's proposed society, we read,

Every man would have a frugal, yet wholesome diet; every man would go forth to that moderate exercise of his corporal functions that would give hilarity to the spirits; none would be made torpid with fatigue, but all would have leisure to cultivate the kindly and philanthropical affections of the soul, and to let loose his faculties in the search of intellectual improvement [II, 806] . . . The narrow principle of selfishness would vanish. No man being obliged to guard his little store, or provide with anxiety and pain for his restless wants, each would lose his own individual existence in the thought of the general good. No man would be an enemy to his neighbor, for they would have nothing for which to contend; and of consequence philanthropy would resume the empire which reason assigns her. Mind would be delivered from her perpetual anxiety about corporal support, and free to expatiate in the field of thought, which is congenial to her. Each man would assist the enquiries of all. [II, 810]

In this community scarcely any can be expected in consequence of their situation or avocations to consider themselves as exempted from manual industry. There will be no rich men to recline in indolence and fatten upon the labor of their fellows. The mathematician, the poet and the philosopher will derive a new stock of cheerfulness and energy from the recurring labor that makes them feel they are men. There will be no persons employed in the manufacture of trinkets and luxuries; and none in directing the wheels of the complicated machine of government, tax-gatherers, beadles, excisemen, tide-waiters, clerks and secretaries. There will be neither fleets nor armies, neither courtiers nor footmen. [II, 821]

From the sketch which has been here given it seems by no means impossible, that the labor of every twentieth man in the community would be sufficient to maintain the rest in all the absolute necessaries of human life. If then this labor, instead of being performed by so small a number, were amicably divided among them all, it would occupy the twentieth part of every man's time. Let us compute that the industry of a laboring man engrosses ten hours in every day . . . It follows that half an hour a day, seriously employed in manual labor by every member of the community, would sufficiently supply the whole with necessaries. Who is there that would shrink from this degree of industry? . . . Is it possible to con-

55. References to these final pages of *Political Justice* will be given in the text of our study.

template this fair and generous picture of independence and virtue, where every man would have ample leisure for the noblest energies of mind, without feeling our very souls refreshed with admiration and hope? [II, 823]

And so on, and so on. Some twenty pages further on, the possibility of a machine to do away with all coöperative labor is discussed (II, 845), and there is a reference (obligatory among Rousseauists) to Lycurgus, the "immortal legislator" (II, 846). We mentioned above that in his principle of benevolence, Godwin out-Rousseaued Rousseau. As if to corroborate our statement, on page 858 we observe that even the barter and exchange of the good Wolmar will be abandoned in Godwin's ideal community, and that, unlike Émile, "no man will learn a trade." Truly, in Godwin's utopia, Rousseau would have been able to return to Les Charmettes.

Now this is very interesting. Godwin's ideal community is no chance slip of the pen. It is a detailed portrait, one hundred pages in length, of the world as he would like to see it. As such, it must come closer to the essential Godwin than the laborious thinking of the preceding pages. Yet it stands in almost complete antithesis to the point of view of the preceding pages, which, as we remember, are extreme in their intellectualism. Godwin's social ideal would seem to be as uncompromisingly emotionalistic as his metaphysics are intellectualistic.

As a matter of fact, there would seem to be little doubt that Godwin was always at heart an emotionalist, and not an intellectualist. In one of the most able essays yet contributed to the study of Godwin, Professor B. Sprague Allen maintains this opinion.[56] Pointing out such traces of emotionalism in *Political Justice* as we have observed, he remarks that Godwin's acceptance of the environmentalism of Helvétius, together with Rousseau's theory of the innate goodness of man, could only fling the doors wide open for sentimentalism. As early as *Caleb Williams* (1794), Professor Allen observes, we hear the reassuring, charitable "He meant well" of the sentimentalist.[57]

Certainly, as the years progressed and Godwin's novels multiplied, Godwin's sentimentalism increased rather than declined. Furthermore, one must not forget that the novels continued to the 1830's, tying up with those of Bulwer-Lytton in *Eugene Aram*, which Bulwer took over from Godwin. Surely, if the assembled tally of a man's writings goes for anything, Godwin belonged rather to the generation that shuddered at *Lenore* than to the generation that found enlightenment in the *Encyclopedia*.

56. B. Sprague Allen, "William Godwin as a Sentimentalist," *PMLA*, XXXIII (1918), 1–29.
57. *Idem*, p. 7.

Professor Allen concludes his article by observing that whether Godwin would have admitted it or not, "the inmost shrine of his philosophy might be entered by way of either the reason or the feelings. The preference," Professor Allen says, "seems to have been for the latter way, if we can judge by the character and writings of some of his most ardent disciples, enthusiastic reformers like John Thelwall and young Shelley. Undoubtedly they conceived themselves as the advocates of a most austere intellectualism, but in reality they were responding to an appeal of a very different order."[58]

58. *Idem,* p. 29.

V

Shelley and the Thought of the Eighteenth Century

1. The Biographical and Bibliographical Facts

AS we undertake to survey the biographical and bibliographical facts connected with *Queen Mab* and Shelley's youthful radicalism, two sobering thoughts must be borne in mind. The first is that as regards this period of Shelley's life we simply do not possess the abundance of information that attends our study of his later years. Shelley's radicalism is an affair largely of 1811 and 1812. It was already on the wane by the spring of 1813 when *Queen Mab* was printed, and, except for the recrudescence in 1817 which we have already noted,[1] it never again occupied the principal place in Shelley's affections. Thus a study of Shelley's radicalism must be conducted without such assistance as is provided by the Journal in the years subsequent to 1814. True, there are the biographies of Hogg and Medwin, but in the matter of specific detail the one is as vague as the other is inaccurate. Furthermore, during the years of Shelley's schooling we do not possess the epistolary check, for Shelley's correspondence scarcely begins before his friendship with Hogg, and does not become a thing of moment until he is corresponding with Miss Hitchener, and then with Godwin. The consequence is that the student of Shelley's radicalism cannot expect to be able to work out so close a relationship between reading and writing as is possible later on in Shelley's career.

The second sobering thought has been well expressed by Professor White, who remarks that most of the philosophical thought in *Queen Mab* is "so much the common property of eighteenth-century radical philosophy, and even sometimes of the ancient Epicureans, that it is futile to attempt to assign it to any one particular source."[2]

The Greek Revival, which we regard as the successor of the French revolutionary philosophy in Shelley's affections, was, in comparison, a relatively narrow current of intellectual interest. Coming into being largely as a result of classical archaeology, it was introduced into European thought by a limited number of individuals, about whom, for the most part, we can be very specific. And as part of the Romantic Movement, the Greek Revival is but one of many strands, indeed but one of many revivals.

1. *Vide supra*, p. 14 *et seq.*   2. *Shelley*, I, 292.

The radicalism of the eighteenth century, on the other hand, was a vast sea of thought. In our preoccupation with the French intellectualists, it is doubtful if we conveyed a true notion of its breadth. Extending from Philadelphia to St. Petersburg, from Edinburgh to Naples, it no more than centered in France. Personalities as diverse as Franklin and Catherine the Great, as David Hume and the Abbé Galiani, added their drop of thought or furnished their bit of example. In fact, the more the historian of ideas seeks to isolate the individual's contribution, the more he is aware of the difficulty of the problem. Brailsford, for instance, after his study of the philosophy of Godwin, finds only the latter's anarchism to be original; the rest to be revolutionary doctrines of the hour.[3] Yet we may ask if even this anarchism did not come from Rousseau, the tenor of so much of whose writings is starkly individualistic and whose influence upon Godwin is an assured fact. Indeed, when the philosophers of the eighteenth century are not borrowing from one another, they seem to be borrowing from their predecessors—from Hobbes and Saint-Évremond and Locke.

Yet, to paraphrase Locke, the candle that is set up for us shines bright enough for our purposes, and if we cannot give so detailed an account of Shelley's radicalism as we can of his Hellenism, at least the general outline is clear. We know when Shelley's thoughts began turning in the radical direction, and through what intellectual influence.

It is clear, for instance, that one of the first intellectual influences in Shelley's life was the influence of science. Before Shelley went to Eton, while he was still at Syon House Academy, he was an enthusiastic attender of Adam Walker's lectures, which, as Professor White remarks, covered every branch of science in which Shelley subsequently showed any interest.[4] Professor White observes, "Immediately after these lectures were delivered we begin to hear of chemical and electrical experiments at Field Place and Syon House and of excited speculation inspired in the schoolboy by the possibilities of telescope and microscope."[5] Nor was the stimulus lost when Shelley went to Eton, for Walker lectured there as well as at Syon House, and must have repeated his course two or three times during the six years that Shelley was at Eton.[6] That the interest thus aroused persisted, few will deny who have read Hogg's inimitable account of the young scientist's quarters at University College. Even a year later, in November, 1811, when Shelley had departed on the road of social and political reform and had acquired a family, we find him writing to Miss Hitchener of lecturing to his womenfolk upon the nature of the atmosphere, and of illustrating his talk by means of experiments

---

3. *Shelley, Godwin, and Their Circle*, p. 87.
4. *Op. cit.*, I, 22.   5. *Idem*, I, 23.   6. Cf. *idem*, I, 40.

with hydrogen gas, the flames of which were seen at a distance and alarmed the countryside.[7] Shelley never lost his interest in science.

Thus one of the earliest and most abiding interests of Shelley's life was one of the earliest and most abiding interests of the eighteenth century. From Mme. du Châtelet to Rousseau, from Father Beccaria to Thomas Paine, an interest in science was almost universal, and Shelley's early experiments show him to have been a precocious but not an unusual boy.

From his earliest years Shelley was also an avid reader of contemporary fiction. Medwin tells of the six-penny novels brought back to Syon House at the conclusion of the holidays, the thrillers of an earlier age, telling of "haunted castles, bandits, murderers, and other grim personages."[8] These Shelley devoured, and when the stock was exhausted the local circulating library was placed in toll. Here the staple was Richardson, Fielding, and Smollett. But Shelley found these authors too realistic, and preferred Mrs. Radcliffe, or such a fanciful writer as Robert Paltock.[9]

At Eton the dearth of information as regards Shelley's reading becomes especially apparent. Shelley was now separated from Medwin and had not, of course, begun his friendship with Hogg. As a result, for the six years of Shelley's stay at Eton we are acquainted with less than a dozen titles, and not all of these can be set down as unassailable fact.[10]

Yet the composition of *Zastrozzi* while Shelley was still at Eton is evidence enough that Shelley's taste for the novel of terror had not diminished. In fact it is clear that until Shelley went to Oxford there are only two intellectual currents in his life worthy of the biographer's regard: an enthusiasm for science and a fondness for Gothic fiction. Not only is this the conclusion to be drawn from such meager facts as we possess with respect to Shelley's reading, but it is borne out by the evidence that comes from vacation time at Field Place. Here the anecdotes are all of home experimentation and of the spell of Gothic romance. Shelley's boyish resolve to adopt a vagrant child Professor White would explain, not as an application of Universal Benevolence, but simply as an imitation of the adoptions romanticized in Robert Paltock's novel *Peter Wilkins*.[11] Nor is the discussion of free love toward the end of *Zastrozzi* at variance with the fiction of the period, which would embrace radicalism as readily as romance, if thereby it could produce a thrill. As Professor White points out,[12] even the radicalism of *St. Irvyne* (which followed *Zastrozzi*) is not unlike that of *St. Leon*, which we know that Shelley read while at

7. Julian *Works*, VIII, 203.
9. Cf. *idem*, p. 25; White, *op. cit.*, I, 24–26.
11. *Idem*, I, 26.

8. *Revised Life of Shelley*, p. 24.
10. Cf. White, *op. cit.*, I, 51–52.
12. *Idem*, I, 90; cf. pp. 52, 577.

Eton, and which is in the full stream of romantic and sentimental fiction.

As a matter of fact it is not necessary to assume an early espousal of radicalism to fill any gap in the story of Shelley's life. Shelley's early partiality for science and for the literature of Gothic terror reflects both sides of Shelley's nature, the intellectual and the emotive, the radical and the romantic, the two sides which strikingly carry their duality throughout Shelley's life. When we add to these two reigning enthusiasms the peculiarities of Shelley's personality, it is clear that no further element is needed to explain the Shelley who went up to Oxford in October, 1810.

It would seem to have been Hogg who turned Shelley's mind in the new direction. This is not to imply that Hogg was any radical himself. But he had no enthusiasm for science, and was more than a little dubious about the amateur experimentation he saw going on in Shelley's chambers. He tells us that he deliberately endeavored to turn Shelley toward ethics, his own favorite study,[13] and Professor White observes that Shelley's interest in the physical sciences waned perceptibly after their first meetings.[14] Thus it would seem to be clear that Shelley's interest in social and political questions dates from the beginning of his university career. In any event, we observe that it was some time after his arrival at Oxford that his attention was directed to that celebrated work which twenty years earlier had appealed to other temperaments of a nature similar to his own. On November 19, Shelley ordered a copy of *Political Justice* from Stockdale, his publisher.[15] That the work made an immediate impression upon him is evident from his letters to Hogg of the succeeding Christmas vacation, which quote Godwin and reveal that Shelley was seeking his address.[16]

The first fruit of Shelley's new interest in the moral rather than in the physical sciences was *The Necessity of Atheism*, which was written early in 1811, not long after Shelley's introduction to Godwin. According to Hogg, Shelley had also been reading Locke and Hume,[17] and we observe that the agnostic thinking of Shelley's pamphlet is built upon the usual empirical objections to revelation and to the assumptions of pure reason. But whether the thinking came directly

13. Hogg, *Life of Shelley* (Wolfe edition), I, 74.
14. *Op. cit.*, I, 80.
15. Julian *Works*, VIII, 19. Those readers interested in conjecturing whether Shelley was acquainted with *Political Justice* before coming to Oxford, and in Shelley's own mystification of the matter, are referred to White, *op. cit.*, I, 577, 620–621.
16. Cf. Julian *Works*, VIII, 25, 46; also White, *op. cit.*, I, 98.
17. *Op. cit.*, I, 163. Hogg reports that he and Shelley read *"Locke concerning Human Understanding* and Hume's *Essays."* By the latter must be meant Hume's *Enquiry*, earlier known as the "Philosophical Essays" and containing the essay "Of Miracles," the argument of which appears in *The Necessity of Atheism*.

from Locke and Hume, or indirectly by way of Godwin, there is nothing either particularly new or particularly interesting in Shelley's use of it.

What is interesting is that Shelley should be directing his empirical arguments toward a religious issue. For the religious problem is not stressed in Locke and Hume, and is conspicuously lacking from the pages of Godwin. Clearly, in Shelley's preoccupation with the problem of the existence of a deity, we are witnessing an intrusion of that subjective element which in the second chapter of this study we avowed as one of the objects of our inquiry. That it was a real preoccupation, Shelley's early letters to Miss Hitchener in the summer of 1811 plainly show. Professor White suggests, in fact, that the shift in the course of this correspondence from religion to politics was at her request.[18]

The shift from religion to politics, first noticeable in the summer of 1811, becomes more marked after Shelley's marriage and the resumption from York of his correspondence with Miss Hitchener. As Professor White points out, Shelley's letters now betray an increasing hostility to soldiers and commerce,[19] and in December comes the first mention of the Irish project.[20]

Yet Shelley did not lose his interest in religion. *Queen Mab* abundantly testifies that the question of atheism remained a burning issue. In fact, we can only conclude that Shelley's persistent interest in the question of a deity's existence reveals an unusual concern for the unseen world, a concern not shared by Locke and Hume and Godwin. Hogg points out that atheism, if it was to be found in Shelley at all, "was only to be found in his words and arguments," that "his turn of mind was towards superstition, by no means towards irreligion and materialism." [21] Southey, no less than Hogg, was impressed by the essential religiousness of Shelley and, as Shelley reported to Miss Hitchener, sought to convince him that he was a pantheist, not an atheist.[22]

Let us return, though, for a moment, to the five-week stay in Edinburgh, which preceded the sojourns in York and Keswick, as these preceded the trip to Ireland.

To us, perhaps the most interesting thing about the stay in Edinburgh is the extension that it witnessed of Shelley's reading to the French philosophers. Hogg, who arrived in Edinburgh a few days after the elopers, tells of the armfuls of books Shelley got from some public or private library. "There were several French books," Hogg says; "some works of the modern French philosophers, and some of

18. *Op. cit.*, I, 147.   19. *Idem*, I, 193–194.
20. Shelley to Miss Hitchener, December 11, 1811, Julian *Works*, VIII, 214.
21. *Op. cit.*, I, 93–94.
22. Shelley to Miss Hitchener, January 2, 1812, Julian *Works*, VIII, 227.

the immortal Buffon."[23] In fact, Shelley formally set about translating a treatise of the latter's.

All this is interesting because it is another item in the accumulation of evidence that *Political Justice* was Shelley's introduction to radicalism. Godwin's work, it would seem, aroused Shelley to go to Godwin's sources, first to Locke and Hume (whom Shelley read while at Oxford), and then to the French writers, whom Medwin observed Shelley consulting in the British Museum in the summer of 1811,[24] and whom Harriet was led to read aloud in the following autumn.[25] Such loosely remembered scraps of information as Shelley's citing Condorcet one day to Medwin (apparently in the *St. Irvyne* period)[26] scarcely alter the general impression that Shelley's acceptance of the French Revolutionary philosophy was the result of his acquaintance with *Political Justice,* and was always viewed through Godwin's eyes.

But let us turn to the excursion to Ireland, which took place in the months of February and March, 1812, and was as logical a consequence of Shelley's continued radicalism as was *The Necessity of Atheism* of his original conversion. By January, Shelley's letters to Miss Hitchener are full of the project, and he is already at work upon the first pamphlet of the crusade, *An Address to the Irish People.*

The unprejudiced observer must be struck immediately by the essential unreality of the whole scheme. And it is not that Shelley was intending merely to conduct a campaign of pamphleteering instead of organizing bands of insurgents or initiating other bold steps of action. Tom Paine, who was much in Shelley's mind as a model, had shown once and for all that it is enough to be a pamphleteer. But Paine had sailed to America before writing his pamphlets—not in messianic fervor, but to better himself, perhaps as a clerk, perhaps as a tutor, perhaps as a surveyor. When his essay against the slave trade appeared in the *Pennsylvania Magazine* in March, 1775, he had had ample time to witness at first hand the slave market in Philadelphia. *Common Sense* was written the next autumn, some six or seven months after Lexington, when the events of the year were crying out for interpretation. The first *Crisis* pamphlet was composed by a soldier who had participated in the retreat to the Delaware. Paine's pamphleteering, we note, was always occasioned by circumstances, and was effective because clearly in answer to the times.[27]

This is just what we do not notice about Shelley's brief career as a latter-day Paine. He approached the Irish question not because it needed him but because he needed it. He went to Ireland because he had generated so much humanitarian fervor that he had to go

23. *Op. cit.,* I, 263.   24. Medwin, *op. cit.,* p. 92.   25. Cf. Hogg, *op. cit.,* I, 373. 26. Medwin, *op. cit.,* p. 50.

27. The facts in this paragraph are taken from Moncure Daniel Conway, *The Life of Thomas Paine* (2 vols. New York, 1892).

somewhere. His enthusiasm was, in fact, at fever pitch before he ever set foot on Irish soil, and the first of his Irish pamphlets was already written. "There is no indication," says Professor White, "that Shelley made anything like a thorough study of the situation before he embarked on his venture. Despite his really remarkable powers of intellectual assimilation he was probably no better informed than all the other English friends of the Irish who, according to their intended beneficiaries, never understood the situation sufficiently to make their aid effective."[28] Nor did Shelley plan, apparently, to offer aid except in the very, very long run. For in the *Address to the Irish People* (of which his second pamphlet is but a recasting) he offers no program save that of cultivation of the moral virtues, from which political reform in due course is supposed to follow. As Professor White observes, "He preached temperance to a people to whom drink was almost the only refuge from reality, and the cultivation of knowledge to a people who were tragically without the means of cultivating it. The great majority of them were unable even to read his exhortation."[29]

But, strangest of all, this new apostle of social and political reform never intended to stay in Ireland more than a few months, less time than would have enabled Paine to discover what the issues were. From Shelley's letters to Miss Hitchener it becomes clear that the whole Irish venture is but an affair of the passing moment, of no more consequence than his scheme for the following summer in Wales, in which he envisions the founding of a revolutionary seminary "in some antique feudal castle whose mouldering turrets are fit emblems of decaying inequality and oppression; whilst the ivy shall wave its green banners above like liberty, and flourish upon the edifice that essayed to crush its root."[30]

Clearly our young radical is more poet than reformer, and after the discouraging results in Ireland, it would not be surprising if he were content to confine his radicalism to poetry.

In other words, as Shelley sails from Ireland to found his revolutionary seminary in an antique Welsh castle, it is necessary to distinguish between a radical and a reformer. The one does not imply the other. The radical, we take it, is simply a man who has gone, or tried to go, to the roots, or *radices*, of things for his view of a new and truer world. He may be a jurist like Bentham, or a psychologist like Condillac. Occasionally he is a reformer like Tom Paine, but not necessarily. No man, for instance, could have been less of a reformer than the Baron D'Holbach, perhaps the most radical thinker of the eighteenth century.

Thus, though the end of the Irish adventure may mark the end of

28. *Op. cit.*, I, 207. 29. *Idem*, I, 215.
30. Shelley to Miss Hitchener, January 26, 1812, Julian *Works*, VIII, 253.

Shelley's career as a reformer, it by no means marks the end, or even signalizes a diminution, of his radicalism. We find him reading the *Système de la nature* immediately after his return from Ireland,[31] and setting about a translation of it in the course of the summer.[32] Before the year was over, he had ordered from the booksellers Hartley, Mary Wollstonecraft, Diderot, Condorcet, and even the French *Encyclopedia* (little realizing, apparently, that it was an affair of ponderous folio volumes, presupposing servants to lug it about as in the tale Voltaire tells of the *souper* at the Trianon). Furthermore, there is the indignant *Letter to Lord Ellenborough,* more radical than either of the Irish pamphlets; and finally there is *Queen Mab* itself, most radical of poems. Clearly the year 1812 saw not a diminution but a growth in Shelley's radicalism.

Yet it is no less clear that Shelley's zeal for reform never recovered from the disappointments and disillusionments of the trip to Ireland. In spite of Daniel Hill's posting Shelley's *Declaration of Rights* on the walls of Barnstaple (and being arrested for it), in spite of Shelley's private dispersal of twenty-five or fifty copies of the *Letter to Lord Ellenborough* (without the name of printer or author), it is clear that the energy which in Ireland had gone into dropping pamphlets from balconies, thrusting them into women's hoods, and giving them by hand to likely-looking passers-by, in Lynmouth was expended in consigning them to the waves in glass bottles and waxed boxes, and to the air in balloons. Clearly publication is now of less importance than composition. Shelley's radicalism has passed from the active to the passive stage. He will print, but he will not publish.

Thus *Queen Mab,* for all its being the culmination of Shelley's radicalism and the veritable Bible of the Owenites after Shelley's death, was pirated but never published. As with the *Letter to Lord Ellenborough,* Shelley sent it only to a limited number of individuals, removing the title page and all signs of authorship and printing. In his entire life not more than seventy copies were distributed.

Will it be any wonder, then, if Shelley's radicalism in its turn tends to wane? It is all very well to resign oneself to the loss of the pleasure of publication, but even to write one needs encouragement—a commodity that the waves and the air are hardly constituted to bestow. To be sure, D'Holbach did not experience the satisfaction (and danger) of receiving credit for his work. But he saw it published and widely circulated. The success of the *Système de la nature* led him to popularize it, and then to write a *Système social* and other radical works. But Shelley did not have the satisfaction even of secret success. He wrote, and that was almost literally the end of it.

31. Shelley to Godwin, June 3, 1812, *idem*, viii, 331.
32. Shelley to Thomas Hookham, August 18, 1812, *idem*, ix, 20.

Furthermore, can we avoid asking ourselves if Shelley was really a radical? Does not radicalism require a certain objective concern for the world? Can a person so subjective as Shelley, for whom the chief need is inner need, really be a radical? It is clear that Rousseau can be called a radical only by an extension of the meaning of the term, that his fundamental message was not outer and practical, but inner and spiritual. We have seen that Godwin's radicalism in the end gave way to something quite different in its implications. Did Shelley possess, we ask, the mental constitution to cope with the oppressions and tyrannies of a real world, and offer a radical solution therefor?

In the hope at least of a partial answer, let us turn to *Queen Mab.*

2. Queen Mab

THE plot of *Queen Mab* is of the simplest. Queen Mab, a fairy, comes to the sleeping Ianthe, a beautiful girl with blue eyes and golden hair, to conduct her to her palace in distant space. The two, in Mab's magic car, voyage through the universe of Newton and Laplace until the earth, far behind, assumes its proportionate place as "the smallest light that twinkles in heaven." Finally they arrive at the fairy's palace, the Hall of Spells, and Mab and Ianthe enter. They proceed to an over-hanging battlement, from which point of vantage they can the better view the universe, and the better conceive of time itself.

The excursion, we perceive, was planned solely to bring Ianthe to a suitable place of instruction, and once the battlement has been attained, Mab plunges into the discourse which was the object of bringing Ianthe hither. Indeed, except for a few interlocutory remarks from Ianthe, the cry of a conscience-ridden king, and the diatribe that Ahasuerus, the Wandering Jew, is summoned to deliver against Christianity, the rest of the poem is a monologue on the part of Queen Mab. There is no further action until the last twenty or thirty lines, when the soul of Ianthe returns to her body, and the united personality awakes to meet the gaze of Henry, Ianthe's lover.

In other words, the poem is a philosophical poem, the most purely philosophical poem that Shelley ever wrote. In *Prometheus Unbound* and *Hellas* there are the conventions of the drama to pay some heed to. In *Adonais* there is the pattern of the formal Greek elegy, while in *Alastor* and *Epipsychidion* there is a theme of narrative and of auto-biographical interest. But in *Queen Mab* everything is subordinated to the philosophic discourse that composes the bulk of the poem. At the very beginning, a position is sought outside of life. The poem will look at life from the grand view, *sub specie aeternitatis*. Yet the poem is also connected with life and presented as the experience of a living being. The soul of a human being voyages outside its body that it may look whence it came, and we may expect that life in its daily as well as in its eternal aspect will be reviewed.

Mab's long discourse, we note, follows a rough plan. She announces that it is to embrace the past, the present, and the future. But the division is not equal. The past is largely covered in the second canto, and although the future receives a greater emphasis, constituting the chief subject matter of the last two cantos, by far the greatest portion of the poem is given over to the present, and to the ideas which the present suggests. In the central four or five cantos of the poem, we find that monarchy, war, commerce, and religion are successively attacked as the chief ills of contemporary society.

Yet this attack on society, though it gave the poem its notoriety, and indeed its popularity among the radicals, cannot interest us particularly. In the first place, coming fresh from a survey of the radical literature of the eighteenth century, we have the sense of having heard it all before. The woes of inequality, the gulf between the luxury of the few and the poverty of the many, the chicanery of priests, the lust for power of kings, the venality of commerce, the curse of wealth—all this we have met, if not on the pages of one writer, then on those of another. In the second place, as philosophical critics of the poem, we may be pardoned if we are more concerned with point of view and tenor of argument than with substance of attack.

EMOTIONALISM

Thus we are much impressed by the fact that at the very beginning of the poem Shelley should have taken up a strongly spiritualistic stand, a stand that he conveys not merely by assertion but by portrayal. Mab and her chariot are pictured as composed of that very substance which Lamettrie, D'Holbach, and the other materialists had denied. As Mab approaches Iànthe, we read,

> The broad and yellow moon
> Shone dimly through her form—
> That form of faultless symmetry;
> The pearly and pellucid car
>   Moved not the moonlight's line:
> 'Twas not an earthly pageant.

I, 79–84

Furthermore, the soul of Ianthe arises from the body, leaving the latter asleep upon its earthly couch. Indeed, as the spirit of Ianthe prepares to accompany Mab, it pauses for a moment that the contrast between the soul and the body may be fully perceived:

> 'Twas a sight
> Of wonder to behold the body and soul.
>   The self-same lineaments, the same
>   Marks of identity were there:
> Yet, oh, how different! One aspires to Heaven,
> Pants for its sempiternal heritage,
> And ever-changing, ever-rising still,
>   Wantons in endless being.
> The other, for a time the unwilling sport
> Of circumstance and passion, struggles on;
> Fleets through its sad duration rapidly:

Then, like an useless and worn-out machine,
Rots, perishes, and passes.

I, 144–156

Thus we are informed that the soul not only exists as a separate substance, but "wantons in endless being." Shelley advances to the extreme spiritualist position, the position that not merely maintains the soul's existence but proclaims its immortality. We recall that this was the position of the emotionalist Rousseau.

Indeed, the full significance of Shelley's stand is perceived only when it is recognized that the materialists were simply the extreme intellectualists of the eighteenth century. Though an antispiritualistic position is by no means the concomitant of intellectualism (as we shall see when we come to Plato), nevertheless in the eighteenth century intellectualists were not given to much credence in the soul. Perhaps Voltaire's well-known letter to Boswell sums up the middle-of-the-road position of eighteenth-century intellectualism as well as any. Voltaire wrote, "You seem sollicitous about that pretty thing call'd Soul. I do protest you I know nothing of it: nor wether it is, nor what it is, nor what it shall be. Young scolars, and priests know all that perfectly. For my part I am but a very ignorant fellow."[33] We recollect, furthermore, that even Godwin, for all his Rousseauism, remained skeptical when it came to the existence of a soul, and as regards the separate existence of thought from matter would only say, "There are various reasons calculated to persuade us that this last hypothesis is the most probable."[34]

In other words, in spite of the long quotations from D'Holbach in the notes to *Queen Mab*, in spite of the intellectualistic influence of Godwin evident throughout the poem, something within Shelley himself must have led him beyond either of these two mentors to the spiritualist position of Rousseau. The fact leads us to examine the subsequent cantos for further evidence of Shelley's psychologic beliefs.

In the fifth canto we are astonished by what we read. The canto is, on the whole, given over to a picturization of the evils of commerce. But, as in the rest of *Queen Mab*, Shelley's basic philosophical interests are not forgotten, and the fifth canto is also one of the most psychologic in the poem.

For one thing, we note that the canto takes up Godwin's emotionalistic war against selfishness. Queen Mab (who utters the whole of the canto) tells Ianthe that suicidal selfishness will decay like the

33. Voltaire to Boswell, February 11, 1765.
34. *An Enquiry concerning Political Justice*, I, 321. For Godwin's spiritualistic skepticism, see Sir Leslie Stephen's "Godwin and Shelley," *Cornhill Magazine*, xxxix, 287 (*Hours in a Library*, No. xx); also his *History of English Thought in the Eighteenth Century* (New York, 1876), II, 266–267.

leaves of the forest, and that out of the decay will spring all virtue, all delight, all love. We note that spontaneous giving will take the place of buying and selling. Mab observes that commerce is

> the venal interchange
> Of all that human art or nature yield;
> Which wealth should purchase not, but want demand,
> And natural kindness hasten to supply
> From the full fountain of its boundless love.

v, 38–42

Not only in her decrial of commerce, but in her championship of benevolence, Mab is clearly at one with the emotionalists.

More interesting, however, is her statement that when all virtue thus springs out of the decay of selfishness, judgment will

> cease to wage unnatural war
> With passion's unsubduable array.

v, 20–21

Thus the conflict between judgment and passion is unnatural, and is profitless in any event, since passion is not to be subdued.

Further on, Mab tells Ianthe,

> Nature, impartial in munificence,
> Has gifted man with all-subduing will.
> Matter, with all its transitory shapes,
> Lies subjected and plastic at his feet.

v, 132–135

Again, she says that not the mind (as Condorcet and the intellectualists had supposed) but the heart "contains perfection's germ." She declares that

> The wisest of the sages of the earth,
> That ever from the stores of reason drew
> Science and truth, and virtue's dreadless tone,
> Were but a weak and inexperienced boy,
> Proud, sensual, unimpassioned, unimbued
> With pure desire and universal love,
> Compared to that high being, of cloudless brain
> Untainted passion, elevated will,
> Which Death : . . might alone subdue.

v, 148–158

Need we quote at further length? There are, to be sure, other references to man's "unchanging will," to his "unalterable will." But they scarcely add to an expression of the emotionalist point of view that is already complete. The very decrial of commerce is enough to tell us that the author belongs to the school of Rousseau and the emotionalistic Godwin, not to the school of Voltaire and Turgot. What especially interests us is that Shelley theoretically states the position himself, sparing us the need. We are told that perfection lies in the heart, that the wisest man who ever drew truth from reason is but a callow youth in comparison with that emotionalist of untainted passion and elevated will whom death alone can defeat. In fact, it is clear that Shelley advances all the way to the emotionalist extreme, to the voluntarism of Rousseau and the Savoyard vicar. The will is free. Matter lies plastic at man's feet.

INTELLECTUALISM

The opening of the sixth canto affords an opportunity for pause in the sweep of Mab's discourse. She has, in fact, spoken without interruption since early in the third canto, and from the beginning of the fourth canto without varying the blank verse that is her favorite medium of address.

But now Ianthe asks,

> O Fairy! in the lapse of years,
>   Is there no hope in store?
>   Will yon vast suns roll on
> Interminably, still illuming
> The night of so many wretched souls,
>   And see no hope for them?

VI, 15–20

After the grim picture painted in the last three or four cantos, we should have asked the question ourselves had not Ianthe anticipated us. It is to be expected that Shelley's answer, as furnished by Queen Mab, will provide much matter for reflection.

The fairy replies,

> Some eminent in virtue shall start up,
>   Even in perversest time:
> The truths of their pure lips, that never die,
> Shall bind the scorpion falsehood with a wreath
>   Of ever-living flame,
> Until the monster sting itself to death.

VI, 33–38

Thus, as in the intellectualist part of Godwin's philosophy, truth is the engine of good, the panacea that will correct the evils of the earth. The difference is that the victory of the above persons "eminent in virtue" will have an effect upon outer nature. For Mab informs Ianthe that contemporaneously with man's coöperation with the spirit of nature, the angle between the earth's orbit and its axis will be erased, and the inequality of the days and seasons thus removed.

Now the thing that is interesting about this statement is that evidently it is to be taken, not as poetical embellishment, but as sober truth. For Shelley, in a learned note, points to the tropical fossils that have been found in northern climates as evidence of the fact that such an occurrence has happened before, and finds "no great extravagance" in presuming that there should be a perfect identity between the moral and the physical world. In other words, it is clear that Shelley really believed that the force that is at the bottom of the physical world is of the nature of mind, and that perfection in the one realm could not be unaccompanied by perfection in the other. Thus the victory of truth in the moral realm will be accompanied by a victory of truth in the physical realm.

But Mab, for all Ianthe's importunity, is unready to dwell upon that golden time. She has not yet pictured the darkest of all abuses upon the earth. Thus she has no sooner uttered her words of encouragement than she turns to describe the last and worst of the ills of man,

> Religion! . . . prolific fiend,
> Who peoplest earth with daemons, Hell with men,
> And Heaven with slaves!
>
> vi, 69-71

From its animistic childhood and polytheistic youth, Mab traces the history of religion to its maturity, when it conceived of the arch-superstition, God.[35] Dotage followed, and it returned to the polytheism of its youth, to the trinity and hagiology (we must suppose) of the Christian church. In fact, this period is the present one, and religion is even now descending to its darksome grave. Luminous only against the dreadful night that has long lowered over the ruined world, its glare is now fading before the "sun of truth."

The Shelley of Oxford days has not changed. For all the emotionalism of earlier parts of the poem, when it comes to the most emotional of human institutions Shelley cannot contain his rage. Religion is the worst of the afflictions of man. Whereas a single canto apiece had sufficed for the attacks on monarchy, war, and commerce, two are necessary for the attack on Christianity. The attack on Christianity represents, in fact, the climax of the poem, and to understand it we must penetrate, as we did with *Political Justice*, to the basic convictions upon which the thinking rests.

It is clear, for instance, that we must draw a distinction between churchly and scientific temperaments. Shelley would seem to have possessed the latter in its most cosmic aspect. As *Queen Mab* abundantly shows, Shelley naturally lodged in the full universe. The gal-

---

35. Professor Barnard points out that Shelley's brief sketch of the history of religion anticipates the three periods of Comte's "theological" stage (*Shelley, Selected Poems, Essays, and Letters,* "Odyssey Series in Literature" [New York, 1944], p. 13).

axy to his imagination was a more harmonious hostel than any dwelling made by man. When he was in York, the minster and its buildings had seemed to him no more than "gigantic piles of superstition," "retardations of the period when Truth becomes omnipotent."[36] That the function of a church might be to separate man from the outside world, that its secular meaning might be its embodiment of man's search for the inner light, that religion might be human rather than natural—of all this Shelley had not the least idea. The loving, Burkian sense of the human past Shelley was totally without. He no more possessed the temperament to understand traditional religion than he did to understand the long years of human history. Shelley naturally roamed away from what was intensely human to what was intensely cosmic. Mab's palace is symbolic of Shelley's real resting place.

In fact, from her palace, Mab now gives the Shelleyan version of natural religion, uttering the passage we have already quoted:

> Throughout these infinite orbs of mingling light,
> Of which yon earth is one, is wide diffused
> A Spirit of activity and life,
> That knows no term, cessation, or decay.
>
> VI, 146–149

Ianthe is told that this Spirit of activity guides the whirlwind, roars in the tempest, cheers in the day, breathes in the balmy groves, strengthens in health, and poisons in disease. Mab adds,

> Even the minutest molecule of light,
> That in an April sunbeam's fleeting glow
> Fulfils its destined, though invisible work,
> The universal Spirit guides.
>
> VI, 174–177

Nor less, Mab says, does it rule all passions.

> Not a thought, a will, an act,
> No working of the tyrant's moody mind,
> Nor one misgiving of the slaves who boast
> Their servitude, to hide the shame they feel,
> Nor the events enchaining every will,
> That from the depths of unrecorded time
> Have drawn all-influencing virtue, pass
> Unrecognized, or unforeseen by thee,
> Soul of the Universe!
>
> VI, 182–190

Finally comes the climactic passage of the whole poem:

36. Shelley to Miss Hitchener, October 16, 1811, Julian *Works*, VIII, 159.

Spirit of Nature! all-sufficing Power,
Necessity! thou mother of the world!
Unlike the God of human error, thou
Requir'st no prayers or praises.

VI, 197–200

In his flight from the intensely human to the intensely cosmic, it is apparent that Shelley believes he has attained an unanthropomorphic spirituality. He goes out of his way to make this clear. Necessity, the mother of the world, is said to be free of the caprice she yet causes in man, free of the changeful passions in his breast that are nevertheless of her doing. She has no love or hate, though she causes both; no revenge or favoritism or desire of fame, though she necessitates each. The slave and the good man, the poison tree and the fair oak, are equal in her sight. All things that the wide world contains are her passive instruments, which she regards impartially, being unsubject to their joy or pain since she has no human sense, and is not human mind. In fact the shrine to Necessity (which will endure when the last altar to the almighty fiend has been swept away) is the world itself, that "sensitive extension" where pain and pleasure, good and evil, join to do her will.

But has Shelley attained an unanthropomorphic spirituality?

Why, if free from caprice herself, should Necessity occasion caprice in others?[37] If she knows not joy and pain, what is the meaning of it in her creatures? If good and evil are equal in her sight, what reality can be given to them in ours? What is the meaning of good and evil in stellar space? If Necessity is the mother of the world, why should there be anything in addition to physical law, anything in addition to the tireless sweep of planet and orb according to astronomical revolution?

It is not enough to say that Shelley is inconsistent. Why is Shelley inconsistent? For he never wrote a more deeply felt poem. A part of the poem, almost as it now stands, appears in the correspondence with Miss Hitchener written from Ireland in the early days of Shelley's messianic enthusiasm.[38] The inconsistency of *Queen Mab* must spring from deeply settled, yet unresolved, elements within Shelley's own personality.

In Canto V, for instance, we noticed a step-by-step progress along the emotionalist path. There was the hatred of commerce, the faith in natural kindness and in the "full fountain of its boundless love," the belief in the power of man's will. In Canto VI there is a step-

37. For a contemporary expression of this opinion, the reader is referred again to Professor White's *The Unextinguished Hearth*, p. 85.

38. Cf. Dowden, *The Life of Percy Bysshe Shelley*, I, 247–248; White, *op. cit.*, I, 208, 630.

by-step progress along the intellectualist path until we attain the final, eighteenth-century stage, not of free will, but of necessity. We noticed much the same conflict in *Political Justice*. But surely the conflict in *Queen Mab* is several degrees more intense.

Furthermore, the conflict is present from the beginning of Shelley's poem. For there can be no doubt that the excursion to Mab's palace is an excursion to the intellectualist world of Newton and Laplace, to the world that Adam Walker lectured about, to the world of cycle and orbit and period and scientific law. Yet Ianthe is selected to take this journey, not because of aptitude or enthusiasm for science, but for purely emotional reasons—because she is good and sincere, because she has struggled with a resolute will, because she has vanquished earth's pride and meanness. The conflict of points of view is present even in Mab's discourse. For, on the one hand, Ianthe is made conscious of the quiet movement of the celestial bodies according to law, and, on the other, she is made to feel with earth-born passion a hatred for the abuses of the world. From the vantage point of Mab's palace, the abuses of human society should have sunk to insignificance. The earth itself is described as a little light, twinkling in the misty distance. The turbulence of its inhabitants ought surely to have been lost to view. One ought to have had from Mab's palace a poetic *Mécanique céleste*, not a poeticized *Rights of Man*. Shelley travels into the celestial world, but when he arrives there he delivers a human, Rousseauistic philippic against the evils of inequality. He travels the intellectualist path to the determinism of D'Holbach, but he travels with a beautiful girl, and though he ends with necessity, it is a necessity that D'Holbach would never have recognized.

The emotionalist watering of necessity had, in fact, been begun by Godwin, to whom Shelley stands largely in debt. Godwin had found in D'Holbach's determinism not so much physical law as Hume's mere constant conjunction of like phenomena. And, not content with this quasi-subjective explanation of outer necessity, Godwin had conceived of a parallel, spiritual necessity to account for human behavior. Entirely overlooking the fact that motives, according to his own explanation, are tied to exterior phenomena, Godwin nevertheless conceives of a chain of motives independently stretching back into spiritual infinity. Shelley, as is clear from his prose note on Necessity, takes over bodily the whole concept. And Shelley further emotionalizes Necessity by making the chain of motives cause both good and ill. Shelley is, in fact, far more conscious of the problem of good and evil than Godwin and the intellectualists, for whom, in reality, it was not so much a problem of good and evil *per se,* as a problem of rationality and irrationality, of truth and error, of right thinking and wrong thinking. But to Shelley, as should be clear even from the brief passages we have quoted, good and evil enjoy a certain existence in their own right. And as undoubted realities, whether of the moral or physical world, they are both occasioned by Necessity.

Now the problem of good and evil is the most narrowly human problem there is. "Good" means good to us, "evil" means evil to us, and the terms have no meaning in stellar space, apart from the haunts and concerns of man. It makes no sense to say that Necessity is without human sense, without human mind, and yet occasions good and evil, which have no meaning apart from human sense and human mind. In other words, it is clear that Shelley, in his flight from the intensely human to the intensely cosmic, nevertheless carried along an intensely human point of view. Consistently, he should have taken along telescope and astronomical tables. Inconsistently, he took only the equipment with which to study man. And the result of his study is that the force that controls stellar space is the force that controls good and evil among men.

We can only suppose that Necessity thus causes good and evil because, on the one hand, Shelley is aware that the problem of good and evil exists, and because, on the other hand, Shelley's intellectualism, which goes back to the days of Adam Walker and Syon House, can conceive of ultimate explanations only in the terms of scientific law. Yet Shelley does not approach the problem of good and evil as a scientist. His awareness of good and evil in the world is shot through with indignation, with a strong subjective intrusion. Yet, curiously enough, this subjective intrusion is unaccompanied by a sense of inner life, of personal experience apart from the experience of the many. Religion in the ordinary sense, as we have observed, is incomprehensible to Shelley. Shelley's subjectivity would appear to be curiously objective in its content.

In other words, it is clear that in *Queen Mab* there is a strange mixture of humanitarianism and science, of intellectualism and emotionalism, of D'Holbach and Rousseau; and that these elements have been relatively unthought out, and are being set down on paper in a man's first expression.

Which is the more fundamental side of Shelley's personality? Which side will win out? Fortunately we are not left in doubt, for the last two cantos of the poem present Shelley's version of the Golden Age. As with Rousseau and Godwin, it cannot but be that this portrait of an idealized world will tell us of the real Shelley, of the real Shelley that exists beneath the clutter of unassimilated elements in the earlier portions of the poem.

UTOPIANISM

Perhaps the most striking thing about the picture of the future that Mab unrolls before Ianthe's gaze in Canto VIII is the physical change that has come over the earth. In truth, we were not entirely unprepared for it, for it is the result of the disappearance of the obliquity of the earth's axis, prophesied earlier in the poem. In the arctic and in the antarctic,

> Those wastes of frozen billows that were hurled
> By everlasting snowstorms round the poles

are now unloosed,

> And fragrant zephyrs there from spicy isles
> Ruffle the placid ocean-deep, that rolls
> Its broad, bright surges to the sloping sand,
> Whose roar is wakened into echoings sweet
> To murmur through the Heaven-breathing groves
> And melodize with man's blest nature there.
>
> VIII, 59–69

In the tropics,

> Those deserts of immeasurable sand . . .
> Now teem with countless rills and shady woods,
> Cornfields and pastures and white cottages,

and in place of human and animal bloodshed, the daisy-spangled lawn smiles

> To see a babe before his mother's door,
> Sharing his morning's meal
> With the green and golden basilisk
> That comes to lick his feet.
>
> VIII, 70–87

More noteworthy, however, than any of these phenomena is what has happened to the trackless deep. In order to avoid the monotony of interminable days, and to soften the tempest-waves that have hitherto swept over the sea, the ocean floor has cast up myriads of islands, so that

> Those lonely realms bright garden-isles begem,
> With lightsome clouds and shining seas between,
> And fertile valleys, resonant with bliss,
> Whilst green woods overcanopy the wave,
> Which like a toil-worn labourer leaps to shore,
> To meet the kisses of the flow'rets there.
>
> VIII, 101–106

This is really remarkable. For it presupposes benevolence rather than necessity as constituting the spirit of the universe. Conceivably, if one rejected Laplace's hypothesis of periodicity to the diminishing obliquity of the earth's axis (and Shelley in his note did reject it), in a couple of hundred thousand years the obliquity would have vanished. It could all be construed as the working of necessary law. But the sea could not be spangled with monotony-relieving islands through any such slow working of natural law, since no such process is in evidence now. Nor could accident account for the phenomena, since the islands have come into being expressly for the sake of human good. Only benevolence can account for the phenomena— benevolence and not necessity on the part of the spirit of nature.

Indeed, in the general felicity, the lion is like the lamb, the nightshade poisons no more, and man, who was marked for some abortion of the earth (judging from his stunted stature and imbecile frame), now stands adorning the earth with taintless body and mind,

> Blessed from his birth with all bland impulses,
> Which gently in his noble bosom wake
> All kindly passions and all pure desires.
>
> viii, 200–202

No longer does man eat flesh, the source of all his woes, and as a result,

> No longer now the wingèd habitants,
> That in the woods their sweet lives sing away,
> Flee from the form of man; but gather round,
> And prune their sunny feathers on the hands
> Which little children stretch in friendly sport
> Towards these dreadless partners of their play.
>
> viii, 219–224

In fact, all creatures have lost their terror, and man stands at last an equal among equals. Happiness and science dawn, though late, upon the earth. Reason and passion cease to combat,

> Whilst each unfettered o'er the earth extend
> Their all-subduing energies, and wield
> The sceptre of a vast dominion there;
> Whilst every shape and mode of matter lends
> Its force to the omnipotence of mind,
> Which from its dark mine drags the gem of truth
> To decorate its Paradise of peace.
>
> viii, 232–238

SOCIAL IDEAL

The import of the concluding cantos of *Queen Mab* is thus unmistakable. It is the emotionalist social ideal carried to an unexampled extreme. What in Rousseau had been limited by a real (if idealized) past, and in Godwin by an immediate (if impracticable) future, in Shelley is freed from all limitations whatsoever. Shelley's paradise of peace is projected into that cosmic future when celestial mechanics and the geologic forces of the earth may safely be imagined to coöperate with the emotionalist desires of man. In Shelley's paradise of peace, as the above lines suggest, truth will serve merely as a decoration. No longer must man acquire knowledge for the mastery of nature. Nature will coöperate with man, and every shape and mode of matter will lend its force to the omnipotence of mind. The result is that man can rest completely from labor and spend all his time enjoying the emotions that perfection brings. Mab declares,

> The souls
> That by the paths of an aspiring change
> Have reached thy haven of perpetual peace,
> There rest from the eternity of toil
> That framed the fabric of thy perfectness.
>
> IX, 18–22

It is true that in Rousseau's Genevan ideal the impression of Maypoles, regattas, and other festivals in the open air is frequently stronger than the impression of the industry of the citizens. Yet Rousseau admits that the Genevese subsist entirely upon the fruits of their labor.[39] And though he represents the peasants of Neuchâtel as idyllically "happy and at their ease, free from taxes, imposts and oppressions," yet he states that they cultivate with all diligence the lands of which the property and produce are their own.[40] The radical rejection of labor as part of the social ideal comes first with Godwin. By Spartan simplicity, he reduces it to half an hour. But Shelley reduces it to nothing. For in Shelley's new world it is perpetual spring and autumn, with the flowering season and the harvest ever at hand. There is no need for man to work at all, and, as we have observed, he can spend the entire day enjoying his emotions.

Furthermore, not only is all industry and commerce erased, but every form of civil or political organization. Godwin had permitted a rudimentary parochial organization, and even allowed an assembly of parishes once a year. But in Shelley's new world, when Falsehood finally committed suicide, she left "the moral world without a law." In this happy state of absolute anarchism, as Mab points out,

> Reason was free; and wild though Passion went
> Through tangled glens and wood-embosomed meads,
> Gathering a garland of the strangest flowers,

39. "Letter to d'Alembert," *Miscellaneous Works* (London, 1767), III, 133.
40. *Idem*, III, 87.

Yet like the bee returning to her queen,
She bound the sweetest on her sister's brow,
Who meek and sober kissed the sportive child,
No longer trembling at the broken rod.

ix, 50–56

Man's true nature is good in an absolute way that Rousseau never dared suppose, and passion brings back her *fleurs du mal* to give to her sister reason, and receives a kiss in exchange.

Needless to say, the buildings and structures of tyranny have long been crumbling into ruins. The thorn that usurped the standard of the palace when the revolution came, is by now an old tree. The cathedral is roofless, and within the moldering courts of the decaying prison children play in the sunlight. Soon even these reminders of the past will have disappeared, their elements being molded to happier shapes and becoming ministrant to all blissful impulses. In the following lines, Mab concludes her picture of the future:

Thus human things were perfected, and earth,
Even as a child beneath its mother's love,
Was strengthened in all excellence, and grew
Fairer and nobler with each passing year.

ix, 134–137

In other words, in these last two cantos, Shelley has endeavored to portray a state of human perfection, a state which, as it turns out, receives its meaning from a state of the emotions. Let us make no mistake about this. Reason and truth are barely mentioned in Shelley's sketch of the future. The picture is entirely subservient to the emotions portrayed, emotions which are shared by nature. As the surges fall on the arctic sands, their echoes mingle with man's happiness, and the waves of the vaster ocean leap ashore to meet the kisses of the flowers on the newly risen islands. The lion, the deadly nightshade, the basilisk—all creatures are now filled with benevolence. Shelley's state of perfection is a state of the feelings, and needs only peace and a bounteous nature to be enjoyed.

CONCLUSION

Thus in Shelley a curious tendency reaches completion, a tendency first noticeable in Godwin. Before Godwin, as we have tried to make clear, notions of perfectibility belonged to the intellectualists. Being aware of the accelerated progress of man's mental development, they looked forward to his rapid improvement. But it must be remembered that they spoke of perfectibility rather than of perfection. Even Condorcet in the Tenth Epoch of his *Historical Sketch*, the epoch of the future, talks only about the *perfectionnement*, or improvement, of human beings. To all the intellectualists, the state of perfection was a limit to be approached rather than attained,[41] and to be approached through a utilization of all man's faculties and all the resources of nature and society. It was Godwin who, as far as we are concerned, gave the doctrine of perfectibility its sentimental cast, and in doing so turned from the full life to the narrow. Shelley completed the distortion of this intellectualistic concept. Perfectibility becomes perfection, and a retreat is made even from Godwin's half-hour of work a day.

How appalling the Shelleyan ideal would be to an intellectualist, we need not mention. Whether one considers a Voltaire or an Adam Walker, a Bentham or a Linnaeus, death from immediate and overwhelming boredom would be the inevitable result of residence in Shelley's "Paradise of peace." The Shelleyan ideal represents, in fact, the emotionalist ideal carried to the absolute extreme.

Thus it is not surprising, though it is remarkable, that necessity is not mentioned once in the course of Shelley's portrait of the future. For necessity (like perfectibility) is an intellectualistic concept, and inharmonious with an emotionalistic view of life. We have seen how perfectibility had to be altered to carry an emotionalistic connotation. And, at that, perfectibility is a concept of result rather than of cause. Being comparatively tangible, it could be changed to represent a desirable, emotionalistic end. But necessity, a concept of causality, summoned as often as not to account for the irrational in human affairs, loses all meaning when the human world attains perfection. Shelley espoused the concept, apparently, as a ground for evil. But in Shelley's utopia there is no evil. The fountain of Universal Benevolence takes over, and no man acts because he is constrained. Indeed Benevolence, with its implications of freedom and inexhaustibility, is antithetical to Necessity, and usurps, not shares, the power of the world.

The fact is, as we have already suggested, that the emotionalistic and intellectualistic elements in *Queen Mab* are thoroughly disharmonious with one another, and in their disharmony can only be treated separately and not combined. From a philosophical point of view, *Queen Mab* is a number of poems, not a single poem. There is no indication of that modification of one or another of its component parts that must precede a welding into a single point of view. Prob-

---

41. It is interesting to note that Sir James George Frazer in his Zaharoff lecture on the *Historical Sketch* (Oxford, 1933), p. 18, says of Condorcet, "The last, and not the least interesting, part of his treatise is devoted to speculations on the course which humanity may be expected to follow hereafter in its progress towards that goal of absolute perfection *which it will continually approach without ever actually reaching.*" The italics are ours, but one should remember that a large number of the French intellectualists were mathematicians (notably D'Alembert and Condorcet), and that one should ascribe to many of their philosophical ideas a mathematical strictness of definition.

ably the issue will hinge upon the problem of good and evil, a problem which, as we have seen, preoccupies Shelley even in Mab's palace, yet a problem for which he offers no solution. For it is not enough to say that Necessity, the mother of the world, occasions both good and evil. For good is good, and evil is evil, and if Necessity causes both, then she is as evil as she is good, and cannot be the object of veneration that the enthusiastic temperament requires. Unless we are much mistaken, Shelley will return to the problem of good and evil.

In the meantime, we must turn abruptly from our present concerns to the current of intellectual interest that was preparing in the eighteenth century to rescue Shelley from his dilemma. According to our preliminary survey, we have reason to believe that the Greek Revival, tentatively in 1815, conclusively in 1817, stepped in to harmonize the differences between intellectualism and emotionalism, between radicalism and idealism, between the determinism of *Queen Mab* and the voluntarism of *Prometheus Unbound*.

The Greek Revival [1]

1. Introduction

IN our brief sketch of the intellectual history of the eighteenth century we followed, in the main, three different trends of thought: the rational, the empirical, and the emotional. We noted that these three trends went back to the seventeenth century (where we rather arbitrarily began our study), and that these trends were by no means isolated one from another. We saw that the empirical tendency (always present in the form of science) came to modify the rational tendency, and that the emotional tendency, even as it reacted from the modified rational tendency, in many ways returned to the original rational tendency. Furthermore we observed that Rousseau and Saussure, although emotionalists, were by no means hostile to science, which may be said also of the romantic poets Shelley and Novalis. In tracing the strands that make up the thought of an age, one is impressed with the fact that they are strands, that they weave and interweave, in and out of a greater fabric.

With these ideas in mind we must now push our thinking farther back than we have yet done—to the beginning not of the seventeenth but of the fourteenth century. For the Greek Revival, even as it appeared in the eighteenth century, cannot really be understood without a comprehension of its appearance in the Renaissance, and its appearance in the Renaissance cannot be understood without an awareness of the role of Petrarch, though for him Greek remained all but a closed door.

It has long been recognized, in fact, that a literary movement may be materially hastened or retarded by the stature of its leaders.[2] In England, though the beginnings of the Romantic Movement may be detected as early as the commencement of the eighteenth century,[3]

1. The reader's indulgence is asked once again for a chapter based upon secondary rather than upon primary sources. It is our opinion that, although the Greek Revival of the eighteenth century directed Shelley's attention to the Greeks, Shelley took his ideas not from the Revival but from the Greeks themselves. Hence we must leave the thought of the Greeks until Shelley became acquainted with the Greeks. Here we can give only the highlights of the movement that presented the Greeks to Shelley.

2. So William Lyon Phelps, *The Beginnings of the English Romantic Movement* (Boston, 1893), p. 47; Henry A. Beers, *A History of English Romanticism in the Eighteenth Century* (New York, 1898), p. 384; and others.

3. Cf. John Philips' *The Splendid Shilling* (1705), Thomas Parnell's *A Night Piece on Death* (published posthumously, 1722), etc.

men of the first literary rank did not appear until the beginning of
the nineteenth century, not until Wordsworth, Scott, and Coleridge.
In Germany the contrary is true. Although the movement started
nearly a half-century later than in England, with the Swiss Controversy, men of genius quickly rallied to the standard, and before the
end of the century the movement's heyday had been reached. In fact,
these men of genius were of such stature that to our astonished ears
the Germans speak of their age as the *klassische Epoche,* in contradis-
tinction to the period that followed, which they term the *romantische
Schule.* Thus the authors of *Werther* and *Die Räuber* are classical
presumably because great; the writers from Hölderlin to Heine romantic presumably because not so great. Yet our interest here is not
in the meaning of terms but in the early and late emergence of men of
genius.

Perhaps the earliest of these men of genius to appear in any age
was Francesco Petrarch. Even Æschylus, though he founded almost
single-handed the drama as we know it, found one actor already upon
the stage and had only to add a second. But Petrarch was without
heralds. Dante, the contemporary of his father and his father's fellow-
exile from Florence, was an interpreter of medieval culture. But Petrarch possessed a different point of view. As has been said so many
times, he was the first modern man.[4]

Indeed, it would be possible to write Petrarch's biography, leaving
out all names and dates, but including all salient facts and happenings,
so that one would think it the life of a great Romantic, rather than
the life of a great Restorer of Learning. There would be trips to
the tops of wild mountains and musings in the presence of woods
and waterfalls. There would be the fire of patriotism, the notion of
a national unity transcending all clefts and divisions. There would
be an illegitimate child or two, and a thirst for notoriety along with a
deprecation of fame and celebrity. Above all, there would be a general inconsistency of conduct and principle, a yearning both for society and nature, a combination perhaps of too many sides of life.

Why, then, in the reaction to medievalism, in the desire for a new
and fuller life, did not all the traits of the later Romantic Movement
spring forth in the Renaissance? That they were present at the start
seems inescapable.

The answer would appear to lie in the conditions of the Renaissance
itself. At its commencement the Renaissance was without the books
of antiquity, without the learning of the past; and the restoration
of this learning proved to be the task not of a man, nor even of a

4. So Ernest Renan, *Averroès* (Paris, ed. of 1861), p. 328; Pierre de Nolhac, *Petrarch
and the Ancient World* (Boston, 1907), p. 5; Irving Babbitt, *Rousseau and Romanticism*
(Boston and New York, 1919), p. 273; and many others.

generation, but of an age. Furthermore, not only did the restoration of this learning prove to be a quest beyond all expectation exciting and absorbing in its own right, but it offered the surest way to that fuller knowledge which must precede any expansion of life itself.

No doubt the moment that attends the discovery of new lands or truths repays the toil and trouble of the search. But at the beginning nò man will toil and labor if he hears that what he wants to know is in a book. Though the quest of new knowledge may prove the most exciting of human endeavors, it only becomes so when one has reasonable assurance that one is leaving the frontiers of the already known. Man's instinct as well as his better judgment prompts him to look first in books.

And so it was with Petrarch. Though his interests ranged from experiments in scientific gardening to *canzonieri* in the vernacular, there is no doubt that the real passion of his life was for books. Toward the end of his life it became his only passion. Then we find him surrounded by half a dozen copyists at a time, and taken up with schemes for a great public library to be built around his private library. Indeed, it is doubtful if the first sight of Laura in the church of St. Claire at Avignon was as memorable a moment in his life as his first sight in Verona of the manuscript of Cicero's letters to Atticus. If his sonnets are filled with the former event, his letters are filled with the latter. For the first time it was possible to look into the life of the ancients. The past took on a reality it had not enjoyed before. Petrarch writes that in after years he kept his copy of the letters on a special lectern in the very entrance of his library.[5] Indeed, the way in which Petrarch's philological interests came to supplant all others may be looked upon as an earnest of the Renaissance to come. Even without the introduction of printing into Europe a century later, there is little doubt that the Renaissance would, in the main, have been literary and bookish. For at Petrarch's death in 1374 the principal job was yet to be done. He had accomplished much in the revival of Latin learning, but he knew almost no Greek, and at his death the greater part of classical literature was still to be restored.

In fact, the psychological determinist would say that the thirst for books led to the invention of the printing press, just as the closing of the trade routes to the East was at the bottom of the discovery of the New World. Be this as it may, there can be little doubt that the invention of printing in the fifteenth century finally determined that the Renaissance should be largely scholarly and literary.

What is more difficult to conceive is the full scope of the bookish and literary quality of the Renaissance. It is difficult now to recognize

5. Cf. Pierre de Nolhac, *op. cit.*, p. 119. M. de Nolhac points out that our sole manuscript for these letters today is a copy of Petrarch's copy.

that men once looked at the past solely through the medium of the printed word; that the ancient world to the people of the Renaissance was a world of report, of opinion, of account; that on the whole the learning which the Renaissance restored was abstract rather than concrete. Yet between the Renaissance viewed as the Restoration of Learning, and the rationalism of the seventeenth century which we have already dwelt upon, it is clear that there is an unbroken continuity, that the two are, in fact, the same current of human thought.

Perhaps a study of anachronism will make the bookishness of the Renaissance more vivid. In our American schools the first experience with anachronism usually comes with the reading of *Julius Caesar*. In the eighth, ninth, or tenth grade the great play is read as an introduction to Shakespeare, and the teacher unfailingly points out that the Romans did not wear hats about their ears, that they did not tell time by clocks which strike, and that their books did not have leaves like our own.

The real awakening, however, comes later. Usually in college, the thoughtful student perceives, almost with a shock, that the past was without a sense of its own past in any realistic way. Perhaps he reads about the jousting outside the walls of Minoan Athens; perhaps his study of the Elizabethan stage makes him aware of the fact that the Elizabethans actually played *Julius Caesar* in ruff and doublet; or perhaps in an old *Cato* he perceives an engraving of that protagonist as portrayed in 1713 in the glory of buckled shoes, knee breeches, and full-bottomed wig. Perhaps a trip abroad takes him to some such curiosity as the great doors of the cathedral at Hildesheim where the crucifixion is rendered with much graphic detail, but where the walls of Jerusalem are turreted as in Grimm's fairy tales, the Marys depicted as so many Brünhildes, and the Roman soldiers given long, tilting spears and medieval visors.[6] The Renaissance may have brought back the literature of antiquity, but it did not alter the conception men had of that antiquity. There is no advance in this respect from Chaucer to Shakespeare, none from the bronze doors of Hildesheim to the stage properties of *Cato*. The movement which had started out as a reaction to the Middle Ages came in many ways to be a continuity of the Middle Ages.

The historical sense was, indeed, not born before the eighteenth century. Mornet tells us that "throughout the 17th century, and at the beginning of the 18th, history was not to be distinguished from eloquence, panegyric, or the diverting and moralizing novel," that until the very end of the eighteenth century many historians continued "to apply the rules of rhetoric rather than those of his-

6. The doors were executed during the episcopacy (992–1022) of Bernward, tutor to Otto III. The above is a travel impression, and may be slightly inaccurate as to detail.

torical research and criticism." He points out that, with the discovery of the ruins of Herculaneum and Pompeii, a real and living Rome replaced the oratorical and bookish Rome of the colleges, and that the Abbé Barthélemy's *Voyage of the Young Anacharsis* is really a *Telemachus* in which historical curiosity and archaeological research have taken the place of moral teaching.[7]

The theater is no exception to the rule. "The drama until about 1750," Mornet observes, "remains as conventional as that of the 17th century. The stage is still encumbered with benches for spectators; the Greeks, Romans, or Turks wear wigs or hoop petticoats and slaves wear most elaborate diamonds." The change occurs after the middle of the century. "On the stage toward 1750–1760," Mornet writes, "the peasants of the comic opera are clad in veritable peasant garb, with simple dresses, aprons, wooden shoes. Mlle. Clairon wears Oriental garments to represent Roxane, chains to represent the slave, Electra. The benches on the stage disappear in 1759."[8]

The change, as we need scarcely point out, is but part of that general empirical trend which we have already described, a tendency that begins with Tycho Brahe, Galileo, and the other scientists of the late sixteenth and early seventeenth centuries. We have seen how this tendency grew until finally it came to modify the prevailing rationalism. It is no accident that at the time when Locke and Newton were directing men's thoughts toward the world of experience, Voltaire, as Mornet points out,[9] should have been turning to unpublished memoirs, documents, and governmental archives as the materials of his histories. The historical sense was born of eighteenth-century empiricism and needed only the impact of the Romantic Movement to give birth in its turn to that dominating idea of nineteenth-century thought, the idea of development.

The Greek Revival of the eighteenth century was part and parcel of the general empirical trend. On the one hand, it was a result of the emergence of the historical sense; on the other, it contributed of its own account to the growth of that sense. Rendered dramatic by the discoveries at Herculaneum and Pompeii,[10] and represented in England by such books as Robert Wood's *Ruins of Palmyra* and the *Ionian Antiquities* of Chandler, Revett, and Pars,[11] the Greek Revival of the eighteenth century restored a classical past that was now in

7. For this paragraph, cf. Mornet, *French Thought in the 18th Century*, pp. 161–163.
8. For this paragraph, cf. *idem*, pp. 166–167.
9. *Idem*, pp. 162–163.
10. The conventional dates are 1738 and 1748. However, the excavations at Pompeii were not systematically pursued until 1763, while after the death of Alcubierre in 1780 those at Herculaneum languished.
11. London, 1753 and 1769. These volumes, although not the most important of the revival, are representative of it. In large, luxurious folio, they show both the scientific tendency to be accurate and the romantic tendency to be nostalgic.

three dimensions instead of in two. In so doing it supplied the dimension of empirical reality to the literature that the Renaissance had already recovered, and thus disclosed, as we need not add, a romantic source of emotion.

But before turning to this eighteenth-century revival it will be necessary to examine more narrowly the Greek Revival of the Renaissance, the revival that, after all, furnished the literature which the second revival could be romantic about.

2. The Greek Revival in the Renaissance

THE Greek Revival in the Renaissance is usually conceived as beginning with the appointment of Manuel Chrysoloras in 1396 as professor of Greek in the University of Florence. It is true that before this, in 1360, Boccaccio had secured the appointment of Leontius Pilatus to the same post. But the appointment had ended in failure—perhaps because the appointee was only a pinchbeck Greek, a mere Calabrian, scarcely qualified to arouse real enthusiasm. We recall that, in spite of a three-year sojourn in Florence, Pilatus left without even having taught his sponsor Greek.

But the appointment of Chrysoloras was a different matter. A member of a distinguished Byzantine family, he had been professor of philosophy and rhetoric at the University of Constantinople, and already, in 1393, had been an envoy of the emperor, Manuel Palaeologus, to the West. After four years at Florence, Chrysoloras moved on to Pavia and Rome. But the seed he sowed took root and flourished, and for a century Florence remained the center of the Greek Revival in the West. In the course of the fifteenth century such distinguished Hellenists as Aurispa, Filelfo, George of Trebizond, and John Argyropulus followed him as professor of Greek at Florence.

From Florence the Hellenic enthusiasm spread to the rest of Italy and led to a great demand for teachers of Greek and Greek manuscripts. In 1423 Aurispa returned from an extended trip to the East with no less than two hundred thirty-eight manuscripts, including the famous Laurentian manuscript of Æschylus, Sophocles, and Apollonius Rhodius. Four years later, Filelfo returned from his eight-year stay in Constantinople with a similar loot. As late as 1492 we find John Lascaris, the agent of Lorenzo, returning with two hundred manuscripts from Mount Athos alone.[12] It is not too much to say that the whole of Greek literature suddenly arrived in Italy in the fifteenth century.

The flood of manuscripts from the East was accompanied by a migration of scholars. Nor was this merely a consequence of the capture of Constantinople. As the late John Edwin Sandys observes, the fall of Constantinople "was in no way necessary for the revival of learning, which had begun a century before. Bessarion, Theodorus Gaza, Georgius Trapezuntius, Argyropulus, Chalcondyles, all had

12. The above facts may be found in any standard work on the Revival of Learning in Italy. For the most part we take them from the excellent article on "Classics" by J. E. Sandys in the Eleventh Edition of the *Encyclopædia Britannica*, VI, 448–461.

THE GREEK REVIVAL IN THE RENAISSANCE 87

reached Italy before 1453."[13] After the conquest of Constantinople, Musurus, Callierges, and Constantine and John Lascaris joined their ranks. The result was that when it came time to print the many manuscripts now in Italy, there was at hand a host of Greek scholars to guide the first editions through the press.

The printing of Greek began at Milan in 1476 with the *Grammatica Graeca* of Constantine Lascaris. The earliest editions of Homer and Isocrates were produced in 1488 and 1493 under the guidance of Chalcondyles at Florence. There also, from 1494 to 1496, John Lascaris was the first to edit the Greek anthology, Apollonius Rhodius, and parts of Euripides, Callimachus, and Lucian.[14]

But it was destined that Venice, not Florence, should be the center from which Greek literature should issue to the world. We recall that Petrarch had dreamed of a great public library to be founded in that city around the nucleus of his private library. His dream was realized a century later, when in 1468 Bessarion presented his unparalleled collection of Greek manuscripts to the republic of Venice.[15] Thus it was inevitable that when Aldo Manuzio became imbued with the desire of preserving Greek literature from further accident by committing it to print, he should choose Venice as the site of his press. Thither he removed in the year 1490. John Addington Symonds writes,

At Venice Aldo gathered an army of Greek scholars and compositors around him. His trade was carried on by Greeks, and Greek was the language of his household. Instructions to type-setters and binders were given in Greek. The prefaces to his editions were written in Greek. Greeks from Crete collated MSS., read proofs, and gave models of calligraphy for casts of Greek type. Not counting the craftsmen employed in merely manual labor, Aldo entertained as many as thirty of these Greek assistants in his family. His own industry and energy were unremitting.[16]

The consequence was the most astonishing succession of first editions that the world has ever seen. Between 1495 and 1498, Aristotle was published in five volumes. In 1496 Theocritus, Bion, Moschus, Hesiod, and Theognis appeared; in 1498, Aristophanes. In 1502 came Thucydides, Sophocles, and Herodotus; in 1503, Euripides and Xenophon; in 1504, Demosthenes; in 1508 and 1509, the minor Greek orators and Plutarch's *Morals;* and finally, in 1513, Pindar and Plato[17]—the latter, appropriately enough, being dedicated to Leo

13. *Idem*, p. 453.
14. *Ibid.*
15. According to Henri Alline, Bessarion's collection contained more than 600 Greek manuscripts (*Histoire du texte de Platon* [Paris, 1915], p. 299).
16. Article on "Manutius," *Encyclopædia Britannica* (11th ed.), XVII, 624.
17. For a more detailed account of Aldo's first editions, as well as of all Greek authors, the reader is referred to the table of "Editiones Principes of Greek Authors" in

X, the son of Lorenzo de' Medici. So seriously, in fact, did Aldo take his self-imposed mission that in 1500, with a view to promoting the study of Greek and the systematic publication of its literature, he founded his "New Academy." Here the rules were written in Greek, the transactions conducted in Greek, and the names of non-Greek members Hellenized. We recall that Erasmus and Thomas Linacre were honorary members.[18]

But before this, a more celebrated academy had been founded in Florence.

In 1439 the Council of Ferrara had removed to Florence, and the emperor, John Palaeologus, with his train of Greek theologians and scholars, had taken up residence in the city that was already the center of Greek learning in Italy. Chief among his attendants was Georgius Gemistus, eighty-three-year-old sage of Mistra, of whose magnetic personality the earlier discipleship of Bessarion is telling proof. As Symonds writes,

The Florentines were just then in the first flush of their passion for Greek study . . . What they wanted, Gemistos possessed in abundance. From the treasures of a memory stored with Platonic, Pythagorean, and Alexandrian mysticism he poured forth copious streams of indiscriminate erudition. The ears of his audience were open; their intellects were far from critical. They accepted the gold and dross of his discourse alike as purest metal. Hanging upon the lips of the eloquent, grave, beautiful old man, who knew so much that they desired to learn, they called him Socrates and Plato in their ecstasy. It was during this visit to Florence that he adopted the name of Plethon, which, while it played upon Gemistos, had in it the ring of his great master's surname.[19]

The result of his conversations with Cosimo de' Medici was the founding of the Florentine Academy, which, as Sandys observes in his *Harvard Lectures*,[20] was the "prototype of all the Academies, that, in process of time, sprang into existence in every town of Italy"—and from Italy, we might add, spread out over the world, even to our faraway New England.

The importance of Gemistus' visit and of the founding of the Florentine Academy can hardly be overestimated. Symonds writes that without the guidance of Gemistus the Florentines might never have made "that rapid progress in philosophical studies which contrasts so singularly with their comparative neglect of the Attic dramatists.

Sandys' *History of Classical Scholarship* (3 vols. London, 1903–08), II, 104–105. It is from this table that we have taken our much-abbreviated list.

18. Cf. *idem*, II, 98.

19. John Addington Symonds, *Renaissance in Italy*, Pt. II, "The Revival of Learning" (London, 1877), pp. 206–207.

20. John Edwin Sandys, *Harvard Lectures on the Revival of Learning* (Cambridge, Mass., 1905), p. 85.

Gemistos Plethon . . . materially affected the whole course of the Renaissance by directing the intelligence of the Florentines to Plato."[21]

In fact, as Henri Alline makes clear in his *Histoire du texte de Platon*,[22] what Gemistus did was to transfer to the West a quarrel that had raged in the East since the beginning of the Byzantine Renaissance. Photius, the father of that Renaissance, had been an Aristotelian, but Constantine Psellus, his great successor in the eleventh century, had been a Platonist; and the controversy thus engendered was continued until Gemistus transplanted it to Italian soil. Spreading to Rome, it woke all Italy to the differences between Aristotle and that Plato whom, as Petrarch had discovered in the *Letters to Atticus*, Cicero had called his God.[23] The controversy was closed only by Bessarion's triumphant apology, *Adversus Calumniatorem Platonis*, in 1469. During the thirty years that it raged, the quarrel prepared an eager public for Ficino's Latin translation of Plato, which was completed in 1482 and enjoyed the greatest success.

The Platonic–Peripatetic controversy that thus held the center of the learned stage in fifteenth-century Italy, and the triumph of Plato, brings us to the heart of the matter. The enthusiasm for Plato, indeed much of the entire Greek Revival, was in no small measure purely reactive. Plato was seized upon because he was fancied to be the opposite of Aristotle, and the Greeks were loved to no small extent because their point of view was conceived to be the contrary of that of the medieval Schoolmen.

This tendency of the Renaissance indeed stems from earlier Byzantine days when, as Alline points out,[24] after the Iconoclastic Controversy, the Eastern emperors and their court reacted sharply against the ascetic hegemony of the Western monks. A consequence was that, beginning with Constantine Psellus, professor in the newly founded University of Constantinople, the expositors of Plato showed an inclination to interpret him from the Alexandrine point of view, a point of view more at variance with that of Aristotle and the medieval Schoolmen. This tendency was carried by Gemistus, the "Proclus of Mistra," to Italy, where by now the reaction to the hegemony of the medieval monks[25] was sharper than it had ever been in the East. Thus we find that the Plato of Ficino, Pico, Colet, More, and indeed of the whole age, is a Plato seen through Neoplatonic eyes.

Nowadays, thanks to the Greek Revival of the eighteenth and

21. Symonds, *op. cit.*, p. 198.   22. Pp. 300–301.
23. Cf. Petrarch to Giovanni Andrea di Bologna, *Familiares*, iv, 15.
24. *Op. cit.*, p. 282.
25. For the practical synonymy of monk (and, by extension, friar) with Schoolman, cf. Maurice de Wulf, *Philosophy and Civilization in the Middle Ages* (Princeton, 1922), Chapters III and IV, and especially p. 160.

nineteenth centuries, we know a Plato more pluralistic than Aristotle, a Plato less mystical than Socrates, a Plato whose forms are to be incorporated into no single teleological or emanatory system. That Plato should be confounded with Plotinus or with Pythagoras seems to us as incredible as that the Bible should be confused with the Koran simply because there are certain features in common. Yet the Renaissance had no notion but what Plato was both Pythagorean and Neoplatonic. Cosimo's Platonic Academy was frankly Neoplatonic, and all over Europe the idea sprang up that Plato was the opponent of Aristotle rather than the precursor and teacher of Aristotle.

Indeed, in their reaction to the arbitrary pluralism of the Middle Ages, the philosophers of the Renaissance were inclined to interpret all ancient philosophies monistically. Furthermore, in their eager desire to recover as much of antiquity as possible, they regarded the difference between Plato and Plotinus as of far less importance than the preservation of both. The Renaissance, as a hundred writers have pointed out, was assimilative rather than critical. The result was a confusion of authors that accompanied the entire Greek Revival down to, and including, the Cambridge Platonists.

Bruno illustrates the Greek Revival in its philosophical aspects as well as anyone. The violence of his reaction carried him beyond Plato to the Neoplatonists, before Plato to the pre-Socratics. His philosophy is a hodgepodge of all Greek elements except the peripatetic. We find he has incorporated the hylozoism of the early Ionian philosophers, the monism of the Eleatics, the mysticism of the Pythagoreans and the Neoplatonists, the infinity and innumerability of the pre-Socratic pluralists. And let us not think that he ascribes each element to its source. J. Lewis McIntyre in his excellent *Giordano Bruno*[26] records that Bruno ascribes one idea to the Pythagoreans, the Platonists, the Magi, Orpheus, Empedocles, and Plotinus; another to Heraclitus, Democritus, Epicurus, Pythagoras, Parmenides, and Melissus!

We dwell upon the confusion of authors in the Greek Revival of the Renaissance because it is important that it be understood for what it is. The phenomenon has nothing to do with purity or corruption of text. As a matter of fact, M. Alline speaks of Ficino's translation of Plato as excellent,[27] and states that we can still admire the work of the second Henri Estienne,[28] who published at Paris in 1578 the edition of Plato which still gives us our pagination, and which was the edition that Shelley read in its Bipontine reprint of 1781–87.[29] The confusion of authors of the earlier Greek Revival is solely an interpretive phenomenon, to be explained by the very nature of the

26. London, 1903, p. 125.   27. *Op. cit.*, p. 302.   28. *Idem*, p. 317.
29. Cf. Hogg, *Life of Shelley*, I, 122.

Renaissance. It was not dissipated until the empiricism of the eighteenth-century Greek Revival threw emphasis upon the individuality and the circumstances of writers, instead of upon their difference from Aristotle, or upon the preciousness of all of them.

Thus the strain of empiricism that dawned late in the sixteenth century, and takes rank with the Reformation and the discovery of the New World as one of the major developments of the Renaissance, must be sharply discriminated from the Renaissance in its aspect as the Revival of Learning. This latter, as we have seen, was from the start "bookish," the progenitor of the later rationalism, and the very opposite of the empirical strain. In fact, the distinction between the New Learning (largely Greek) and the New Science is essential to any understanding of the period. Without the explanation that it affords it is impossible, for instance, to understand Tycho Brahe's rejection of Copernicanism and Bruno's enthusiastic acceptance thereof. The explanation is that once again Copernicus' *De revolutionibus* belongs to the Greek Revival, to the Renaissance in its bookish aspect, and not to the Renaissance as the commencement of modern science.

Nor is this merely a conjecture based upon a reading of Copernicus' treatise. As a young man of twenty-four, Copernicus made the journey to Italy, and was there for nearly ten years. Arriving in 1497, five years after Ficino's translation of Plotinus, he plunged, as Francis R. Johnson observes, "into an intellectual atmosphere surcharged with neo-Platonic ideas. During his stay south of the Alps," Mr. Johnson goes on to point out, "Copernicus not only became acquainted with the postulates of Pythagorean philosophy but also made himself thoroughly familiar with early Greek astronomical speculations, in so far as they were then known in Europe. His friend and teacher at the University of Bologna, where he studied for several years, was Domenico Maria da Novara, an ardent neo-Platonist who fully subscribed to the Pythagorean doctrines."[30] Moreover, in the course of his treatise, Copernicus refers to the Greeks who preceded him, to Heraclides and Philolaus and Aristarchus. In fact, as with Bruno, when one segregates the old from the new, it is but to observe how greatly the old preponderates over the new. The assumption of the earth's rotation is to be found in Heraclides, the assumption of heliocentricity in Aristarchus. In Copernicus only the mathematical demonstration is new. Thus one still finds in Copernicus the eccentrics and epicycles of Ptolemy, the sphere of the fixed stars at the bounds of the universe, and the Greek notion of the circle as the perfect figure. As Mr. Johnson points out,[31] *De revolutionibus* is based upon no new evidence,

30. Francis R. Johnson, *Astronomical Thought in Renaissance England* (Baltimore, 1937), p. 96.   31. *Idem*, p. 111.

nor did Copernicus ascertain any new evidence. Between his system and Ptolemy's there is more rather than less in common.

Is it any wonder, then, that Tycho Brahe, the observer of novae and comets, the compiler of tables, and one said never to have been surpassed as a practical astronomer—is it any wonder that Tycho should have viewed the theorizing of Copernicus with suspicion? The two belonged to completely different streams of thought, as different as those separating Descartes and Locke, as different as those separating Voltaire and Rousseau. Tycho belonged to the new century, Copernicus to the old.

Indeed, Bruno, who was burned at the stake for his heresy in 1600, closes the sixteenth century and the Greek Revival as a living, expansive force. Hereafter, the Revival of Learning becomes a matter of classical scholarship, and the interest in things Greek shifts to an interest in things Latin. The whole business becomes a minor concern, and the seventeenth century is principally taken up with affairs of the present or with affairs of the future. In Cartesianism, the seventeenth century witnessed an independent development of philosophy, and in the science of Galileo, Huyghens, and Newton, the further growth of that empirical strain we have already noted.

3. The Greek Revival in the Eighteenth Century

IT IS to be hoped that our exposition of the bookish aspect of the Renaissance has not been taken as a disparagement of the Renaissance, or of the Greek Revival that the Renaissance contained. Half our emphasis has been only to distinguish the early revival from the late. Though it is true that the revival of the Renaissance required correction, and that our knowledge of classical antiquity would never have been complete had not the romantic revival of the eighteenth century rounded out the revival of the Renaissance, yet it would take a hardy soul to maintain that the "rounding out" is the most important part of a process, and the fact remains that the first revival was the more essential of the two.

The first revival restored the thought of the Greeks to modern times—restored it so that, as we have seen with Copernicus, it might enter the fabric of modern thinking. The second revival, thanks to the emergence of the historical point of view, was able to clarify that thought. But it hardly did more than clarify it. The thought was already present, if confused and imperfectly distinguished as regards author from author. The second revival made contributions from archaeology and travel to Greece itself, but its contributions hardly rank with the restoration of the entire body of Greek literature.

Thus the Greek Revival of the eighteenth and nineteenth centuries, though it inspired Byron and Shelley and Keats and led to the independence of modern Greece, strikes us as the lesser of the two revivals. It rectified the conceptions produced by the earlier revival, but it did not produce comparable conceptions. It filled out a picture that sadly needed to be filled out, but it did not sketch that picture in the first place. To the romantic Greek Revival we owe our present-day ability to regard Plato as Plato—a philosopher enjoying a distinct individuality, a Plato that can be known and appreciated without giving a thought to Plotinus and the Neoplatonists. But to the Renaissance we owe the fact that we have Plato at all.

We have mentioned that the Greek Revival of the eighteenth century made contributions to the knowledge of antiquity from archaeology and travel to Greece. Undoubtedly these influences occasioned the movement in its popular aspect. But the interesting thing is that the eighteenth-century revival really begins in the realm of classical scholarship, whither the earlier revival had retreated in the seventeenth century. Of the seventeenth century and its awakening, Sandys says, "On the whole, it was a century of multifarious erudition rather than minute and accurate scholarship, a century largely concerned with the exploration of Latin rather than Greek Literature. But a new age of historical and literary criticism, founded on a more intelligent study of Greek, was close at hand with Bentley for its hero."[32]

It is a pity that most students of English literature know Bentley only through the caricatures in the *Dunciad* and the *Battle of the Books*. As it happens, in the Phalaris controversy, which produced the latter, Bentley was right and Swift was wrong. But what is more interesting is that Bentley proved the epistles of Phalaris spurious, not through recourse to learned citation, or by ingenious conjecture, but by the simple use of facts. He showed that towns and individuals mentioned in the epistles were in reality not yet in existence when the historical Phalaris lived, that the epistles betrayed a knowledge of literature a century later in date, and that even the dialect and coinage were Attic instead of the Sicilian Doric they should have been. Bentley's *Dissertation on Phalaris* (1699) is far more important in the history of classical scholarship than in the Phalaris controversy. In its pages, for the first time, a classic is regarded *per se,* and not for what can be done with it or got out of it. The friend of Locke and Newton, Bentley belongs to their generation, and brought into the world of classical learning the influence they infused in the worlds of philosophy and science. Appearing in the same decade as the *Essay concerning Human Understanding*, the *Dissertation on Phalaris* in its field wielded a comparable influence, which is to say very nearly the greatest influence of modern times. In spite of the greater drama of the discoveries at Herculaneum and Pompeii, the Greek Revival of the eighteenth century must be said to begin with Bentley.

In the realm of classical scholarship, the influence of Bentley not only dominated England until the middle of the nineteenth century, but extended, as Sandys points out,[33] to the Continent as well. In an age that thought textual criticism pedantry and useless labor, Bentley turned to textual criticism with indisputable results, and in so doing founded, single-handed, modern historical philology. In particular, the English school of Hellenists was his creation. Thus Dawes, Markland, Taylor, Toup, Tyrwhitt, Porson, Dobree, Kidd, and Monk all work in the vein he suggested, and acknowledge him as master.[34] Unfortunately, limitations of space prevent our giving them an adequate treatment.

Only Porson, the greatest of them, demands a word in passing. He assisted in the Grenville *Homer* (1801), which, as we have seen,[35]

32. *History of Classical Scholarship*, II, 370 (with slight change in punctuation).
33. *Idem*, II, 409.
34. For much of this summary, we are indebted to the unsigned article on "Bentley" in the *Encyclopædia Britannica* (11th ed.), III, 752.
35. *Vide supra*, p. 21.

was Shelley's text; and he shows how far the school had gone in preparing the texts and kindling the classical enthusiasm that Shelley was to inherit. The Renaissance confusion of authors has by now been completely eliminated. Now the classical authors are read for themselves rather than for learned quotation, and their works are available in good, legible editions that lack only the final touch of nineteenth-century, scientific manuscript collation to resemble our texts today. To be specific, it was Porson who assisted with the Herculanean papyri and who restored the Greek inscription of the Rosetta stone. He participated in the Glasgow *Æschylus* of 1795, and issued memorable editions of Euripides himself. He was the friend of Dr. Goodall at Eton, headmaster for most of Shelley's stay, and in many ways brings the history of classical scholarship to the period when Shelley was to reap its fruits. It is interesting that Porson, as Professor Bywater observes,[36] should have been a student of Plato when Plato was little read in England. Thus once again Porson carries the scholarly side of the Greek Revival to that period when Shelley himself was to take a romantic, but nevertheless scholarly, interest in Plato and the Greeks.

We dwell upon the scholarly side of the Greek Revival of the eighteenth and nineteenth centuries more than is customary in the various studies of the movement[37] because it is our opinion that the Greek Revival came to Shelley chiefly in this way. We have already expressed the opinion that the person who communicated the enthusiasm to Shelley was Peacock;[38] and, as we shall see, with Peacock the Greek Revival was largely scholarly—largely a matter of texts and commentaries, of ideas and learning—and but slightly an affair of Greek archaeology or travel, or, finally, of modern Greek independence.

Nevertheless, classical scholarship in the eighteenth century, in spite of its progress along the empirical road, and in spite of its production in England and on the Continent of texts that compare favorably with those of today, was itself subject to the increasing vogue of Hellenism rather than the cause of it. It is doubtful if scholarship alone could have produced that enthusiasm which was the mainspring of the movement, and which was shared by Peacock—an enthusiasm for the Greeks as a people who had once been very much alive, and who consequently possessed a message for the generations of today. Such an ardent conviction could have come only from the land of the

36. Ingram Bywater, *Four Centuries of Greek Learning in England* (Oxford, 1919), p. 18.
37. For instance, Bernard H. Stern in his *Rise of Romantic Hellenism in English Literature* (Menasha, Wis., 1940), to which on other counts we are much indebted, does not dwell upon the scholarly side of the Greek Revival at all.
38. *Vide supra*, p. 14.

Greeks, from a recovery, almost in a literal sense, of the time and place of ancient Greek civilization. The Greek Revival that was finally, in distant America, to dot the hillsides with Greek temples and to compete seriously with the Bible as a source of given names found its essential origins not in the scholar's world but in the world of travel and archaeology—in fact, on the shores of the Mediterranean itself.

Yet, as it happens, the new enthusiasm was first aroused not by excavations or explorations on the soil of Greece, but by the remarkable disclosure in the 1730's and 1740's of the buried towns of Herculaneum and Pompeii.

It is still possible to recapture an element of the excitement that attended the original discoveries of Alcubierre at Herculaneum in 1738. Scholars from all over Europe hastened to see the statues of the Balbi and the paintings on the walls.[39] By the 1750's, when the Accademia Ercolanese was founded and the Abbés Barthélemy and Winckelmann, chief apostles of the Greek Revival in France and Germany, visited Naples, it was clear that a movement comparable to the discovery of Greek literature in the fifteenth century was at hand. As the reposing Hermes, the drunken Silenus, the sleeping Faunus, the dancing girls, the bust called Plato's, the two discoboli, and other reproductions of Greek art issued from the pits at Herculaneum, learned monographs appeared in every language, not the least of which were the *Sendschreiben* and *Nachricht* of Winckelmann, which came forth in 1762 and 1764 respectively. For a thousand years the ancients had been thought of as characters in a tale. Now it was possible to look at their daily lives, to see their art in quantity and in color. When we reflect that the historical spirit had already been born in the world of classical scholarship, we may well believe that the effect of Herculaneum and Pompeii was overwhelming. The ancient world had come alive.[40]

From Herculaneum and Pompeii the movement spread out like the ribs of a fan, passing directly from the Mediterranean to the various countries of the North. Barthélemy and Winckelmann, as we have observed, were its principal bearers to France and to Germany. The Dilettanti carried it to England. Furthermore, the movement quickly spread to Greece itself. By 1748, ten years after the discoveries at Herculaneum, Stuart and Revett were issuing in Rome their *Proposals for Publishing an Accurate Description of the Antiquities of Athens*. Three years later they journeyed to Athens, as a result of financial

39. The student of Shelley will recall Shelley's visits to Pompeii and Herculaneum, and his mention of the equestrian statues and the wall paintings. Cf. Shelley to Peacock, January 24, 1819, Julian *Works*, x, 22.

40. For the archaeological facts of this paragraph, cf. the article on "Herculaneum" in the *Encyclopædia Britannica* (11th ed.), xɪɪɪ, 342–344.

assistance from various Dilettanti in Italy. With the publication of their justly famous *Antiquities of Athens* in London in 1762, the Greek Revival came of age in England, as it did two years later in Germany with the publication of Winckelmann's *History of the Art of Antiquity,* and as it finally did in France in 1789, when Barthélemy at long last published his *Voyage of the Young Anacharsis.*

Indeed, the independence of the Greek Revival in the various countries of Europe is no less remarkable than its essential Hellenism from the start. For apparently from the beginning there never was a doubt that it was ancient Greece that had been discovered rather than ancient Rome. Nor is this to be explained by the fact that much if not most of the ancient art discovered at Herculaneum was Greek either in fact or in inspiration. Apparently the reaction to the Latinity of the neoclassical age would have carried the upholders of the new art to the shores of Greece no matter where the first classical archaeological discoveries had been made. Thus Winckelmann and Barthélemy, who never set foot on the soil of Greece, are more ardent, if anything, in their Hellenism than their English counterparts who actually went there. It is Greek art that Winckelmann holds up to the admiration of his countrymen; it is ancient Greece itself that Barthélemy describes so sympathetically in his novel of the fourth century before Christ.

But, much as an enthusiasm for the lyrics of André Chénier, or for those of Hölderlin, might tempt one to pursue the fortunes of the Greek Revival on the Continent, the fact remains that the Greek Revival which led to Byron, to Shelley, and to Keats was independent in its origins.[41] In fact, not only was it independent, but it antedated the movement abroad. We have already remarked the rise of Bentley, far in advance of his time. It is interesting to note that the Society of Dilettanti was founded half a dozen years before the discoveries at Herculaneum in 1738.[42] Two years later, in 1740, Horace Walpole visited the excavations, and before Barthélemy and Winckelmann had departed for Italy, Stuart and Revett, to say nothing of Robert Wood, were back in England from their travels to Greece itself.[43] Indeed, Wood had already published his *Palmyra* (1753), the first of the many architectural volumes that were to appear in the course of the Greek Revival in England, and the ancestor (at least in inspiration) of Peacock's poem *Palmyra,* which Shelley greatly admired in 1812.

Thus it is clear that the Greek Revival in England in no small way epitomizes the larger Romantic Movement of which it was a part.

41. Cf. Stern, *op. cit.,* pp. 16, 85.

42. The Society was probably founded in 1732, records being kept from 1736. Cf. *idem,* pp. 18–19.

43. Stuart and Revett returned to England early in 1755; Barthélemy and Winckelmann left France and Germany for Italy later in the same year.

True, its architectural volumes are second to none, and in this respect the revival in England may be said to have reached a timely and distinguished maturity. But in literature, the same delay in the emergence of genius that characterizes the Romantic Movement as a whole is clearly evident. Though the literature of the Greek Revival in England begins in the 1730's, with Thomson's *Liberty,* and continues through the eighteenth century, yet, as Professor Pierce makes clear,[44] it is not until 1812, not until the publication of *Childe Harold,* that any genius of the first rank appears in the revival in England.

In Germany the exact opposite obtains. In 1766, two years after the publication of Winckelmann's great *History,* Lessing's *Laokoon* appeared, and in 1769 this brought forth Herder's *Kritische Wälder.* Before the century was over, Goethe, Schiller, and Hölderlin had all shown their allegiance to the Greek Revival and had in particular taken up the Laocoön theme.

How different this is from the situation in England a glance at the leisurely appearance of the successive volumes of the *Antiquities of Athens,* or of the *Ionian Antiquities,* will reveal. We have mentioned that in 1762, with the first volume of the former, the Greek Revival came of age in England. Yet the second volume did not appear for more than twenty-five years, not until 1789, the year after Stuart's death. A third volume, by a different editor, came out in 1794, and a fourth in 1816. As for the *Ionian Antiquities,* the second volume did not appear until 1797, nearly twenty years after the first, and the third, not until 1840!

Yet these volumes are superb. It is no wonder that they led to a vogue of Grecian architecture in St. James's Square, and inspired men to build latter-day Parthenons on America's "templed hills." In many ways they seem to anticipate even the movement that took place in English poetry between 1812 and 1822. In fact, to understand anything of the fullness of the Greek Revival in the English-speaking countries, it is necessary to turn over the pages of one of the volumes itself. Even in the first volume of the *Antiquities of Athens,* both the romantic and the scientific tendencies of the age are clearly present. The romantic tendency is represented by the frontispiece to the work and by the initial plate to each of the five chapters. Here the impression is all of the general scene, not of details of architecture. The frontispiece to the book, for instance, is a double-page panorama of Athens as viewed from Mount Anchesmus. Turkish figures are seen in the foreground, and in the background is a sweep of cloud, sea, and mountain appealing to a soul seeking escape from the constraints of European civilization. In the center

---

44. Frederick E. Pierce, "The Hellenic Current in English Nineteenth-Century Poetry," *Journal of English and Germanic Philology,* xvi (1917), 105 *et seq.*

rises the Acropolis, its altitude enhanced, its buildings partially seen in the distance.

The five chapters of the work are each given to a particular monument of architecture, to a Doric portico, to the Ionic Temple on the Ilissus, to the Octagon Tower of Andronicus Cyrrhestes,[45] to the Choragic Monument of Lysicrates, and to a stoa, thought to be that of the Temple of Jupiter Olympius. In each case, the first plate of the chapter shows the ruin as a ruin, with tree and vine and human figure and all the picturesque details of the living reality. The effect is thoroughly romantic. An air of peace and calm pervades the scene. In the Arcadian sunshine that suffuses the world, gone are all suggestions of Turkish conquest and barbarism. The Turks have brought peace and rest. Life is better there than at home.

But more remarkable are the plates that follow. Here the romanticist gives way, and the student of architecture takes over. No longer is one conscious of the sad sweetness of far-off times and places, but of the structures it is possible to build in the future. Here all is restored, and restored with accurate and loving care. Exact measurements are given of every flute and curve. Sections are furnished of roof and peristyle. The elevations resemble those submitted for a *Prix de Rome*. The sheen of newness glistens from every page, and the effect is altogether intoxicating. One wonders that any other style was ever tolerated.

Yet the volumes are interesting in more ways than the purely architectural. For one thing, they offer visible proof that the scholarly revival, the revival of Bentley and the English Hellenists, had been incorporated in the architectural and archaeologic revival. The *Antiquities of Athens* is provided with an array of footnotes in Latin and Greek referring to nearly every author of classical antiquity. Sometimes the notes fill half the folio page, and one is led to exclaim that there was never a more learned book on architecture. Furthermore, in 1764, two years after the success of the *Antiquities of Athens*, when it came time to dispatch to the Orient the authors of the *Ionian Antiquities*, the Society of Dilettanti chose as their leader Richard Chandler, brilliant young classical scholar and an authority on the Arundel, now the Oxford, Marbles.

Moreover, as the eighteenth century progressed and passed into the nineteenth, it is clear that the romantic element in the volumes

---

45. It is unnecessary to point out that the *Antiquities of Athens* does not possess a nice discrimination between architectural periods, between what is Graeco-Roman, Hellenistic, and truly Periclean. As with the Restorers of Learning in the Renaissance, the essential thing to Stuart and Revett was the recovery of Greek antiquity. To its first discoverers it was all of it precious, and all of it more or less confused. Later, when it had been brought within men's ken, there would be time to distinguish between period and period.

increased. Though the accurate architectural drawings remain as before, it is noticeable that the sketches of the ruins in their setting multiply. In the second volume of the *Ionian Antiquities,* which appeared in the year before the *Lyrical Ballads,* there are nearer two dozen of these than the mere half-dozen in the original volume of the *Antiquities of Athens.* To the student of Shelley, this second volume of the *Ionian Antiquities* is perhaps the most interesting of all. In some of the plates it seems as if the dream isle of *Epipsychidion* had come to life a generation before the poem.

It makes no difference whether one looks at the "Ruin near the Port of Aegina" or at the "Temple of Minerva at Sunium" or at the "Ruins near the Lake of Myüs, or Baffi." In each of the drawings,

> The halcyons brood around the foamless isles;
> The treacherous Ocean has forsworn its wiles.
>
> *Epipsychidion,* 412–413

In each of the drawings one also gains glimpses of the

> pastoral people native there,
> Who from the Elysian, clear, and golden air
> Draw the last spirit of the age of gold,
> Simple and spirited.
>
> *Epipsychidion,* 426–429

In fact, in the "Ruin near the Port of Aegina," one of the three figures in the drawing is a shepherd reclining with his crook over his shoulder and his dog at his feet. In the "Ruins near the Lake of Myüs, or Baffi," one sees what might easily suggest

> a lone dwelling, built by whom or how
> None of the rustic island-people know:
> 'Tis not a tower of strength, though with its height
> It overtops the woods.
>
> *Epipsychidion,* 484–487

Over the ruin hangs the "roof of blue Ionian weather," and in the background are seen both the "meadows" and

> The mossy mountains, where the blue heavens bend
> With lightest winds, to touch their paramour.
>
> *Epipsychidion,* 544–545

Had Shelley looked at this second volume of the *Ionian Antiquities?* Who knows? The historian of ideas would be inclined to add, Who cares? For if Shelley had not looked at this particular volume, he had looked at others. And if he had not looked at others, he had read books in the Hellenic vogue, or been spurred by conversation, or by his own thoughts, to imagine Grecian scenes that were similarly romantic and alluring. The Greek Revival had been long in the air, and the fact of the matter is that the Odes of Keats, with their loving mention of Hippocrene, Tempe, and Arcady, are prefigured in Thomson and Akenside before the turn of the eighteenth century.

Although in passing from the *Antiquities of Athens* and the *Ionian Antiquities* to the literature of the English eighteenth-century Greek Revival we descend from the first-rate to the third- or fourth-rate, yet some attention to this literature must be given before we end this brief sketch. Inferior as most of it is, it nevertheless forms part of the entire picture, and mention of it must be made to complete a survey of the Greek Revival that led to Shelley.

The literary Greek Revival in England begins with Thomson and includes nearly all the minor poets of the eighteenth century. In the article of Professor Pierce's which we have already cited, there is a list of their various works, from Thomson's *Liberty,* the first part of which appeared in 1734, to Wright's *Horae Ionicae,* which was published only three years before *Childe Harold.* We note in the list Home's *Agis,* Glover's *Leonidas,* Akenside's *Hymn to the Naiads,* Falconer's *Shipwreck,* and many more. But, as Professor Pierce says, "Who outside of specialists as much as hears their names?"[46]

Yet these Grecian works of these minor poets are interesting if for no other reason than that they indubitably show that the movement was a whole, that the point of view of the scholarly, of the archaeologic, and of the literary Greek Revivals was one and the same.

Thus we note that as early as Thomson's *Liberty,* the primary interest of the revival is less in the art and literature of the Greeks than in the circumstances of their civilization. To Thomson the art and literature of the Greeks was a secondary phenomenon, the result of their political liberty, and the loss of that liberty, the reason for their moral and intellectual decay. Similarly in Glover's *Leonidas,* the struggle between the Greeks and the Persians is the struggle between free men and slaves, and the outcome a foregone conclusion because of the inherent advantages of liberty. Indeed, as Stern points out,[47] the notion that the glory of Greece was the result of its social and political liberty is a fundamental tenet of the Greek Revival of the eighteenth century, and as such is to be found wherever one looks, whether in England or abroad.[48] Thus Stuart and Revett, in the dedication of the first volume of their *Antiquities of Athens,* particularize Athens as "once the most distinguished seat of Genius and Liberty"; and Winckelmann in his early *Reflections,* the pamphlet which he wrote before leaving for Italy and which brought him his fame—

46. *Op. cit.,* p. 104.   47. *Op. cit.,* p. 92.
48. In England, Stephen A. Larrabee in his *English Bards and Grecian Marbles* (New York, 1943), pp. 66, 76, traces the doctrine back to Shaftesbury and Addison.

Winckelmann declares, "Art claims liberty . . . In Greece, where, from their earliest youth, the happy inhabitants were devoted to mirth and pleasure, where narrow-spirited formality never restrained the liberty of manners, the artist enjoyed nature without a veil."[49] Liberty, that watchword of the eighteenth century, becomes, in fact, a watchword of the Greek Revival, and when Byron, musing on the plain of Marathon, dreams that "Greece might still be free," he but echoes, at long remove, Thomson and Glover and their successors.

The newness of this interest in the circumstances of Greek civiliza-tion can only be appreciated by those who come to it from a reading of the Greek Revival of the Renaissance. In the latter, the tie with life had become more and more tenuous until finally, with the Cam-bridge Platonists, it had completely disappeared. With these latter, even the ascription of thought to thinker is largely conventional, and one is at sea in a world of unattached reflection without chart or compass. In the eighteenth century the opposite obtains. An interest in the thought of the Greeks comes only after an interest in their civilization, and in the beginning the interest was entirely in the civilization—in the social and political life of the Greeks, in their literature and art, in the Grecian scene itself.

Thus in Thomson's *Liberty* we read of Hymettus, the mountain to the southeast of the Attic plain. We learn that Athens lies between the Ilissus and the Cephissus, the rivers that flow respectively from Hymettus and Pentelicus. Similarly Akenside asks the Genius of Greece to guide his way

> Through fair Lyceum's walk, the green retreats
> Of Academus, and the thymy vale,
> Where oft enchanted with Socratic sounds,
> Ilissus pure devolv'd his tuneful stream
> In gentler murmurs.
>
> *Pleasures of Imagination,* I, 591–595

Again, in Thomas Warton's *Pleasures of Melancholy,* the poet gazes on the Attic plain from "Hymettus' brow" and reflects upon a land-scape threaded by the Ilissus and "resounding once with Plato's voice." In his *Newmarket,* Warton thinks again of the "laureate al-leys of Ilissus" and of Plato walking in his "oliv'd Academe." Sim-ilarly in William Mason's *Isis,* Plato is no vague label for even vaguer thoughts, but a philosopher who was once very much alive, a phi-losopher whose steps marked a glade adjacent to the Ilissus. True, it was the Cephissus rather than the Ilissus that the glade actually bordered, but the interesting thing is that by now Plato is universally

49. *Reflections on the Painting and Sculpture of the Greeks,* translated from the German original of the Abbé Winckelmann, by Henry Fusseli (London, 1765), p. 9.

associated with the olive grove of his Academy rather than with abstractions such as his Theory of Ideas.

Indeed, it is unnecessary to explore further the literary Greek Revival in England, and in so doing recover bit by bit the Grecian countryside. By the end of the century every feature of it was familiar, and it would have been impossible for a reader of the literature not to have been acquainted with the fact that, of all philosophers, Plato was the one who taught under the most romantic circumstances.

Thus in the Greek Revival of the eighteenth century, Plotinus, Plato's great rival in the Renaissance, was at a hopeless disadvantage. Had he stayed in Egypt, conceivably, some circumstantial lore might have become attached to him. But Plotinus wandered about the ancient world, finally taking up his residence in Rome, where no single hill or river or philosophic grove became associated with his name. In fact, as we bring our sketch of the Greek Revival to a close, it would seem to us predetermined that a romantic poet who was also interested in Greek thought would be led straight to Plato, and to Plato alone.

VI

Shelley and the Thought of the Greeks

1. The Biographical and Bibliographical Facts

THE story of Shelley's conversion to the Greek Revival begins with the summer of 1812, when Shelley was most certainly not a Hellenist and when he had not yet met Peacock. He had not met Godwin either. But he had been corresponding extensively with him for half a year, and in the summer of 1812 they were discussing the value of classical studies. In his letter of July 29 from Lynmouth,[1] Shelley tells Godwin that in his opinion "the evils of acquiring Greek and Latin considerably overbalance the benefits," and that he does not perceive "how one of the truths of *Political Justice* rests on the excellence of ancient literature." Shelley concludes his remarks on the subject by asking, "Did Greek and Roman literature refine the soul of Johnson, does it extend the thousand narrow bigots educated in the very bosom of *classicality?*"

Shelley's position in 1812 is so plain about Greek and Latin, both as to language and literature, that we may question the veracity of the impression that Hogg gives of Shelley's classicality at Oxford. As we need not point out, having read Xenophon in the original by freshman year by no means constitutes a classicist, and a translation of a translation of Plato hardly deserves more than mention in a person's general reading.[2] In spite of Hogg's protest that "it would be tedious to specify and describe all the reflected lights borrowed from the great luminary, the sun of the Academy, that illumined the path of two young students,"[3] we may wish that Hogg had specified and described them. For all we have from Hogg is a general impression, almost certainly colored by his love for making a fine sentence and by the Hellenism of his later years. Furthermore, it is plainly at variance with the known facts. The positive evidence all points to a preoccupation on Shelley's part during his early years with Gothic romance, natural science, and French and English revolutionary philosophy.

But the seeds of Shelley's future Hellenism were even then being sown, a year before the publication of *Queen Mab*, when Shelley was still largely given over to radical ideas and to schemes for reforming the world. For three weeks later, on August 18, Shelley wrote to

1. Julian *Works*, IX, 10–14.   2. Cf. Hogg, *Life of Shelley*, I, 121.
3. *Ibid.*

Hookham,[4] thanking him among other things for two volumes of Peacock's poetry received the night before, and praising the conclusion to *Palmyra* as the finest piece of poetry he had ever read.[5] Thus Shelley, before he ever met Peacock, was disposed to give him respect and admiration.

The meeting between the two poets (for Peacock had already published three longish poems and as yet no novels)—the meeting between the two poets occurred the following autumn during the Shelleys' six-weeks' stay in London. We have no firsthand information of the meeting, but Carl Van Doren points out that in Shelley's book orders of the next December appear Lord Monboddo's *Origin and Progress of Language,* Sir William Drummond's *Essay on a Punic Inscription,* and Horne Tooke's *Diversions of Purley,* books which were favorites of Peacock's at the time, and which were out of the range of Shelley's interests.[6] We have already mentioned that the book orders also included (perhaps as a result of Godwin's arguments) a generous sprinkling of classic authors, although with the proviso that they contain English translations of the text.[7]

Our real interest, however, begins with the summer of 1813, when Peacock was visiting in Leicestershire and when as yet the Shelleys were little more than acquaintances of his. Peacock was already a confirmed Hellenist, and in the evenings, when he had returned from his long, solitary, paper-boat-sailing rambles across the countryside, he would read Greek for pleasure, a dramatist in one hand and a commentator in the other, to the no small wonder of the local farmers, who marveled that a man should read two books at one time.[8] Peacock was at this time in his twenty-eighth year, and the principal enthusiasms of his life were already clearly marked: a passion for walking and boating, and a love for all things Greek.

When Peacock returned to the neighborhood of London from his excursion to Wales and Leicestershire, he found the Shelleys established at Bracknell, and there visited them at their invitation. In October he accompanied them on their second trip to Edinburgh,

4. Julian *Works,* ix, 18–20.

5. Mr. A. Martin Freeman points out in his *Thomas Love Peacock* (London, 1911), p. 49, that Shelley's eulogium is of the entirely changed and vastly improved conclusion to the revised version of *Palmyra,* and that this should color our opinion of Shelley's judgment. The 1812 revised version of *Palmyra* was apparently not reprinted until 1927, in Volume vi of the Halliford Edition of Peacock's works (10 vols. London and New York, 1924–34).

6. Carl Van Doren, *The Life of Thomas Love Peacock* (London and New York, 1911), p. 56.

7. *Vide supra,* p. 20.

8. The anecdote is told in the *Autobiography* of John Arthur Roebuck, who as a boy witnessed the incident, and as a young man was introduced to India House and Benthamite circles by Peacock. Cf. H. F. B. Brett-Smith, Biographical Introduction to the Halliford Edition, i, liii–liv.

which certainly must have strengthened the growing friendship, since it is well known that travel in twosome or in threesome either ripens friendship or terminates it. From this Edinburgh visit, in a letter to Hogg,[9] comes the first real indication of a new interest in the classics on Shelley's part. In addition to reading Tacitus, Cicero, and the *Odyssey,* Shelley reports translating Plutarch's two essays *On Flesh-Eating,* which he had read before with Hogg (but in connection with his vegetarianism, we may be sure), and which he had cited in the notes to *Queen Mab* (viii, 211–212).

In fact, Hogg's mention of the two-volume Grenville *Homer,*[10] one volume of which was continually in Shelley's hand, and of Shelley's devouring the text by firelight until his cheek was roasted like an apple—this mention must be of the winter immediately succeeding the trip to Edinburgh, when the Shelleys were living at Windsor. Hogg's *Life* is surely one of the least chronological ever written, and it would be a confident reader who essayed to date many of the vague anecdotes related in it. But in this case we can be fairly sure since, the winter before, the Shelleys had been in Wales and away from Hogg, and since Hogg's *Life,* as it stands, comes to a close in the spring of 1814. Thus Shelley's new enthusiasm for Homer (we have heard nothing of it before) must date from the trip to Edinburgh, and be attributable to his association with Peacock.

This influence of the new friend, a greater influence than Hogg ever possessed, should not surprise us. Whereas Hogg was but a few months older than Shelley, Peacock was seven years Shelley's senior, thus possessing a greater age-differential than many a schoolmaster possesses over his students at the beginning of his career. In the winter of 1813–14 Peacock was twenty-eight to Shelley's twenty-one, and furthermore a man whose point of view was unusually mature, a man whose Hellenism was a settled habit.

Unfortunately, the information to be gleaned from a study of Peacock is of the meagerest. In the Halliford Edition of his works no letters are given at all between April, 1811, and May, 1818, and only some fifty to account for the remaining forty-five years of his life.[11] Thus we do not wonder that Hogg accused Peacock of being one "who never writes to anybody,"[12] nor that for the years of Peacock's relationship with Shelley Peacock's biographers depend largely upon Shelley material. Indeed, the student of Shelley discovers that it is Shelley who throws light upon Peacock, rather than Peacock upon Shelley. Nevertheless there are a few independent facts to be ob-

9. Julian *Works,* ix, 80–82. *Vide supra,* p. 20.
10. Hogg, *op. cit.,* ii, 59–60. *Vide supra,* p. 21, note 41.
11. Halliford Edition, viii, 157–260.
12. Letter of October 22, 1826, from Hogg to Peacock; given in Walter Sidney Scott, *The Athenians* (London, 1943), p. 80.

tained from a reading of the various biographies of Peacock, one of which is that in 1809 Peacock made an earlier excursion to the headwaters of the Thames, thus suggesting that if he was not the proposer of the Shelleyan excursion of 1815 he was at least the willing guide. In fact, one consents to proceed with the investigation of Peacock's influence over his younger friend because the information, though scanty, all points in one direction, and the investigator is saved the task of having to manipulate any of it.

The fact, however, that dwarfs all others (at least as regards Peacock's Hellenic influence upon Shelley) is that the periods of Shelley's increasing enthusiasm for the Greeks exactly coincide with the periods of his settled relationship with Peacock.

The first of these periods is the autumn and winter of 1813–14, when Shelley saw much of Peacock in Edinburgh and Windsor. Unhappily, we have presented all the available facts.

The autumn and winter of 1814–15 were far less settled than the year before, with sometimes almost daily shifts of quarters to avoid the bailiffs. Shelley's intellectual pursuits were constantly interrupted, and, as White points out,[13] for nine whole months Shelley set pen to paper in creative composition only twice. Shelley's association with Peacock was not nearly so regular as it had been before, and for two months it lapsed entirely.[14] Hence it is not surprising that the reading list for 1814 (that is, from July 28) contains four Latin authors but no Greek ones. Yet one cannot pass over a curious juxtaposition of items in the various Journals that the Shelleys kept in September, 1814. On September 18, five days after the Shelleys were back in England from their trip to Switzerland, Peacock called, and on that day, as she records, Mary received her first lesson in Greek. Before the week was up, Claire had begun her study of Greek, and Shelley had resumed his.[15] Unfortunately, the first week in England, with its Hellenic forecast, was not an earnest of the year to come.

The spring of 1815, however, saw Shelley's financial settlement with his father, and by August, after a trip to Torquay and Clifton, Shelley and Mary were established in Bishopsgate. The excursion to the headwaters of the Thames toward the end of the month put Shelley in excellent health. Peacock had moved to Marlow before the Shelleys came to Bishopsgate, and as the winter wore on there were many walks, which Hogg came out from London to join, and much, much Hellenism. Writing of the winter forty years later (and recalling a reminiscent letter of Hogg's[16]), Peacock declared, "This winter was, as Mr. Hogg expressed it, a mere Atticism. Our studies were exclu-

---

13. *Shelley*, I, 405.   14. Cf. *idem*, I, 387–388.
15. The items are given in *idem*, I, 366–367.
16. Letter of April 29, 1819, given in Scott, *op. cit.*, p. 55.

sively Greek."[17] Accordingly it is not surprising to find that, whereas the reading list for 1814 shows no Greek authors, the reading list for 1815 reports Euripides, Hesiod, Theocritus, Herodotus, Thucydides, and Homer. The autumn and winter of 1815–16 thus constitute the second of the periods of Shelley's close association with Peacock.

But, curiously enough, even this second exposure to Peacock's Hellenism didn't "take." For in May, 1816, the Shelleys departed for Switzerland, and, if one thing more than another may be said of the summer's reading and thinking, it is that it was no more Hellenic than Latin or French or German or English. To be sure, according to Medwin, Shelley translated the *Prometheus Bound* of Æschylus for Byron,[18] and the Journal records that in August he read a little Plutarch. But Rousseau would seem to have received the chief emphasis of the summer, and along with Rousseau went German *Spukgeschichte* (in French translation), Pliny, Tacitus, Lucretius, Milton, and Wordsworth.

The same lack of bent continued to characterize Shelley's intellectual interests after his departure from Switzerland. In England there were occasional visits, either by Shelley alone or by Shelley and Mary together, to Peacock in Marlow. But for the most part the Shelleys resided at Bath, giving themselves over to their reading, which then, as so often, was the chief occupation of their daily life.

Here, if ever, it will pay to look at the Journal itself.[19] Because of the hiatus in its pages from the middle of May, 1815, to the end of July, 1816, it covers only the last month of the Shelleys' stay in Switzerland, and is then an account of activity rather than of reading. But in Bath there was little to do, and the record of the Shelleys' reading is unusually full. As an indication of Shelley's frame of mind in this period before the return of his radical enthusiasm, the importance of the Journal's day-by-day account of his reading is not likely to be overestimated.

By September 28 the visitings to Marlow and London were over, the Shelleys were established at Bath, and we find Shelley reading "Peter Pindar's book" aloud. On September 29 he finished Lacretelle's "History of the French Revolution," begun the day before he left Switzerland, and also read a little Lucian. Then, on October 1, the Journal records that he spent the whole day reading aloud the "Life of Holcroft"—apparently the *Memoirs*, published that year by Haz-

17. Peacock, *Memoirs of Shelley*, ii, 341.
18. Medwin, *Revised Life of Shelley*, p. 161. The statement is borne out by Byron's *Prometheus* and by the inclusion of the Æschylean play in the 1816 reading list. But Medwin's other statement, that the Greek dramatists were Shelley's great study at this time, is at variance with all the known facts and is surely unfounded.
19. It seems scarcely necessary to observe that the Journal of the Shelleys is chiefly available through copies of *Shelley and Mary*, twelve of which were printed in 1882 for private circulation by Lady Shelley. For further details, see White, *op. cit.*, i, 680–681.

litt. A few days later he was reading Tasso to himself, and on the evening of the seventh began the reading of *Don Quixote* aloud, which for a month (with occasional intermissions) constituted the evening's entertainment for the Shelleys. On October 13 (after the interruption of Fanny's death) Shelley read a "Life of Cromwell," and from October 18 until November 10 was busied with Montaigne, whom he finished on the latter date "to his great sorrow." On October 21 Shelley also resumed the reading of Lucian, which occupied him, with various lapses, until November 14. Then followed Locke, Plutarch, Curtius Rufus (the biographer of Alexander), Godwin's *Political Justice,* Shakespeare, and finally Roscoe's *Life of Lorenzo de' Medici.* As for the Shelleys' oral reading, *Castle Rackrent* followed *Don Quixote* for an evening, after which came *Gulliver's Travels* and *Paradise Lost.* The latter was finished on November 22, and after a brief try at *Pamela* (Shelley evidently could not stomach the novel, since Mary was obliged to finish it alone) the Shelleys read Gibbon, a chapter an evening, until the fifth of December, when Shelley departed for Marlow and the itemized record breaks off.[20]

The above is the complete record of Shelley's reading at Bath. We have omitted no item, nor changed the order of any. We have only summarized the daily jottings as they occur in the Journal. Now the one conclusion we should wish to draw from this summary of Shelley's reading is that it is clearly without determinate bias. Clearly there is no bent to be perceived, either toward literature or philosophy, toward the essay or the novel, English or French, Latin or Greek. Perhaps only it shows, in its very absence of unity, the reading of a man aware of his lack of bent, and striving to discover one. Or perhaps it shows no such thing.

Tragedy and happiness came together to Shelley in December, 1816, for Harriet's death was closely paralleled by his new friendship with Hunt; and his marriage with Mary at the end of the month repaired the estrangement with Godwin. Thus it is not surprising that the Journal shows a different Shelley in 1817. To be sure, there is the lawsuit over the children on his hands; but there are more comings and goings of a purely social nature. Typical is the entry for February 9. In the morning Mary, Shelley, and Hunt walk to Brougham's, and after supper there is a discussion until three in the morning with Hazlitt concerning monarchy and republicanism. Between the new year and February 23, when another lapse occurs in the Journal until April 10,[21] there is but one reference to Shelley's reading, and that is

20. The facts of this paragraph have been taken directly from *Shelley and Mary,* I, pp. 142–166.

21. The last entry, that of February 23, attempts to make up for the lapse, and records of the ensuing interim that Shelley read *Waverley, Tales of my Landlord,* and several of the works of Plato.

of the *Arcadia*. By April 10 Shelley was at work upon his new poem, *The Revolt of Islam*, as it subsequently came to be called.

As we have already suggested,[22] the renewed interest in radicalism which this poem shows is probably to be attributed to the radical, or at least liberal, group of friends to which Shelley had been admitted. In his spare moments we find Shelley turning again to Lacretelle's "History of the French Revolution." In the evenings, to get the rhythm of his new poem, he read Spenser aloud, and, as White observes,[23] the two items run through the Journal like a refrain until July. Occasionally there are other notations of Shelley's reading, but until the latter part of June they are without significance.

Of greater significance is the "Athenian" letter from Hogg to Shelley which the Journal includes.[24] We say "Athenian" because the letter properly belongs with those other Hellenic letters recently gathered together by Mr. Walter Sidney Scott (whose wife is the great-niece of Hogg) in his remarkable little collection called *The Athenians*, to which we have had occasion to refer already,[25] and from which we are presently going to quote at length. This letter of Hogg's we shall give in its entirety, not only because of its brevity, but because it shows in a firsthand way the pressure to which Shelley was being subjected to join the new cult.

London, May 5, 1817

Dear Shelley,

If you are not reading Plutarch's Lives, I will thank you to send them forthwith to me; if you are, Lucian will do as well. I have finished Euripides, and indeed all my small stock of Greeks, except some parts of Xenophon and the whole of Isocrates, which must wait until some more worthy authors are disposed of, and Pindar, who requires powerful and expensive machinery. I do not know whether you have read "Ion"; the chorus, v. 82, which describes him sweeping the Temple of Apollo at sunrise with a branch of laurel, sprinkling the pavement with water, and driving away the birds, is exquisitely beautiful. The incident of the Dove (v. 1210) is as charming as that in Tasso, "Gerus." 1. 18, st. 49. I am quite void of news of all things but of Law, Greek, Health, and Content. Remember me to all whom I know at Marlow, and accept my good wishes for yourself and them that the Gods may so far shake off their Epicurean laziness as to impel you all to the reading of as much Greek as external circumstances and the incessant showers of colliding atoms will allow.

Yours truly,

T. Jeff. Hogg

1, Garden Court, Temple

Hogg, who would seem to have become a Peacockian convert to the Greek Revival during the "Attic" winter of 1815–16, and who has

22. *Vide supra*, p. 15.   23. *Op. cit.*, I, 527.   24. *Shelley and Mary*, I, 200.
25. *Vide supra*, pp. 106–07, notes 12 and 16.

all the zeal of a new disciple, seems totally unaware of the fact that Shelley is at the moment engaged upon a long philosophical poem of a radical nature. Through the month of May and for a good part of June there is no evidence that Shelley felt the impulsion of the Epicurean gods.

After a desultory toying with Homer on the second and third of June, the Journal records that Shelley read Arrian from the eighteenth to the twenty-fourth. But our eye is arrested by an item that Professor White has taught us to regard with significance.[26] On the thirtieth of June we read, "Shelley reads Homer. He is not well." On July 1 we read, "Shelley very unwell; he reads Homer," and on the second, "Shelley reads Homer. He is better." Whatever the coincidence signifies, the fact remains that Shelley now read Homer not desultorily but persistently, reading him nearly every day through the thirteenth of July, when he turned to Æschylus. By August 5 he had finished the plays of Æschylus, and on the thirteenth was reading Plato's *Symposium*. On the seventeenth he read the *Œdipus* of Sophocles.

But let us turn directly to some of the correspondence given in Mr. Scott's *Athenians*. We have already outlined the disintegration of the optimistic mood with which Shelley began *The Revolt of Islam*.[27] Let us now see the faith that was waiting to count Shelley as a member, the enthusiasm that had long been urging him to join its ranks.

The correspondence of particular interest to us belongs to the year 1817, and we notice, in a letter of July 14 from Hogg to Peacock, the rather revealing remark that Hogg is "glad S. is so sensible to the wonders of the Iliad." The letter from Peacock to Hogg in reply, dated the sixteenth of July, makes no report on the progress of Shelley's Hellenism, but is interesting for the evidence it affords of Peacock's having read the *Symposium* three or four weeks before Shelley. Peacock observes,

I am reading the Συμποσιον of Plato, in which I have found one passage perfectly wonderful. I did not think there was such a combination of επεα πτεροεντα in the world, not even in Greek.

A letter from Hogg to Peacock, written from his home in Durham on September 8, deserves to be quoted at greater length.[28] We read,

26. *Vide supra*, p. 16, note 29.
27. *Vide supra*, pp. 15–16.
28. The learned nicknames in the following letters reveal a side of Shelley's Marlow period that should not be overlooked. There was fun among the Marlow friends as well as seriousness. "Conchoid" for Shelley needs no exegesis, and Professor F. A. Pottle suggests that Godwin is meant by "Demogorgon." "La Caccia" is of course Hunt, author of *The Story of Rimini* and chief protagonist, according to Professor Beers (*A History of English Romanticism in the Nineteenth Century*, p. 107), of the Italian Revival.

I have long wished to enquire after you, the Conchoid, Demogorgon & my other Marlow friends . . . Except in the five last & most divine Iliads, which my brothers read to me & by which I measured their knowledge of perfecta act. pars. & med., with a very satisfactory result & in a few pages of Plutarch, I have in no respect bettered my condition as an Athenian, but my mind's boat has remained moored just above the falls of All-evils weir under the arch of Gt. Idleness bridge unpainted, unswept & untrimmed, nor have I towed her one inch higher up the stream of Greek with the line of Scapula, or even set the sails of Translation & attempted to make questionable way by tacking with the Western or Latin wind . . . If I have been in practise less loyal to Greece than usual I am not without this apology, that in heart I am more a Grecian than ever.

Peacock's reply to Hogg is the gem of the collection, and should be given in full. It graphically conveys the atmosphere with which Shelley was surrounded when in the company of his two Athenian friends.

My dear Hogg

My conscience reproaches me δεινοτατως for not having written to you long before but I have been inebriating myself with copious draughts of classico-poetical punch of which Theocritus has been the sweet, Aristophanes the acid, Pindar the spirit and Homer the water, on the principle of αριστον μεν ὑδωρ. Pindar has grown into great favor with me. The walnut-shell of his meaning often exacts the whole energy of the Scapulistic crackers, but the kernel is well worth the trouble.

I walk about the woods with him & strictly meditate the flight of his ωκεα βελη φωναντα συνετοισιν. Aristotle & Herodotus were welcome guests. I have deposited the study of the former till the days of mist & snow. I have not yet been able to attain any intelligence of Demogorgon. The Conchoid is well. A Conchoidion or little hermitess has just stept forth upon the stage of the world. La Caccia and his wife have been passing four or five days at the Hermitage, and a Mr. Baxter from the Highlands, with whom I have taken some long walks. La Caccia & his cara sposa went to town yesterday. They exerted their energies and walked to Beaconsfield. I saw them off by the Wycombe stage at 3 minutes & a half past 4 P.M. & walked back to Marlow through an agreeable Scotch mist. The mornings had been particularly beautiful & they were delighted with the valley of the Wye. Perhaps a due mixture of tea, Greek & pedestrianism constitute the summum bonum. I shall comfort myself in the course of the short days with the prospect of our conjointly exploring some more radii of the 90 mile circumference in the course of the next long ones. I hope you may have a day or

---

"Scapula" and "John" throughout the correspondence refer to the *Lexicon Graeco-Latinum Novum* published in 1580 by John Scapula, who was an employee of the second Henri Estienne and piratically abridged his master's great thesaurus. One would like to know which particular reprint was in use among the Athenian friends. Perhaps it was the two-volume Glasgow edition of 1816, which had the advantage of being in quarto rather than in folio.

two to spare for Marlow between your return from the north & the commencement of term.

The Conchoid is in town at present. He has been sometime talking of writing to you. Let me hear from you soon and believe me yours most sincerely

T. L. Peacock

Marlow Sept. 26. 1817

T. J. Hogg esqr.
Norton, near Stockton upon Tees, Durham

We shall quote from but one more letter, an undated one from Hogg to Shelley. It evidently closely follows the preceding letter from Peacock to Hogg, and is interesting for the schoolmasterish air that it assumes.

My dear S.

I confess my negligence in not having once written to you from the North, & by addressing you immediately after my arrival in Town. I came here on Wednesday. Peacock mentioned the addition to your family. I heartily congratulate you & I sincerely hope the young lady may prove everything you can desire.

Hitherto I have been idle but from this time I propose to myself serious application. You can do no more for the future, but of the past you can doubtless give a better account. You had in July nearly finished Aeschylus; Sophocles has I conjecture been read thro' attentively; you have made some progress in Euripides, & have perhaps become acquainted with two or three of the Comedies of Aristophanes.

Peacock is, I trust, climbing upon some steps in his Poem & a new Novel nearer to honour & profit . . . I shall be glad to hear that you have enriched your *purple* room with a Scapula.

When you did not esteem the Classics ('pace vestra,' let me use so impious an expression that there once was a time when you preferred the Ghost seers of Germany to the Philosophers of Greece.) I was anxious that you should see your error, but not very anxious for I knew that such an error could not be lasting, so great & *not greater for the same reason* is my present wish to overcome your distaste for the society of John. I do not hold that the turning over of dry brown mouldering leaves can teach the antient languages, for if that were so the autumnal wind would before the 8th of Nov. have become an admirable linguist; nor that if we can find the meaning entire in the translation we ought to seek it piecemeal in the Lexicon, but I maintain that the meaning cannot be found in the translation. I do not deny that the rude meaning of Homer might be learnt from Clarke's translation, as for instance that Achilles slew Hector, or even enough to shew that the Iliad is the most sublime production the world ever saw. I deny that the exact, full & just meaning can be learnt from a translation . . .

In the Lexicon we see the origin & composition of the word in what passages of the same author and what other authors it is used in the same or in a different sense, & also all cognate words. We meet the individual not once in public but behold him in the bosom of his family, with his parents & kindred who eagerly enumerate his various talents, his services, & when & where he distinguished himself; thus we form an intimacy not with one solitary being, but with a numerous, powerful and closely-united clan.

Perhaps we shall be taken to task for quoting from this last letter of Hogg's at such great length. But we have scarcely given the half of it, especially if one includes the long quotation from Cicero with which it closes, and it is better to have a sample of what was going on among these Athenian gentlemen than a mere statement as to the effect. No doubt the cult of the Greeks as Peacock presents it is the more attractive article. In any event it has been our contention from the beginning that Shelley's interest in the Greeks stemmed from Peacock. That Hogg also became a convert, and in so becoming caught the letter of the enthusiasm rather than the spirit, should not surprise us. What is remarkable is that on this score Shelley's two oldest friends should have presented a united front.

Before Hogg's letter was received, however, the third and last period of Shelley's settled relationship with Peacock had come to an end. On the twenty-third of September, as the Journal tells us, Shelley finished his poem and went up to town with Claire. From then on, until his departure from England the next March, Shelley's life was anything but settled. This we have already gone over,[29] and need not do so again. The record of Shelley's reading bears out what we know of his life. There are no notations for October,[30] and almost none for November, and though the account is more complete for December, it appears then to be mere random reading. *Mandeville* is followed by the *Rights of Man*, and the *Biographia Literaria* by Hume, Berkeley, and Lady Morgan's *France*, three of these items being current publications.

In March, 1818, Shelley left England for a third time, and for a third time his departure for the Continent followed at greater or at lesser length a period of close association with Peacock. Probably we should also speak of Shelley's association with Hogg. But what is more to the point, and indeed the most significant thing that we have to record, is that this time the Hellenism of Shelley's friends "stuck."

On May 9 the Shelleys arrived in Leghorn, and the next day, according to the Journal, Shelley began the reading of Euripides. On June 2 he turned to Sophocles, the *Philoctetes*, *Electra*, and *Ajax*

29. *Vide supra*, pp. 16–17.

30. There are none for September, either. But here the lack of record must be attributed to the birth of Clara on the second of the month, and to Mrs. Shelley's inability to keep track of her husband's reading although she was able to record her own.

following in rapid order. From June 13 to June 17 Shelley was engaged with the *Memorabilia* of Xenophon, and from June 17 until July 6 with Aristophanes. In addition, he read the *Anacharsis* of the Abbé Barthélemy, a sure sign of allegiance to the Greek Revival. Then on the ninth of July Shelley began his translation of the *Symposium*, which occupied him, according to the Journal, until the seventeenth. Yet even before he was finished with this labor, Shelley began the reading of Herodotus, which engaged him until the second of August. On the third of August he read the *Persae* of Æschylus, and we are much interested to observe that on the fourth and fifth he read the *Phaedrus*.

Thus, within a couple of months of the commencement of *Prometheus Unbound*,[31] Shelley had read the two dialogues which chiefly expound Plato's philosophy of love. Indeed, not merely had Shelley read them, but he had worked with one of them as only the translator is obliged to work in his attempt to put the thought of one language into the words of another.

On October 17, after the first act of *Prometheus Unbound* had been written,[32] and during the estrangement between Mary and Shelley that Clara's death had occasioned,[33] Shelley wrote to Byron asking for his Plato.[34] Perhaps in the troubled state of his mind it was to Plato that he turned for the stability and certainty that seemed to be slipping away from him in the world of concrete fact. At any rate, the Plato must have come, or Shelley must have picked it up (since both Shelley and Byron were in Venice), for the Journal records that on the twentieth Shelley began reading the *Republic*. From entries recorded as of Ferrara and Bologna, it may be assumed that the *Republic* was Shelley's reading on the journey south to Naples.[35]

Shelley returned to the *Republic* the next year in Florence, whither he and Mary had gone to await her last confinement. The Journal notes that Shelley began reading the dialogue on the very day they arrived, the ninth of October. Shelley's second reading of the *Republic* thus belongs to the same period as the fourth act of *Prometheus Unbound*, which was composed also in Florence. Until November 9, when the Journal breaks off a few days before the birth of Percy Florence, the *Republic* figures steadily in the record of Shelley's reading. Indeed, Shelley's continued devotion to the great Platonic dialogue constitutes one of the chief justifications for calling him a Platonist. It is one thing to read the *Symposium* and the *Phaedrus*, which belong as much to literature as to philosophy. But the *Re-*

31. According to the Journal, Shelley was at work on *Prometheus Unbound* by September 5.

32. Cf. White, *op. cit.*, II, 557.   33. *Vide supra*, pp. 17–18.

34. The letter is given in White, *op. cit.*, II, 460.   35. So *idem*, II, 59, 565.

public is another matter, and Shelley's continued interest in the great work shows an enthusiasm for Plato that is not an affair of the passing moment. In September, 1820, Shelley returned to the *Republic* again.

But it is not our intention to carry the account of Shelley's Greek reading to the end of his life. In spite of further items in the Journal, and a notation of Shelley's reading the *Phaedo* in May, 1820, that very much interests us, the Journal as a record of Shelley's reading becomes less and less satisfactory. Besides, Shelley's Hellenism during the years in Italy is not a thing that needs to be proved. There are no dissenting witnesses, and it is borne out by Shelley's writings, up to and including *Hellas,* the last major poem Shelley lived to complete. Our "bridge" is finished. We have every reason for undertaking a study of "Shelley and the Thought of the Greeks."

Yet the phrase reminds us that there is a last stumbling block to be removed before the journey can be prosecuted. We have entitled the present chapter "Shelley and the Thought of the Greeks," and it follows our brief history of the Greek heritage as the romantic generation received it. Yet specifically it is the influence of Plato which we intend to study, and even our references to Plato will be limited to the particular dialogues that Shelley is known to have read.[36] This possible inconsistency in our position calls for an explanation before we set forth on our journey.

Fundamentally, the explanation is to be sought in the preceding chapter, the point of which was that not until the eighteenth century were the ancient Greeks themselves restored to modern consciousness. Their books had been recovered by the Renaissance—imperfectly according to modern standards, but sufficiently for all practical purposes. The body of Greek literature had been provided for subsequent generations to think or to feel about. But the Greeks themselves, the Greeks as human beings who had lived on the earth under widely different historical conditions from ours, the Greeks as the authors of their literature—these individual Greeks had either been totally abstracted or, perhaps what is worse, looked upon as mere prototypes of the modern man.

We have seen that the Greek Revival of the eighteenth century brought the historical Greeks back to men's thoughts and discovered their descendants to be still alive, under the yoke of the Turk.

Now it should be clear, even from the slight glimpse of Peacock that we have given, that to Peacock the ancient Greeks were, in just

---

36. The Journal records Shelley's reading of the *Symposium, Phaedrus, Republic,* and *Phaedo.* From letters of February 15 and October 22, 1821, to Peacock and Hogg respectively (Julian *Works,* x, 234; vii, 311), there is specific information as to Shelley's reading the *Ion* and *Gorgias.* Finally, from the translated fragment of the *Menexenus* and the brief comment on the *Crito* which appear in the 1840 volumes of Shelley's prose, we may infer that Shelley had also read these latter dialogues.

this way, a people who had once been very much alive. There can be little doubt that he took them as a standard of the way in which human beings ought to live, and tried his best to be a Greek himself. Right from the publication of *Headlong Hall*, written during the Bishopsgate period, Peacock's contemporaries set him down as a latter-day Epicurean;[37] and until the end of his life, when he protested to the Anglican clergyman that "by the immortal gods" he would not be moved,[38] Peacock lived up to the fiction. Nor can there be any doubt that when it came to the Greeks Hogg shared Peacock's opinion.

Though the quality of Shelley's imagination was too impersonal, or perhaps too universal, to allow him to identify himself with the ancient Greeks, yet that he too came to regard them as a people who had lived in most certain, three-dimensional veritability, indeed in an age that was almost if not quite the Golden one—that Shelley followed Peacock and Hogg in their veneration of the ancient Hellenes must be apparent to all who have read the Preface to *Hellas*. That Shelley in addition looked upon Plato as the spokesman of his people, rather than as a member merely of the kingdom of thought, is clear from the fragments connected with his translation of the *Symposium*.

Immediately upon the conclusion of his translation, Shelley set to work upon his *Discourse on the Manners of the Ancients Relative to the Subject of Love*.[39] Although this *Discourse* remains but an essay of some 2,500 words and is one of those prose fragments that we can by no means be sure Shelley would have permitted to be published had he remained alive, yet, as always, the fragment is not without biographical value. It comes fresh from the Platonic mood of Shelley's translation of the *Symposium*, and was in some way intended to introduce or accompany or apologize for the latter.[40] It is an indication of the way Shelley was thinking in the summer of 1818 at the Baths of Lucca.

Thus it is rather a startling confirmation of our theory to find that in Shelley's *Discourse* Plato is not mentioned once, and that Pericles and Aristotle serve chiefly to mark the boundaries of the Periclean

37. Cf. *The Critical Review* for January, 1816, p. 69, where Peacock is called "a sort of laughing philosopher."

38. The anecdote is furnished by Edith Nicholls, Peacock's granddaughter, in her Biographical Notice to the Bentley Edition of Peacock's works (London, 1875), I, l–li.

39. According to the Journal, Shelley finished translating the *Symposium* on July 17, 1818. A week later, on July 25, he wrote to Godwin, telling him that he had been "excited . . . to attempt an Essay upon the cause of some differences in sentiment between the Ancients and Moderns, with respect to the subject of the dialogue" (Julian *Works*, IX, 317). On the same day Shelley wrote Peacock that he was at work on a "prefatory essay" (*idem*, IX, 315).

40. In her preface to the 1840 volumes of posthumous prose, Mrs. Shelley says of the *Discourse* and prefatory essay simply that they "form an introduction to *The Banquet* or *Symposium* of Plato" (*idem*, v, viii).

age. Though the *Discourse* was occasioned by a dialogue of Plato's, the impression the reader receives is not of Plato but of the age in which Plato lived. As Shelley emerged from his ardent study of the *Symposium,* it is evident that his generalizations are of the Greeks as Greeks. We read,

The history of ancient Greece is the study of legislators, philosophers, and poets; it is the history of men, compared with the history of titles. What the Greeks were, was a reality, not a promise.[41]

Again we read,

The Greeks of the Periclean age were widely different from us. It is to be lamented that no modern writer has hitherto dared to show them precisely as they were. Barthélemi . . . never forgets that he is a Christian and a Frenchman. Wieland . . . refrains from diminishing the interest of his romances by painting sentiments in which no European of modern times can possibly sympathize. There is no book which shows the Greeks precisely as they were; they seem all written for children, with the caution that no practice or sentiment, highly inconsistent with our present manners, should be mentioned, lest those manners should receive outrage and violation.[42]

Yet, though the sense of the Greeks was probably always stronger with Shelley than the sense of Plato, this is not to imply that Shelley was unaware of Plato's individual greatness. To Shelley Plato was no less than chief among the Greek thinkers, as appears from the even more fragmentary Preface that he wrote to accompany his translation of the *Symposium.* There Shelley tells us that he selected the *Symposium* for translation "as the most beautiful and perfect among all the works of Plato," and he declares that "Plato is eminently the greatest among the Greek philosophers."[43]

The truth of the matter is that Plato came to represent Greek thought to Shelley, the thought of that civilization to which, as Shelley says,[44] we owe our civilization. It would be a mistake to entitle the present chapter merely "Shelley and Plato." The implications are greater than that. The influence of Plato was an influence bearing connotations of the whole of Greek civilization. In fact, it would seem that the premature periods of Shelley's Hellenism were premature because Shelley did not have Plato to inform them, and that after Shelley went to Italy it was Plato who permitted the noticeable expansion of Shelley's interest in the Greeks. Furthermore, we must remember that whether we look at the unfinished *Prince Athanase,* or at *Prometheus Unbound,* the first Greek influence in Shelley's

41. *Idem,* VII, 226.   42. *Idem,* VII, 227.   43. *Idem,* VII, 161.
44. In the Preface to *Hellas.*

poetry that is not superficial has a distinctly Platonic cast. Hence it seems not too much to say that Shelley's seekings for a faith to take the place of his radicalism were not answered, that the exertions of his friends to enroll him as a fellow Athenian were not successful, until Plato came to stand for the Greeks.

2. The 1816 Hymns

So much for the general picture of Shelley's espousal of the Greek Revival. It is our turn now to examine the poetry that came out of this espousal. But first we must go back to the 1816 Hymns which, though composed before Shelley became a Hellenist, yet show his latent idealism, an idealism only waiting to receive a Hellenic cast to become the dominant as well as the basic thing in his life.

In our second chapter we outlined the circumstances that must have led to the groping and disillusion of *Alastor*. These circumstances did not ameliorate as 1815 passed into 1816. The disenchantment that seemed to overtake most of the human beings in whom Shelley placed his trust deepened rather than abated. In spite of the little William Shelley, Godwin's namesake, the philosopher remained inflexibly estranged. At the same time, his demands for financial assistance became more urgent. Because of legal developments in the settlement between Shelley and his father, Shelley was unable to pay Godwin the second thousand pounds in November, and the subsequent bickering between the two men (not on speaking terms) forms one of the most distressing chapters in either of their lives. On Shelley's good health and spirits the protracted quarrel was an ever-increasing drag, and as early as February, 1816, flight, whether to Scotland or to the Continent, seemed to be the only way out. In April came the scornful reviews of *Alastor*. And in April came Claire's request that the Shelleys journey to Switzerland instead of to Italy, whither they had decided to go with Hogg.[45]

The events of the summer in Switzerland are the common property of all lovers of English literature. Except for the fellowship of Wordsworth and Coleridge at Nether Stowey, no other association of poets has so caught the imagination of literary posterity as that of Byron and Shelley on the shores of the Lake of Geneva. The setting, with its trips to Chillon, the wood of Julie, and Mont Blanc, would have memorialized the comradeship even of minor poets. A result is that we know the events of the summer almost hour by hour. We know that Shelley "dosed" Byron with Wordsworth.[46] We also know that with Shelley it was still the slack water between tides, that he was occupied with no major creative work, that even his reading was without particular direction.

Thus, as we approach the two poems of the summer of 1816, the

45. For the facts of this paragraph, see White, *op. cit.*, I, 426–436.
46. Cf. Medwin, *Conversations of Lord Byron* (2nd ed. London, 1824), pp. 293–294.

Hymn to Intellectual Beauty and *Mont Blanc*, two facts emerge as of major importance. The first is the lack of change in the unsettled condition of Shelley's life, so that we should expect, if anything, the poetry of the summer to reveal a deeper subjective stratum than *Alastor*. The second is the looseness of the criticism that has been showered upon the idealism of this poetry, as indeed upon all of Shelley's idealistic verse.[47] Plato and Berkeley, as our note would indicate, appear to be the favorite putative sources, but Spinoza and Sir William Drummond are never far off stage. In fact, so much has been asserted on this score that a survey of the various idealisms upon which Shelley's poetry is said to rest is sooner or later an inevitability in an ideological study of Shelley. Since Shelley's debt to Plato is to be the main topic of the next section of this chapter, it need concern us here no more than in passing. But there could be no better opportunity than the present for a brief survey of the various modern idealisms with which Shelley's poetry has at one time or another been connected. The survey can stand at the same time as a clearinghouse for our discussion of the 1816 Hymns.

In this survey of the philosophy of Shelley's own age we shall lean upon the unusually able article on "Metaphysics" contributed to the *Encyclopædia Britannica* by the late Thomas Case, President until 1924 of Corpus Christi College, Oxford.[48] In the course of this article, President Case synopsizes the chief metaphysical systems of modern philosophy. From Descartes to Schopenhauer (who forms a hithermost limit to this Shelleyan study), President Case finds that the distinguishing mark of modern philosophy is its *psychologic* idealism. Descartes conceived that we know nothing but mental objects, that our sole justification for believing outer objects to exist is our faith in the integrity of God, who would not willingly deceive us. Even Spinoza, who approaches closest to an ontological philosophy—even Spinoza grants no existence to things apart from ideas. To Spinoza things and ideas are parallel manifestations of the same reality, with

---

47. Professor Beach states in his *Concept of Nature in 19th-Century English Poetry* (p. 243), "The influence of platonism is vaguely felt in *Alastor* (1815). It is more obvious in the *Hymn to Intellectual Beauty* and *Mont Blanc* (both 1816)."

Professor White says of *Mont Blanc*, "Its hint that experience is simply the universe flowing through the individual mind reflects the philosophy of Berkeley" (*op. cit.*, I, 455).

On p. 390 of *The Romantic Quest*, Professor Fairchild says of Shelley, "The *Hymn to Intellectual Beauty*, written in the summer of 1816, a little less than a year after *Alastor*, plainly reflects his devotion to Plato."

In *The Magic Plant* (Chapel Hill, 1936), p. 180, Professor Grabo says, "In the poem *Mont Blanc*, written during Shelley's second visit to Switzerland in the summer of 1816, the Platonism is more copious, more elaborately reasoned, than in the *Hymn*."

48. President Case contributed his article originally to the Tenth Edition (London, Edinburgh, and New York, 1902–3). It was slightly revised for the Eleventh Edition (Cambridge and New York, 1910–11), but was dropped from the Fourteenth Edition.

ideas being the closer of the two to that ultimate substance that is the goal of knowledge and of our lives.

However, of all the major philosophers from Descartes to Schopenhauer, it is Berkeley who most signally brings out the psychologic, or epistemologic, character of modern philosophy. Berkeley's famous phrase from the third paragraph of the *Principles* that "*esse* is *percipi*" is heard throughout the eighteenth century, and made plain to everyone just where he stood. Indeed, it is clear that in his idealistic divergence from the ordinary realism of common sense Berkeley went farther than the German philosophers who followed him a century later. For Berkeley cheerfully advances to the solipsistic extreme of psychologic idealism, admitting that "all the choir of heaven and furniture of the earth, in a word all those bodies which compose the mighty frame of the world" have no existence save as they are known by individual minds.[49] There is not one sun but many suns, Berkeley preserving the logic of his paradoxical position by the conventional Christian hypostasis of a unitary God who speaks to all of us at once. The Germans, as we have said, never went so far as this. Though to them, as to Berkeley, the sun existed only as it is known, nevertheless they kept its unity by hypostatizing a unitary mind in all of us to perceive it. But not so Berkeley, who became a prelate of the Church of Ireland, and was all his life an upholder of Christian doctrine.

Now the historian of ideas will not admit a philosophical influence unless there really is a philosophical influence—unless, that is, there is a transference of some or all of a philosopher's main ideas. If there is a Spinozistic influence, it should be apparent that the individual is looking at the world as a correlate of thought, indeed as knowledge rather than as fact. To the Spinozist the way to truth is not through observation, and then through interpretation of that observation, but through contemplation of the mind's own innate ideas—those ideas that lead to the idea of ideas, to the law of laws, to the substance without predicate. Similarly, if there is a Berkeleyan influence, it should be apparent that the individual is looking upon the world as mental phenomena, as *his* mental phenomena. To the Berkeleyan, just as the fact of vision (if properly considered) is but a language of signs and significates, so the whole order of the universe is but our perception of the language of God as He speaks to us and to other human beings. Even with the divine spokesman left out, as with Hume and Sir William Drummond,[50] we should expect the individ-

49. The quotation and the thought come from the sixth paragraph of the *Principles of Human Knowledge* (Dublin, 1710).

50. This will be nearly our last reference to Sir William Drummond. His volume of *Academical Questions* (London, 1805) is entirely derivative, and he is without mention in any standard history of philosophy. Yet one does not wonder at Shelley's regard for

ual showing a Berkeleyan heritage to view the world as perception, personal perception, and not as fact.

But let us examine the actual thought content of the two poems in
question.

In the first stanza of the *Hymn to Intellectual Beauty* we are informed of a Power of which we perceive only the effects, and perceive these only in glimpses. For, though the shadow of this Power
is ever present, it visits both the "various world" and the "human
heart" most inconstantly,

> Like clouds in starlight widely spread,—
> Like memory of music fled.
>
> 9–10

Far from being inherent in the world of outer fact, or in the world
of inner consciousness, the Power is but an occasional visitor of either.
In the second stanza the Power is defined as the spirit of Beauty, and
is declared to consecrate whatever of human thought or form it shines
upon. Yet in its very shining upon something other than itself it reveals its separateness, and indeed only too frequently fails to shine
at all, passing away and leaving the world "vacant and desolate."

Why is the spirit of Beauty so inconstant? In the fourth stanza the
poet recognizes what so many others have recognized before him,
that were divine Beauty to dwell permanently in the heart of man
he would be "immortal and omnipotent." In other words, the incon-
stancy of the spirit of Beauty is a circumstance of man's mortality,
which is an ultimate datum, a thing to be accepted and not explained.

Then, in perhaps the most memorable stanzas of the poem, the
poet tells of the moment in his youth when the spirit of Beauty fell
upon him. Perceiving that the reality of things is beautiful, he dedicated himself to the Loveliness that is truth, trusting that it would
free the world from its dark slavery. Finally, in the last stanza, the
poet beseeches the spirit of Beauty, which thus came to him in
youth "like the truth of nature," to supply its calm to his onward
life.

That the poem is idealistic, that it recognizes the chief reality of

the work. The first of its two books is an "introduction to philosophy" quite in the usual
sense, with a general criticism of philosophic ideas from the Berkeleyan point of view.
The second book is a history of modern philosophy, beginning with Descartes, and devot-
ing chapters to Bacon, Newton, Spinoza, Hartley, Leibniz, and finally to Kant and to
Reid. The work is well written, with an unusual clearness of style, and as a textbook is
entirely adequate. There can be no doubt of Shelley's indebtedness to the volume. In
fact a good deal of his scientific knowledge must have come from it, just as (judging
from the carry-over of exact phrases) it must also be the source of the ridicule of Kantianism found in Peacock's *Nightmare Abbey*. Yet, since the *Academical Questions* is clearly
a textbook and can only have helped Shelley to other men's ideas, it falls outside the
province of this study. Only if it were the source of erroneous thinking (as would be
the case with Spinoza) would it come within our scope.

things to be spiritual, or "intellectual," goes without saying. But that the poem in any way suggests Spinoza, Berkeley, or any other modern idealist, simply is not borne out by an examination of the poem's thought. Its ontological presuppositions are those of the Greeks, of Christian dogma, and of common sense. There is the "various world" of ordinary fact, there is the "human heart" standing apart from the world, and there is a greater, spiritual power standing apart from either. There is not the slightest suggestion that the world of fact may be no more than our knowledge, or that the greater, spiritual power speaks to us in the language of our knowledge, or that our knowledge is but a form that this spiritual power takes. It means absolutely nothing in a Berkeleyan sense that Shelley speaks of "life's unquiet dream." He might just as well have spoken of "life's fitful fever," except that Shakespeare used the phrase before him. From time immemorial the strivings and disappointments and illusions of human endeavor have suggested a similar phraseology. If one is to show the influence of any post-Cartesian philosopher in the poetry of Shelley he must point out, not that the world is insubstantial, or that it takes the chief reality from some participating spiritual power, but that it exists, either chiefly or entirely, as we know it.

It is doubtful if such an idea is conveyed in Shelley's poetry before the composition of *Hellas*. Certainly no such idea is expressed in either of the two poems in question.

The belief in Shelley's Berkeleyanism apparently comes from Mrs. Shelley's unfortunate remark that "Shelley was a disciple of the Immaterial Philosophy of Berkeley," which occurs in her preface to the 1840 volumes of Shelley's prose, and is apropos of the fragment *On Life*.[51] Mrs. Shelley's remark is unfortunate because it is doubtful if it can be applied to any of Shelley's poetry, and because, even as regards the prose fragment in question, it can be uttered only with reservations. For though in the fourth-from-the-end paragraph we read, almost in Berkeley's words, "Nothing exists but as it is perceived," yet before the paragraph is finished we also read, "The words *I, you, they,* are . . . merely marks employed to denote the different modifications of the one mind."[52] Then, in the next paragraph, we are told that this is not to imply that the individual is that one mind, but that he is merely a portion of it. Now we need not add that such a Fichtean thought as this would have been anathema to the Bishop of Cloyne. In fact, such a thought could have come only from Shelley's own time, and not from the eighteenth century at all.

It is a pity that so few of Shelley's critics have themselves been serious students of philosophy—that is, students of philosophy not for Shelley's sake but for philosophy's sake. Had they been, they

51. Julian *Works*, v, ix.   52. *Idem*, vi, 196.

would have had an explanation for the metaphysical prose fragments which, even if undemonstrable as fact, would at least have deterred them from giving the fragments more than the biographical value they deserve. For students of philosophy, face-to-face with a difficult doctrine such as Hegel's theory of the concrete universal, or Kant's deduction of the categories, invariably take paper and pencil and attempt to work out the doctrine for themselves, paraphrasing the philosopher in question and putting into their own words the philosopher's thoughts. Such essays have nothing to do with one's own considered philosophical position. They indicate only one's general interest in philosophy. To the student of philosophy it is difficult to regard the fragment *On Life* in any other light. The number of direct, unrhetorical questions, the preponderance of the first person, suggest to him his own wrestlings with various philosophical conundrums, and make him recognize in Shelley a kindred soul.

Yet there can be no question as to the biographical value of the fragment *On Life*. For it shows beyond cavil that Shelley understood the ideas of modern philosophy and hence, presumably, could have expressed them in his poetry had he wished. It will avail nothing to say that Shelley unconsciously implies them, that he is a Berkeleyan or Spinozist *malgré lui*. We must assume that if he could specifically and clearly set down these ideas in prose he could have done as much in poetry. Even if we recognize with Dowden,[53] and more recently with Professor Notopoulos,[54] that the prose fragment *On Life* should be dated not earlier than 1819, we still have testimony that Shelley as early as 1813 was clear as to the import of modern philosophy. For, in the letter of November 26 from Edinburgh to Hogg, Shelley writes, "I have examined Hume's reasonings with respect to the non-existence of external things, and, I confess, they appear to me to follow from the doctrines of Locke. What am I to think of a philosophy which conducts to such a conclusion?"[55]

Shelley was clearly aware of the meaning of modern philosophy, but it was remote from the cares and occupations of the summer of 1816. That the essential Shelley was idealistic we have never doubted. But it seems no less certain that Shelley's essential idealism was of the world rather than of the mind, was ontologic rather than psychologic. We may well ask if it would ever have permitted of a psychologic, Berkeleyan cast. Certainly the poetry of the summer of 1816 does not express a psychologic idealism, and from the lack of predilection to the summer we may assume that the poetry of the summer is expressive of Shelley himself rather than of a reigning enthusiasm.

53. Dowden, *The Life of Percy Bysshe Shelley*, I, 534 n.
54. J. A. Notopoulos, "The Dating of Shelley's Prose," *PMLA*, LVIII, 489–491.
55. Julian *Works*, IX, 81.

There still remains the problem of the Platonism of the *Hymn to Intellectual Beauty* to be disposed of, although biographically, there is nothing to show that Shelley had thought of Plato for years.[56] Nevertheless the poem has been dubbed Platonic with a frequency that suggests either that the term has no meaning or that the critics of the poem have written from general recollection, without submitting themselves to the discipline of rereading Plato and Shelley before writing. For in the *Phaedrus* it is distinctly stated that, of all the ideas, beauty alone receives an adequate embodiment in the material world. We read, "This is the privilege of beauty, that being the loveliest she is also the most palpable to sight. Coming to earth we find her . . . shining in clearness through the clearest aperture of sense."[57] As we shall see, beauty to Plato is the immediate aspect of good, the aspect that appeals to us directly through the emotions instead of indirectly through reason. Yet in Shelley's *Hymn* beauty is fleeting and evanescent. Far from shining through the clearest aperture of sense, it is only occasionally to be perceived, and then by its effects rather than by itself.

But it may be averred that Shelley is not speaking of individual beauty but of universal beauty. Let us turn, then, to the *Symposium*, where Plato ascends from the individual to the universal, to beauty "pure and clear and unalloyed, not clogged with the pollutions of mortality and all the colors and vanities of human life," to "true beauty simple and divine."[58] Perhaps here there are grounds for regarding Shelley's *Hymn* as Platonic. Let us look, then, at what Professor Gingerich has to say upon the subject. We read,

Shelley's approach to Beauty is almost diametrically opposite to Plato's. For Plato urges the advocate of Beauty to . . . proceed as on steps from the love of one form to that of two, and from that of two to all forms, point by point through a self-discipline of the mind. . . . Shelley on the contrary, without any "former labor" upon which Plato lays so much stress, arrives, by a sort of instantaneous conversion, suddenly into a full sense of the meaning of the absolute Beauty.[59]

As Professor Gingerich makes clear, Shelley's approach to absolute beauty is romantic and emotional, not disciplined, rational, and Platonic. Shelley's conception of ideal beauty is not "intellectual" in the strict meaning of the term, which implies an approach by means

56. The last evidence of Shelley's concern for Plato comes from the book orders of December, 1812. Professor White in his *Shelley* gives no reference between then and the summer of 1817, and Professor Notopoulos states of the *Hymn*, "There is no evidence in Shelley's letters or Journal that he had been reading Plato shortly before or at the time of the composition of the poem" (*op. cit.*, LVIII, 582).
57. *Phaedrus* 250 DE, rearranged from Jowett's translation.
58. *Symposium* 211 E, Jowett's translation.
59. *Essays in the Romantic Poets*, pp. 212–213.

of the thinking faculties. To be sure, the phrase "intellectual beauty" occurs only in the title of the poem,[60] and by its use Shelley probably intended only to convey that the supreme beauty he had in mind was abstract rather than concrete. Yet with Plato, the abandonment of the concrete is the very signal for the intellectual faculties to take over control, while with Shelley, even in its ideality, beauty is still a business of the feelings rather than of thought. Shelley's *Hymn to Intellectual Beauty* is, in point of sober fact, not Platonic at all.

Let us look, however, at *Mont Blanc*, in many ways the more interesting, as it is the longer, of the two poems. The general content of the poem is simple enough, and is indeed composed of the thoughts and feelings that anyone might have on viewing the ravine of the Arve and Mont Blanc for the first time. Yet the poem opens with a metaphysical passage and closes with another, which together have produced many an interpretation not borne out by the thought of the poem as a whole, or by the historical position that Shelley's intellectual development had reached in the summer of 1816.

Thus the poem begins with the statement that the "everlasting universe of things flows through the mind" and there receives its tribute from the "source of human thought." The passage has received one knows not how many Berkeleyan and Platonic and Spinozistic constructions from various critics. Yet why it should be given other than the plain and simple interpretation is hard to understand. That the world in some way flows through the mind has always been an assumption of common sense and of naturalistic science. Today it is assumed that the human individuality is literally bombarded by light waves and sound waves and heat waves and, in fact, many waves that it has no means of picking up. That to the world's message the mind adds its own—this too is an age-old assumption. Even the pantheistic notion that the two messages in reality come from an identical source is hardly new, and is, as everyone knows, the central thought of Wordsworth's "Tintern Abbey."

But all this is ontologic and far removed from the connotations of modern philosophy. If the lines in question mean that the universe in its entirety flows through the mind (as seems to have been assumed),[61] then we may ask, What is the mind through which it flows? And what is that extra-universal source from which the contributions to its entirety are made? An epistemologic interpretation of the passage is fraught with difficulties of the highest order.

On the other hand, in the very next stanza, where Shelley has abandoned metaphysics for sheer contemplation of the ravine of the Arve,

60. Professors White and Notopoulos have shown that Shelley may have picked up the phrase whole-cloth from his reading (*Shelley*, I, 701; and *PMLA*, LVIII, 583–584).
61. *Vide supra*, p. 121, note 47.

the phrase "universe of things" is again used, and used in a context that admits of no unusual interpretation. Here Shelley speaks of his "own separate phantasy," of his "own . . . human mind, which . . . renders and receives . . . influencings,"

> Holding an unremitting interchange
> With the clear universe of things around.
>
> 39–40

In other words, the metaphysical presuppositions of *Mont Blanc* are exactly those of the *Hymn to Intellectual Beauty*. There is the "clear universe of things around," there is the "human mind," and there is a superior, spiritual Power which

> in likeness of the Arve comes down
> From the ice-gulfs that gird his secret throne.
>
> 16–17

Well might that supreme spectacle from the valley of the Arve have moved Shelley to contemplation of the Power that lies behind the forces of nature. In the ravine of the Arve Shelley witnessed the forces of erosion at work, and foresaw the consequences of what he perceived. He writes,

> The glaciers creep
> Like snakes that watch their prey, from their far fountains,
> Slow rolling on; there, many a precipice,
> Frost and the Sun in scorn of mortal power
> Have piled: dome, pyramid, and pinnacle,
> A city of death, distinct with many a tower
> And wall impregnable of beaming ice.
> Yet not a city, but a flood of ruin
> Is there, that from the boundaries of the sky
> Rolls its perpetual stream; vast pines are strewing
> Its destined path, or in the mangled soil
> Branchless and shattered stand; the rocks, drawn down
> From yon remotest waste, have overthrown
> The limits of the dead and living world,
> Never to be reclaimed. The dwelling-place
> Of insects, beasts, and birds, becomes its spoil;
> Their food and their retreat for ever gone,
> So much of life and joy is lost. The race
> Of man flies far in dread; his work and dwelling
> Vanish, like smoke before the tempest's stream,
> And their place is not known.
>
> 100–120

From the last three or four lines it would appear that Shelley divined what science now demonstrates—that the inevitable cycle of denudation and erosion will eventually reduce the whole massif of the Alps to the level of the sea, scattering the race of man afar, and of his mountain cities leaving not a trace. Perhaps we are reading into the passage more than it contains. But at least we are following the logic of the lines. The observations and assumptions they make are those of natural science. In fact, the scientific assumptions of the greater, central portion of the poem should have carried over to the beginning and end, where Shelley is less scientific and more purely metaphysical.

For in the final stanza Shelley returns to the speculative interest of the opening stanza. Out of his thinking emerges the idea that there is a permanence behind the ruin and destruction. Behind the forces of nature carving out the valley of the Arve there is a constancy of law, a power for change that is both "still and solemn." Shelley is impressed with the fact that the processes of nature are independent of the human onlooker (thus betraying a point of view the opposite of Berkeleyanism). He says,

> In the calm darkness of the moonless nights,
> In the lone glare of day, the snows descend
> Upon that Mountain; none beholds them there.
>
> 130–132

To Shelley the human observer is unnecessary, since the force that controls human observation is the force that controls Mont Blanc. To Shelley

> The secret Strength of things
> Which governs thought, and to the infinite dome
> Of Heaven is as a law, inhabits thee!
>
> 139–141

Not only is the human observer unnecessary to Mont Blanc, but Mont Blanc is unnecessary to the human observer. The whole is the ground of its parts, not its parts of one another. Shelley finally asks,

> And what were thou, and earth, and stars, and sea,
> If to the human mind's imaginings
> Silence and solitude were vacancy?
>
> 142–144

For, since the force of thought is the force of nature, the mind's very instinct to conceive of independent objects is a guarantee of their existence. Berkeley to the contrary, the human mind shows no tendency to regard absence of sensation as absence of existence. To the mind's imaginings, silence and solitude are not vacancy. Rather are they reminders of the Power that is greater than either object or perceiver. Indeed, Shelley's fundamental conviction is simply that there is

> A motion and a spirit, that impels
> All thinking things, all objects of all thought,
> And rolls through all things.
>
> Wordsworth, "Tintern Abbey," 100–102

It is not apparent why there should be recourse to philosophy to explain the source of these poems. As Dowden suggests,[62] the *Hymn to Intellectual Beauty* is as obviously aroused by the landscape of the Lake of Geneva as *Mont Blanc* is aroused by the mountains of Chamonix. In the one poem the ultimate spirituality of the universe which Shelley had always believed in, and which we have observed from the days of *Queen Mab,* appears as Beauty. In the other poem it appears as Power, or Law. If one must have a source for the thought of the poems, the rule of parsimony (as applicable to literature as to philosophy) forbids us to go farther than Wordsworth, whose poetry we know Shelley was reading in the summer of 1816, and indeed employing as a gospel with which to evangelize Byron.

62. *Op. cit.,* II, 31.

3. *Prometheus Unbound*

INTRODUCTION

As we come to *Prometheus Unbound,* to the period of Shelley's maturest poetry and indubitable Hellenism, it would be wise to gather up the loose threads of our previous thinking and to look, for a moment, at the poet Shelley himself.

In our second chapter we declared the personal element to be an important factor in the history of literature, whether one looks at the man or at the movement. We cannot believe that the Greek Revival was a revival any more than in part. It is our conviction that Shelley was stronger than any or all of his influences. Hence we shall be circumspect in our search for Platonic ingredients in Shelley's poetry. To expect a wholesale carry-over of the Theory of Ideas, or of the political philosophy of the *Republic,* or of the life and times of fourth-century Athens, would be contrary to the assumptions upon which this study rests.

Indeed, it is our opinion that the personal element is particularly strong in Shelley, and this whether we consider Shelley's life or his work. Byron, perhaps Shelley's greatest rival for individuality, though a truant from Harrow for a term,[63] nevertheless went back, and was never so pitted against the school mores as was Shelley at Eton. Though he was always at odds with his mother, Byron's quarrel with her never developed into the irreparable breach that occurred between Shelley and his father. Though a dissolute young peer at Cambridge if there ever was one (what with the mistress in male clothing, and Jackson and Angelo, the boxing and fencing gentlemen),[64] Byron was never so completely at variance with the university world as was Shelley at Oxford, and was, of course, never expelled. Shelley's intransigence is certainly extreme, whether we look at the early days of school and college, or at a period so late as the final months in England.

Of this later period Mr. W. E. Peck says,

In a year which had witnessed the suspension of the *Habeas Corpus* Act, and the enactment of the Suit in Chancery which had deprived him of the custody of his children on the grounds of his moral, political, and religious beliefs, exemplified in his actions, is it not surprising that Shelley should dare again to bait the lion of the law by portraying, in *Laon and Cythna,* a brother and sister living in the relationship of lovers?[65]

63. Cf. André Maurois, *Byron* (New York, 1930), pp. 55–56. Translated from the French by Hamish Miles.　　64. Cf. Maurois, *op. cit.,* pp. 83–84.
　65. Walter Edwin Peck, *Shelley, His Life and Work* (Boston and New York, 1927), II, 3–4.

To answer Mr. Peck's rhetorical question, we should reply, "No, not at all surprising." Indeed, as Medwin declares (and Mr. Peck quotes), Shelley "would have undergone the martyrdom he depicts in *Laon and Cythna,* rather than have renounced one tittle of his faith."[66]

The same strength of the personal element is evident throughout Shelley's poetry. From *Queen Mab* to *Hellas,* there are the same symbols and mannerisms of style, the same figures of speech taken from experiences that Shelley has imagined but not undergone, the same favorite ideas, the same supernatural machinery of a lively fancy. The car that carries Asia and Panthea on their travels in *Prometheus Unbound* comes from the same manufactory as the car that bears Queen Mab and Ianthe. The Temple of the Spirit in *The Revolt of Islam* is modeled on the Hall of Spells in *Queen Mab.* The Phantom of Mahomet in *Hellas* betrays a common lineage with the Phantasm of Jupiter in *Prometheus Unbound.* Indeed, to a student but tolerably acquainted with English poetry, it would be necessary only to half-breathe such an obscure line as "Like clouds inwoven in the silent sky"[67] to have him shout back, as Coleridge of Wordsworth, "Shelley!"

In fact, such an obscure line as we have quoted introduces us to one of the most individual aspects of Shelley's poetry, an aspect which we might call Shelley's ultra-Wordsworthianism. *Prometheus Unbound* offers a spectacle of rock and ice and stars and clouds and crystals hardly equaled by any other poem of similar length in English literature. In Shelley the cult of wild nature reaches a logical extreme. Whereas the nature that Wordsworth describes is usually the home at least of a solitary shepherd, in Shelley a nature is pictured to which man contributes nothing and from which he draws only aesthetic pleasure. The beauty of external nature comes to exist in its own right, and as such is sung with great lyrical splendor in *Prometheus Unbound.* How far this ultra-Wordsworthianism is from Plato we need not mention. Readers of the *Phaedrus* will remember that the chief use the Platonic Socrates had for the fabled Ilissus of song and poetry was to cool and bathe his feet. Wisdom to the Platonic Socrates was not to be derived from the vernal wood, even less from rock and glacier (which he never saw), but from the market place, the gymnasium, and the drinking party. Thus, as we approach the philosophical aspects of *Prometheus Unbound,* one of the first ingredients to be shaken through our sieve is the romantic, ultra-Wordsworthian cult of nature. It is wholly modern, thoroughly un-Platonic, and indeed entirely Shelleyan. We shall enjoy it as we read the play, and recognize that it constitutes one of the play's chief

66. Medwin, *op. cit.,* p. 438.   67. *The Revolt of Islam,* l. 3568.

beauties. But we shall not suppose that it forms part of any philosophy that may be traced to Plato.

Again, it has been borne upon us that the essential Shelley was always an idealist. We noticed that as early as *Queen Mab*, when it came to describing the universe apart from priests and kings, Shelley always took for granted that at heart it was spirit. In *Alastor* it need not be mentioned how much more important the spiritual world is than the concrete. Finally, in the 1816 Hymns, where circumstances conspired to give expression to the essential Shelley, we observed that once again the reality at the center of the world is assumed to be spiritual, not material.

This essential idealism, it seems to us, is to be attributed to a still more fundamental trait of Shelley's personality. To Shelley the subject was so much stronger than the object that it is questionable, at times, if the object existed at all. The object, in fact, had a habit of dropping from his hands the moment he attained it. The trips to Killarney and the Lakes in 1813 are instances of this;[68] but most conspicuous is the elopement to Lucerne in 1814. The Shelleys headed straight for the lake, one of the most beautiful in the world, the scene of Fleetwood's association with Russigny,[69] and a spot hallowed by William Tell. Yet no sooner had Shelley got there than he shut himself up in his room to write, and the next day decided to return to England.[70] Furthermore, it is not a question of the reality's failing to live up to expectation. No matter how lively Shelley's expectation, it is not likely that the Lake of Uri would have disappointed him. No, the point is that in the very moment of the dream's becoming reality, in the very moment of the subject's passing into object—in that very moment it ceases to charm, and in that moment it becomes necessary to create a new subject. This intense subjectivity is clearly the basis of Shelley's instinctive idealism. For, if conception is stronger than perception to a person, it will be odd if the world too does not seem to be conception rather than fact.

The strong probability that Shelley's intense subjectivity led to his instinctive idealism calls attention to a last peculiarity of Shelley's personality. For we recollect from our study of the 1816 Hymns that in 1816 Shelley's idealism was objective and ontologic. Hence it is not surprising to find that in content Shelley's subjectivity was thor-

68. For the facts, see White, *op. cit.*, i, 286–287, 320.

69. In his mention of Shelley's persistent desire to settle in a place with a summer-house similar to the one in Charles Brockden Brown's novel *Wieland*, Peacock called attention in his *Memoirs of Shelley* (ii, 327–328) to an amusing trait of Shelley's personality. But it remained for Professor White to show how strong in Shelley's life such patterns taken from third-rate fiction could be. Apparently Godwin's *Fleetwood* again and again actually determined Shelley's course of action. (See White, *op. cit.*, i, 229, 320, 357.)

70. For the facts, see White, *op. cit.*, i, 357.

oughly objective. It is the simple truth that though the world of
Shelley's imagination all but swamped the world of outer fact, yet
the world of outer fact was the subject of Shelley's imagination. As
the events of his life clearly show, Shelley was almost without self-
knowledge, and indeed unconcerned with his own or anybody else's
psychology. This alone, we observe, would have prevented him
from granting final allegiance to Berkeley or any other eighteenth-
century, psychological philosopher. In fact, Shelley shows the same
lack of interest in the subject coupled with a conception of the world
in terms of the subject that characterizes the philosophy not of the
eighteenth but of the nineteenth century. This is something to concern us later on. At present we must content ourselves with observing
that this peculiarity of Shelley's is responsible for the paradox of his
being one of the most impersonal of poets in his choice of subject matter, yet one of the most personal in his handling of that subject matter.[71] In his life, it explains the "semidelusions" described by Peacock.[72] In his life, Shelley's selflessness impressed everybody from
Hunt to Byron. Yet, even on the *Don Juan*, Shelley would bury his
nose in a book, in the world of the subject, instead of giving himself
up to the sun and air and blue Mediterranean.

Thus, partly from a study of Shelley's poetry, partly from a review
of the facts of Shelley's life, certain broad characteristics of the
man and poet have emerged. The personal element is by now well
shadowed forth, and will assist us in our further differentiation of the
native from the acquired, of the romantic from the Greek, in Shelley's poetry. It will allow us to center more purely upon the intellectual content of the poems in question. Indeed, before plunging into
the philosophical problems of *Prometheus Unbound*, it will be necessary to bestow a glance upon *The Revolt of Islam*, halfway between
the 1816 Hymns and *Prometheus Unbound* and anticipating the
ethical concerns of the latter poem. And here our differentiation of
the personal element will greatly help.

For we shall waste no time upon the dreamy, impractical, subjective
quality of Shelley's longest poem. It is present, and we have accounted for it. Of greater interest is Shelley's return to the problem
of good and evil. In *Queen Mab*, Shelley assigned both good and
evil to the agency of necessity, though necessity, as we observed,
was antithetical to his more deeply held faith in benevolence. But
now some four or five years have passed, and in his own peculiar way

71. A. C. Bradley in his "Shelley and Arnold's Critique of his Poetry" (*A Miscellany*
[London, 1929], p. 147) points out the lack of reminiscences of earlier writers in Shelley's style. Shelley's style is, in truth, suggestive only of himself. Yet, as regards subject
matter, even such an autobiographic poem as *Epipsychidion* is impersonality itself in
comparison with a poem like *The Prelude*.

72. *Op. cit.*, II, 323, 343.

Shelley has come closer to the problems of real life. The necessitarian brush-off of good and evil is hardly satisfying any longer. It has become increasingly apparent to Shelley that life is not so simple as it seemed, and his return to the problem of good and evil is the reason for our giving a prefatory glance to *The Revolt of Islam* before turning finally to *Prometheus Unbound*.

THE REVOLT OF ISLAM

The first canto of *The Revolt of Islam* is a real introduction. Not only does it introduce the two principal characters, but it epitomizes the forces that will be seen at work upon their lives. The struggle between the serpent and the eagle anticipates the coming action and represents the forces of good and evil locked in mortal conflict. Lest there be any doubt as to the ultimate significance of the episode, the woman who conducts the poet to the Temple of the Spirit expressly explains it, recounting the struggle of good and evil from the beginning of the world.

Thus the theory of good and evil that the poem recognizes is the ancient, dualistic one that conceives of the two as equivalent in power. It has been popular with critics of the poem to call this theory Manichaean[73] (though Albigensian would do as well). Actually, the doctrine as Shelley entertained it, if it came from any outside source at all, probably stemmed from the Zoroastrian fancies of John Frank Newton, which, we recall, infected Peacock for a time.

Be this as it may, the touch-and-go struggle between the eagle and the snake aptly symbolizes the ceaseless alternation of good and evil fortune in the poem. The abduction of Cythna and the imprisonment of Laon immediately follow Cythna's avowal of discipleship and the moment of their closest sympathy. When Laon is at death's door the Hermit rescues him, and, as we recall, in the midst of an earthquake that shatters her cavern and lets the ocean pour in, Cythna is miraculously preserved. But the forces of evil are ever lurking in the rear. No sooner have the liberated multitudes carried everything before them, and held a solemn celebration of their victory, than the mercenaries of the foreign despots arrive to turn the scales in favor of ill. Even at the last, when the disguised Laon is addressing the Senate and converts the younger members, the older members rise up to stab the converts in the back, and a slave is ready to drag the corpses out, "each to its bloody, dark, and secret grave."

Now the point we wish to make is that such a theory of good and evil, though it goes back to the ancient Persians, represents as far as Shelley is concerned an advance over the necessitarian theory. True, Shelley's new theory does not explain what good and evil are. But it

73. So Peck, *op. cit.*, ii, 13; and Fairchild, *op. cit.*, p. 392.

discriminates between them. In *Queen Mab* Shelley's theory had deprived good and evil of all meaning. Not only was the strictly human aspect of good and evil lost in the cosmic view of things, but even the difference between them was neglected in attributing evil to the same agency as good. As an ethical thinker Shelley is advancing.

Yet one wonders if ethics and radicalism really mix, if Shelley's advance as a moralist is not a sign of his permanent decline as a radical. For it is noticeable that the belief in the parity of good and evil takes the punch out of the radical speeches of Laon and Cythna.

The true radical is without a theory of evil. Evil, if he thinks at all, is simply an ulcer, an imposthume, on the body of the state, which needs but to be excised to be forgotten. "*Écrasez l'infâme!*" Voltaire said to the eighteenth century, with the implication that once the infamous thing was crushed, that would be the end of it. Indeed, the radical would scarcely cut off an aristocratic head if he believed that, Hydra-like, two would spring up to take its place. It is clear that a belief in the inevitable resurgence of evil denies the essence of radicalism at the start.

Yet this belief, if not in the minds of the central characters of the poem, is clearly present in the mind of Shelley.

Cythna's speech to the sailors who rescue her from her Andromedean rock after the earthquake is the chief radical speech in *The Revolt of Islam*—as it is also the beginning of the bloodless revolution which the poem portrays. She opens it with a common thought of eighteenth-century radicalism—that the human species is single. She says,

> Ye all are human—yon broad moon gives light
> To millions who the selfsame likeness wear,
> Even while I speak—beneath this very night,
> Their thoughts flow on like ours, in sadness or delight.
>   3222–3225

Cythna returns to this theme again and again, speaking of giving "to all an equal share of good," exclaiming, "Let all be free and equal," and observing, "We have one human heart."

Accordingly, "priests and kings" represent an anomaly in the order of things, and to make their untenable position secure must invent all kinds of lies and superstitions. In the diagnostic part of her speech, Cythna is at one with eighteenth-century radicalism. But in the remedial part we notice a weakening of the radical fervor, a recourse to supposition unknown to the true radical. The true radical is an *esprit simpliste*. He fails to see why the potential mood should be used at all. "Off with their heads! To the lantern! Stamp out the infamous thing!"

Yet in the most exhortative part of her speech, Cythna can only say,

> This need not be; ye might arise, and will
> That gold should lose its power, and thrones their glory;
> That love, which none may bind, be free to fill
> The world, like light; and evil faith, grown hoary
> With crime, be quenched and die.

3334–3338

And again she says,

> But the dark fiend . . . would o'er the heads of men
> Pass harmless, if they scorned to make their hearts his den.

3375–3378

Whether it is Cythna's own experiences with the hirelings of Othman and with Othman himself, or whether it is the Ahrimanic sense of evil portrayed in the opening canto of the poem that is guiding the poet's hand, the punch is gone from Cythna's speech just where it should be inserted. Her exhortation is placed in the conditional mood and turns out to be a suggestion rather than a command. Furthermore, we are given to understand in any event that her success as a revolutionary is to be attributed to the charm of her personality rather than to the force of her words.

In Laon's speeches, which all take place after the revolution has occurred, and are occasioned in each case by fresh outbreaks of evil, the plaintive note is in greater evidence. To the advocates of Liberty who would massacre the assassins that had crept among them and murdered ten thousand of their fellows, he says,

> Oh wherefore should ill ever flow from ill,
> And pain still keener pain for ever breed?
> We are all brethren—

1810–1812

Finally, to the Senate (filled with the Instruments of Darkness) he mourns,

> O, that I whom ye have made
> Your foe, could set my dearest enemy free
> From pain and fear! but evil casts a shade
> Which cannot pass so soon, and Hate must be
> The nurse and parent still of an ill progeny.

4355–4359

Laon's speech to the Senate, from which this is taken and which is his last in the poem, might be described as one long lament at the recrudescence of evil.

Thus we notice in *The Revolt of Islam* a new awareness of the problem of evil. It is present both to Shelley and to his characters. It is present, however, as a stumbling block, and receives no solution. Its presence, as a matter of fact, invalidates most, if not all, of the radical thinking of the poem, and gives the poem its peculiar quality of belonging neither to the radical world of *Queen Mab* nor to the ideal world of *Prometheus Unbound*.

PLATO: THE *Symposium*, THE *Phaedrus*

It is our belief that Plato offered Shelley the solution that is lacking in *The Revolt of Islam*. Close to the essence of Plato is an articulate, highly reasoned, idealistic theory of good and evil, and we can only assume that it came to Shelley in answer to a great intellectual need. Never again did Shelley lapse into the primitive, Zoroastrian notion of the equivalence of good and evil. It is true that in the years that followed, Shelley's thought progressed beyond the stage of *Prometheus Unbound*. Whether owing to forces of his own mind, or to those of the age in which he was born, Shelley came to believe in a monism that is alien to the metaphysics of Plato. Furthermore, he only temporarily accepted Plato's intellectualist point of view. But never again did Shelley believe that evil was a factor in life of equal importance with good.

Let us look, then, at Plato's theory of good and evil, which we declare to be close to the essence of his philosophy. And let us look at it as Shelley looked at it, first through the medium of the *Symposium* and the *Phaedrus,* and then through the medium of the *Republic*. Without venturing to meddle with the voluminous literature that has to do with the dating and sequence of the dialogues of Plato, we note that the above is the order in which Professor Shorey groups the three dialogues in his invaluable *What Plato Said.*[74] Indeed, the student of Plato will look in vain for three dialogues that show a closer kinship of thought and style. The *Symposium* and the *Phaedrus* form the perfect, logical introduction to the *Republic;* the *Republic* is the perfect, logical continuation of the *Symposium* and the *Phaedrus*. Now we have seen that Shelley's first reading of the *Symposium* followed Peacock's in the Marlow summer of Hellenic enthusiasm. And after the *Symposium,* the other two dialogues would have followed in natural course. But we cannot help remarking that had a specialist in Plato been selecting the three dialogues which might best represent the heart of Plato, he could scarcely have picked other than the three dialogues which Shelley read and reread in the years 1817, 1818, and 1819.

The *Symposium,* as everyone knows, is primarily about love. When

74. Paul Shorey, *What Plato Said* (Chicago, 1933).

at the beginning of the particular banquet described in the dialogue it is decided that conversation rather than music shall be the entertainment of the evening, it is decreed that the speeches are to be about love, a subject (or god) hitherto neglected.

Most of the speeches need concern us here but slightly. The first suggestions of Plato's theory of good and evil, of the great ethical doctrine that will find not even the canvas of the *Republic* too large, occur in the colloquy between Agathon and Socrates—in that colloquy which follows Agathon's speech and prepares the way for the tale of Diotima that Socrates offers modestly in place of a speech of his own. In this colloquy it is made clear that love characterizes the lover rather than the beloved, and is the emotion engendered by the beautiful. Finally, it is stated that love wants and has not beauty, and that in wanting beauty love wants also the good, since the beautiful is the good (201).[75] Thus the immediate object of love is the beautiful; the good is seen by implication. With thus much out of the way, Socrates plunges into the doctrine he professes to have learned from Diotima.

Diotima's representation of the discipline by which the vision of absolute beauty may be attained is the best-known and concluding part of her counsel to Socrates. But fully as important, if not more important, is her amplification of the meaning of the beautiful, under aspect of the good.

The good is seen to be that which bestows happiness, the object of desire of all men. Thus love, to Diotima, takes on a greatly extended meaning. It is the universal desire for human benefit, and to Diotima includes money-making, gymnastics, and philosophy. That the word has been restricted to a relationship between animate beings, she points out, is nothing but the specialization of language, where poetry, though actually meaning "making" in general, has nevertheless been restricted to the making of verse. Thus merchants, athletes, and philosophers, though not called lovers, are still seekers after happiness and the good, and betray the general aspects of the emotion (205).

Furthermore, men desire to possess the good permanently, so that Diotima finally defines love as of the everlasting possession of the good. She shows that the desire for offspring and for fame is but a manifestation of this thirst for permanence in one's possession of the good. She also points out that in our procreative desire for permanence of the good we instinctively fall in love with the beautiful, knowing that only out of the beautiful can proceed the good (206).

75. To avoid the useless accumulation of notes, in our exposition of Plato's philosophy the references to the Stephanus pagination will be given, as far as possible, directly in the text. If passages are quoted, they will be quoted from the Jowett translation without further reference.

But perhaps most important of all the many assertions that Diotima and Socrates make between them is the statement that all men naturally desire the good (205 A). For it follows from this that when they pursue evil it is from a mistaken idea of good, from ignorance of the true idea of good, and that the commission of evil is thus involuntary. This is expressly stated in the *Republic* (577 E), but is implied as early as the *Symposium,* and is indeed one half of Plato's theory of good and evil. Evil proceeds from ignorance, its perpetration is involuntary, and if we could but perfect the education of men so that they could see their own true good, evil would vanish from the face of the earth. Whether expressed or only implied, this attitude is never far removed from Plato's ethical thinking, and goes far to explain his great emphasis upon education.

The *Phaedrus* is the strong link between the *Symposium* and the *Republic,* not only affording a connection between the ethical doctrines of the two, but introducing us to the metaphysics and psychology of the latter. Love, treated in the *Symposium* as the generic desire toward the creation and preservation of the good, now becomes man's aspiration toward truth and the realm of ideas. Thus love is regarded in the *Phaedrus* as a kind of madness, an emotion of divine origin, which overwhelms us when we recollect, in the presence of beauty in the flesh, our former vision of beauty in the abstract (249 D). The emotion of love, thus engendered, leads to the dialectical recovery of the other ideas. The philosopher becomes a "lover of wisdom" in the realest sense, and man's quest after truth is portrayed by the procession of the gods to the summit of heaven to gaze upon the realm of true being (247).

The *Phaedrus* also introduces us to Plato's conception of the pyramidal[76] structure of the soul—that is, to Plato's notion of the soul as resting upon the broad base of the appetites, as making use of the emotions on the way up, and as being controlled by reason residing in the apex. We recall that in the *Republic* the entire ideal state is expressly conceived as an analogy of this tripartite soul.[77] In the *Phaedrus* the conception is brought to our attention by means of the well-known myth of the charioteer and his two winged horses, the one horse so much less obedient than the other.[78]

The deaf, shag-eared, dark-colored horse is the steed of the ap-

76. We use the word "pyramidal" deliberately, for we are impressed with the genuine kinship between Plato's views on the structure of the soul and those of the pyramidal school of modern psychologists led by Dr. Eugen Kahn.

77. The analogy is proposed in *Republic* 368 D *et seq.* Observing the advantage for the short-sighted of first reading a sign in large letters, Socrates proposes that the search for justice in the individual be begun by looking for it in the state, where there is "more" of it.

78. The myth forms the substance of Socrates' second speech on love, *Phaedrus* 246–256.

petites; the white and noble animal is that of the emotions; and the charioteer, as we need not add, is reason. Reason thus drives the soul; and we notice that in Plato's psychology there is a complete identification of the intellect and the will.[79] In fact, Professor Shorey observes that it is unprofitable to inquire whether Plato taught free will or determinism, since the modern controversy arises out of conceptions remote from Plato's concern—out of notions of the infinite foreknowledge of God, and of the absolute continuity of physical causation.[80]

Hence the voluntarism taught by Plato is of the most sweeping kind, since an alternative is not even considered. Not only is it presupposed that reason controls the soul, but it is assumed that the soul is capable of wisdom. For, according to the Platonic legend of the reincarnation of souls, it is the express condition of a soul's inhabiting the human form that it must previously have looked upon the realm of true being, upon the world of ideas (249 E). Finally, we observe that in the *Phaedrus,* as in the *Symposium,* evil is looked upon as want, as ignorance—in particular, as forgetfulness (248 D).

Thus, as we leave the two dialogues that Shelley had immediately read before he began the composition of the first act of *Prometheus Unbound,* we observe that Shelley must have been acquainted with the basic ideas of Plato's philosophy. Though wisdom, for example, has not yet been defined as the quality of the intellect which enables it to do its particular work of controlling and counseling the soul, nevertheless the attainment of wisdom is clearly posed as the end of life, and the intellect is clearly the driver of the steeds of emotion and appetite. The failure of the team to attain the summit of heaven is expressly stated to occur through the ill-driving of the charioteer (248 B), and the responsibility for evil is clearly made to rest on man himself.

That much of this is implied rather than expressed, and put in the form of myth or figure, is all the greater assurance that Shelley knew it. For the value of myth and figure is that it arouses one to work out the implications. Would to heaven that Aristotle, with all the rest of his genius, had possessed a gift like his master's for analogy and extended figure! For, in spite of his greatness, it is Aristotle who is largely responsible for the tissue of abstractions that philosophy has so often since become, instead of the gorgeous web of life and thought

79. We cannot forbear pointing out again the similarity between the conceptions of Plato and those of modern psychology. In his justly celebrated chapter on the "Will" in his *Principles of Psychology,* William James finds that the essence of the will is effort of attention, that once an idea of action is entertained by the mind's undivided consciousness, action follows inevitably unless physically impossible. Plato has gained, not lost, stature with the advance of modern science, and the fact should give us a more vivid sense of the strength of his influence over Shelley.

80. Paul Shorey, *The Unity of Plato's Thought* (Chicago, 1903), pp. 9–10.

to be found in Plato. To Shelley, the poet and man of letters, Plato's gift for analogy and figure must have possessed a particular charm. The ideas of Plato's philosophy must have come to him with an especial force, which is why we find ourselves impatient with those who would confine their study of Plato's influence on Shelley to the mere externals of literary suggestion. By common consent, Plato is one of the great thinkers of all time, and among those who can contest his primacy he is clearly the most eloquent. Hence to suppose that the result of an association between a reader like Shelley and a writer like Plato is to be found only in parallelisms of phrase and borrowings of constructional details—to suppose this is completely to miss the potentialities involved.

Prometheus Unbound: ACT I

As we come, then, to the first act of *Prometheus Unbound*, our concern will be for essentials rather than for superficials, for thought rather than for words. The theme of the drama is evidently going to have much in common with *The Revolt of Islam*. Once again the story is to be of oppression and the oppressed, of a tyrant and of a champion of mankind. But at the outset one observes that the action has been removed to the world of the charioteer and his winged horses. In *The Revolt of Islam* the hero and heroine had been natives of contemporary Greece; they had journeyed to Constantinople, or the Golden City; and in the end Laon had pleaded that Cythna be allowed to carry her fortunes to the infant United States of America. But in *Prometheus Unbound* the action takes place not even in the realm of historical myth, but in the realm of Platonic myth, where the action is designed to represent thought.

From his Preface it is clear that Shelley was familiar with the historical legend of Prometheus. This chronicles the reconcilement of Prometheus with Zeus, Prometheus atoning for his presumption, and the primitive Greek balance thus being restored. In this form it is supposed to have furnished the matter of the lost Æschylean play. But in the century separating Æschylus from Plato, Greek morality had advanced to quite other notions of right and wrong, and one looks in vain in the pages of Plato for the doctrine of retributive justice. To Shelley, who may be said to have been an idealist by birth, and who had now been avidly acquainting himself with the Platonic ethics, the ending of the Æschylean play was thoroughly repugnant. In the Shelleyan play it is clear that the Champion of mankind will wholly triumph over the Oppressor, and triumph not because of the requirements of the plot, but because of the inherent superiority of good to evil.

Yet the historical legend of Prometheus, for all its unidealistic ending, contains elements that must have appealed powerfully to Shelley. For in the legend Prometheus is a culture hero, a dispenser of knowledge, a person whose very name means "Foresight." In the historical legend it is significant that even Prometheus' bargaining point with Zeus is a secret, a bit of knowledge that he alone possesses. Thus fresh from his reading of Plato, where virtue is knowledge and vice ignorance, Shelley must have been doubly attracted to this champion of mankind who was also wise. It is doubtful if Shelley could elsewhere have found in Greek mythology a fable so suitable to his purposes. Prometheus can figure as a regenerator of mankind more successfully than Laon. For whereas Laon simply attempted to restore mankind bodily to its primitive innocence, and failed because of the resurgence of the physical forces of evil, Prometheus, as Mrs. Shelley observes in her Note to the 1839 edition, will use knowledge as the weapon with which to defeat evil. He will seek to accomplish the same thing as Laon, but on a higher, more spiritual plane.

Indeed, upon reading the first act of *Prometheus Unbound*, one is struck by the wholesale transposition of the action to the intellectual plane. Prometheus is the seer, the possessor of the hidden knowledge of the universe. With his characteristic generosity he imparted, in the early days, his knowledge to his nephew, even as he imparted to man a knowledge of fire and of the primitive arts. But though Prometheus thus gave to Jupiter knowledge of the physical forces of nature, particularly of the supreme force, of lightning, he did not extend to him knowledge of the psychical forces—neither knowledge of self nor knowledge of other beings. In the curse he laid upon Jupiter, now repeated by the latter's phantasm, this is Prometheus' specific statement, as in the following lines:

> O'er all things but thyself I gave thee power,
> And my own will.

I, 273-274

We can only assume that Prometheus' failure to extend to Jupiter this knowledge came from the fact that he had not attained to it himself. It would have been alien to his nature to hold anything back, and from the beginning of the play his insistence is upon the development that has taken place within himself. In his first speech (the opening one of the play) he says,

> I speak in grief,
> Not exultation, for I hate no more,
> As then ere misery made me wise. The curse
> Once breathed on thee I would recall.

I, 56-59

The lines clearly inform us that spiritual knowledge has come to Prometheus since he was transfixed to the Caucasus and cursed Jupiter in return.

Yet it is also clear from the curse that the notion of good, if not the possession of wisdom, was present to Prometheus at the time of his transfixion. For a portion of the curse is that Jupiter shall be damned by beholding good as infinite as are his evil deeds. No doubt the notion of good came to Prometheus through the unexpected misuse to which Jupiter put the knowledge that Prometheus had given him.

But there is a vast gap between one's first conception of good, and wisdom such as Prometheus evidences in the course of the play. In the Platonic period of three thousand years[81] that has intervened between the uttering of the curse and its revocation in the first act of the drama, suffering has changed hate to love within the soul of Prometheus, and revealed to him that Jupiter is to be pitied for what he misses. As much as anything, it is pity for evildoers in their deficiency that causes Prometheus to revoke his curse, just as it is the pity he exhibits at the end of his tortures that leads the last of the Furies to quit him.

With Prometheus' revocation of his curse, the machinery of his liberation is set in operation (though unbeknownst to him), and we are forced to look at the action on the severely intellectual plane. There is no ordinary causation between the words of Prometheus and the events we are shortly to witness in the succeeding acts of the play. The subsequent action can only mean that with the revocation of his curse Prometheus has attained to the level of absolute good, where good, no matter how wretched, pities evil, no matter how prosperous. Then goodness loses its impotence, and evil its power, and Jupiter in sober truth topples through the chasm to the yawning abyss below.

PLATO: THE *Republic*

It is interesting that the ethical thought thus implied or expressed in the first act of *Prometheus Unbound* should point to the very dialogue of Plato's which Shelley was next to take up. Prometheus' finding all hope to be vain but love (or aspiration toward the good), his recognition of the incompatibility in any sense of good and evil, his attainment to the conception of absolute good, all point to the *Republic*, where these ethical and metaphysical considerations are given a final and comprehensive treatment.

Hence we shall pause here, between the first and second acts (even as Shelley paused for five or six months), to consider the

81. For the significance of the number cf. *Phaedrus* 249 A.

thought of the great dialogue that Shelley read in the interim. As we have seen,[82] Shelley came back to the work with a frequency vouchsafed to no other dialogue of Plato's.

For one thing, the *Republic* probably accommodates itself to re-reading better than the other dialogues. Not only is it so long that the reader is unlikely ever to discover all its excellences, but it naturally falls into four or five sections which readily lend themselves to independent reading. In fact, learned theories have been advanced to the effect that the tenth book is an appendix; the fifth, sixth, and seventh books a metaphysical interpolation; and the first book a "minor" dialogue, after the fashion of the *Charmides*, the *Laches*, and the rest.[83]

However this may be, Shelley read the dialogue and reread it, and it is up to us to see what the dialogue contains.

Undoubtedly the most striking doctrine in the *Republic* is the analysis it offers of the human soul—of its functions and qualities, of the societal organization it gives rise to, of the education it suggests for individual and state. This, the most thoroughly discussed topic of the dialogue, is not entirely absent from any part of it. One is struck by the residuum of truth it still contains. At the base of the soul, it is held, lie the appetites, which cannot perform their function without restraint, without moderation. It is premised that the individual cannot eat too much, or drink too much, without impairing the working of his organism as a whole. Then come the emotions, which cannot perform their function of carrying out the commands of the will without steadfastness. Whether it is a question of love or of ambition or of simple bravery, the emotions attain their ends by holding out, by perseverance. Then comes the intellect, the function of which is to direct the entire organism, and which cannot properly do this without wisdom, its peculiar quality (or virtue). Finally, that all parts of the soul may work together, it is found that justice, or right order, is necessary. Justice thus becomes the virtue of the soul as a whole.[84]

When the individual is magnified and looked at politically, it is seen that the virtues which characterize the functions of the soul characterize the working, defending, and ruling classes of the state, and that the state as a whole is qualified by justice or injustice.

Yet the above is far from being the simple classification it may seem.

82. *Vide supra*, pp. 115–16.

83. Shorey touches upon the matter in his discussion of the *Republic* in *What Plato Said*, pp. 208–258, 557–564.

84. The theory upon which this paragraph is based will be found in the fourth book of the *Republic*, from 427 D to the end. Plato works the doctrine out, first of the state, and then ascribes it to the soul. But the soul is uppermost in his mind from the beginning. *Vide supra*, p. 140, note 77.

It is doubtful if the Greeks ever nourished an *esprit simpliste* among them. Far from looking at things as mere dichotomies of black and white, of 1 and 2, they always saw the gray between the black and white, and furthermore regarded 2 as containing 1. Thus we observe that temperance, in its essence the virtue of the working class, is premised of each of the higher classes; and that courage, properly the attribute of the guardians, is also an attribute of the rulers, since these are selected only from the bravest and most intelligent of the guardians. Thus 2 includes 1, and 3 includes 2 and 1. Furthermore, even as the Pythagoreans regarded 2 as the oblong of 1, and 3 as the triangle of 1, we are asked to look upon justice as the additional implication of the three virtues already specified.

But, though these theories afford important psychological and political truths, more important from an ethical point of view is the doctrine presented in Book IX of the happiness involved in being a just or unjust man. And most important from a metaphysical point of view is the theory of reality developed in Books V, VI, and VII.

To take up the first of these matters first, we observe that the well-known three proofs of Book IX which seek to establish that only the just man is truly happy—that these three proofs sum up the argument of the entire *Republic*. For the issue at point is the issue of the whole dialogue, and is unequivocally posed at the beginning of Book II by Adeimantes, Plato's brother. He asks Socrates to prove not only that justice is better than injustice, but that the one is a good, the other an evil, whether seen or unseen by gods and men (367 E).

The rest of the *Republic* may be regarded as Socrates' endeavor to demonstrate just this. As Professor Shorey says in his *Unity of Plato's Thought,*

Plato himself was haunted by the thought of the unscrupulous skeptic who sought to justify his own practice by appeals to the law of nature or theories of the origin of justice in a conspiracy of the weak against the strong. His imagination was beset by the picture of some brilliant young Alcibiades standing at the crossways of life and debating in his mind whether his best chance of happiness lay in accepting the conventional moral law that serves to police the vulgar or in giving rein to the instincts and appetites of his own stronger nature. To confute the one, to convince the other, became to him the main problem of moral philosophy. It is a chief duty of the rulers in the *Republic* and the *Laws,* and the Socrates of the dialogues is at all times ready and equipped to undertake it.[85]

Thus the three proofs of Book IX give expression to Plato's strenuous conviction that justice is an unqualified good, that injustice is an unqualified evil, and that any kind of tampering with right and wrong simply does not pay.

85. *The Unity of Plato's Thought*, p. 25.

The first proof epitomizes the analogy between the individual and the state. Since the city is but the collective citizen, the unjust man will experience a misery comparable to the misery of the unjust city, and this, "whether seen or unseen by gods and men" (576 C– 580 C). The second proof is the recapitulative one. The lower pleasures are included in the higher, and are known to those who enjoy the higher. Only the latter individuals are in a position to judge, and their rejection of the lower pleasures indicates the inferiority of these (580 D–583 A). The third proof is the chief one and is based upon the metaphysics of the dialogue. It recognizes the insubstantiality of material things, the reality only of the ideal. The happiness of the man given over to the things of sense is dependent upon appearance and illusion, and is unreal and insecure (583 B–588 A).

But how will the rulers of the state bring about the justice upon which its happiness depends? Justice, as we have seen, is not a first determination, but a second, or a third. How will the rulers make their myriad decisions so that at third or fourth remove these will produce the fine flower of communal happiness? How will the individual regulate his own life so that he too will enjoy the justice that brings happiness and is its own reward? The matter obviously depends upon the right use of the intellect, which is the sole directive faculty. And the right use of the intellect depends upon wisdom. But how will the individual know what is really wisdom, and what is only opinion?

Thus all threads of inquiry lead to the doctrine that is central in the *Republic,* to the theory of the Idea of Good.[86] In striving after justice and its attendant happiness, the individual must act according to the Idea of Good, even as the rulers of the ideal state must consult it in their deliberations (540 A). It is the source and explanation of all thought, and is indeed that absolute beauty referred to by Diotima, now looked at under aspect of ethics, politics, and metaphysics. It is what remains apart and above the flux of time and circumstance, and enables us to rise superior to the accidents of existence. It is the object of love in its broadest sense, and is the determiner of justice. Without the Idea of Good, there could be no happiness.

Plato does not define the Idea of Good (506 E). In fact Plato does not define any of the hypostatized concepts. As Professor Shorey points out,[87] Plato says only that they are, not what they are. When something further is desired, it is his custom to resort to myth or figure. Here he uses the analogue of the sun. The sun is the cause of visibility and of vision. As the source of light, it spreads the world

---

86. The doctrine will be found, in the main, from 504 to 521, but it is present throughout Book VII.

87. *The Unity of Plato's Thought*, p. 28.

before our eyes in a visual pattern—a pattern that is the purpose of our having eyes. Furthermore, as the source of warmth, it is the impulse of generation and growth, indeed of human existence (508–509).

Plato's theory of the Idea of Good, we perceive, is much the same as Aristotle's doctrine of Form. Indeed, the Aristotelian notion would appear to be once again but a gloss upon the Platonic, a gloss that in this case appreciably clarifies. For the Platonic conception, as Professor Shorey suggests,[88] is in reality *design, purpose,* and *ideal,* which is but saying that it exhibits the formal, final, and efficient aspects into which Aristotle analyzed the idea of Form. The chief difference between the Platonic and Aristotelian conceptions is that, as always, the Platonic conception carries ethical connotations,· and thus is closer to the every-day reality of man's individual and social life. Aristotle's Form may be looked upon simply as the metaphysical implications of the larger notion of Good.

For the notion of Good is more comprehensive than the notion of Form. It includes the latter, and relates it to the concerns of man. The world itself could hardly have formed a home for man had not it possessed the Idea of Good. As for the institutions of human life, if they are to have meaning at all they must exhibit the Idea of Good. In the present year of 1945, we are witnessing an attempt to found a new world order. We observe that in its essence it is springing from the threefold Idea of Good. It embraces much design, or planning; it is being formulated to achieve a distinct end (that of world confederation); and it is motivated by a pronounced ideal (that of lasting peace). Finally, we observe, the whole business is one of human betterment and justice.

PLATO: SUMMARY

Thus, as we come to the end of our brief survey of the three dialogues Shelley is known to have read either shortly before or during the composition of *Prometheus Unbound,* the impression borne upon us is not only of a philosophy that must powerfully have attracted Shelley, but of a philosophy that is as unified as it is imaginative. Whereas in Aristotle there is the deep cleft between the nominalism of his ontology and the realism of his epistemology, the deep cleft pointed out in the last century by Zeller[89] and more recently by Professor Taylor,[90] in Plato there is a singleness of conviction that extends to everything he ever wrote. Plato profoundly believed that the real

---

88. *What Plato Said,* p. 232.

89. In Pt. II, sec. 2, of his *Philosophie der Griechen,* available to English readers as *Aristotle and the Earlier Peripatetics* (2 vols. London, 1897). Translated from the third German edition by Costelloe and Muirhead.

90. In his *Aristotle* (London and New York, 1912), pp. 26–35.

world is both spiritual and intelligible. To Plato the real world was of the nature of mind and could be apprehended by the mind. Man thus becomes not the measure of all things but the knower of all things, a being capable of knowledge equal to a god's.[91] In Plato's philosophy a world is assumed superior to the world of flux and change, and man is given all but the highest place in it.

Now there are two aspects of this philosophy that must have appealed particularly to Shelley: one, the future it holds out for man; the other, its harmony with the scientific point of view.

As for the first, the fact remains that not even such perfectibilitarians as Condorcet and Godwin ever showed a greater perfectibilitarianism than Plato. In Plato's view not only man but the universe itself is so constituted that man may attain to perfect knowledge, which gives rise to perfect justice, which is the cause of perfect happiness. Plato does not maintain that the reign of justice is around the corner. He does not guarantee that it will ever come at all. But he makes clear that its attainment is within man's grasp, that its consummation depends not upon external forces but upon man himself.

As for the other aspect, the significant thing is that Plato achieves the above without the paradoxes of Berkeley, without the sentimental assumptions of Godwin, without the monistic subtleties of the German idealists. Professor Lovejoy has pointed out that Plato is relatively free of the monistic pathos,[92] and Professor Shorey has made clear that Plato's hypostatization of concepts was no more than was absolutely necessary if he was successfully to combat the cynical and skeptical tendencies of his age.[93] Against the materialists and hedonists and relativists of his time, Plato set himself to declare only what science has always declared: that there is a structure to matter and energy, that there is a system to the universe, that there is an organization to life. Indeed there is no more deeply held faith today. No one doubts in our own age that science will continue to reveal the intelligibility of the world, and no one doubts—least of all the scientists—that this is really true.

Plato's peculiarity—and greatness—is not that he held this scientific faith, nor that he was a perfectibilitarian along with countless other well-wishers of the human race, but that he combined the two in a unified, reasoned body of philosophy.

Hence it is that we may say that of all philosophers who ever lived Plato was best suited to speak to Shelley. Shelley's youthful and never-

91. This is the plain significance of man's joining with the gods in the procession to high heaven (*Phaedrus* 248–250). Note particularly *Phaedrus* 248 C: "And there is a law of Destiny, that the soul which attains any vision of truth in company with a god is preserved from harm until the next period, and if attaining always is always unharmed."
92. *The Great Chain of Being*, p. 38.
93. *The Unity of Plato's Thought*, pp. 27–30.

abandoned[94] interest in science, his hopes for the betterment of the human race, his innate idealism, his metaphysical propensities, all found their prototype in the great Greek philosopher. Furthermore, only Plato could have helped Shelley in the principal intellectual problem of his life, in the resolution of the determinism and voluntarism, of the necessity and benevolence, that are found together in *Queen Mab*. Only Plato with his scientific, even mathematical, point of view could have overcome the mechanistic philosophy which Shelley had acquired from the eighteenth century, itself based upon the mathematical science of the seventeenth century. When one adds to Plato's idealism, perfectibilitarianism, and scientific outlook the fact to which we have already alluded, that he is one of the great writers of all time, it is not difficult to see that his influence over Shelley would be unique.

Prometheus Unbound: ACT II

But to return to *Prometheus Unbound,* we observe that the miraculous events attendant upon Prometheus' renunciation of his curse commence with the second act. The refrain of Panthea's dream, as well as of Asia's, is now heard coming from outer space, as the words "Follow, Follow!" echo from the cliffs around. Further echoes, and then choruses of spirits, take up the cry and between them conduct the sisters through forest and mountain to Demogorgon's realm.

These external events which follow the internal act of Prometheus' renunciation remind us again that the subsequent action of the drama is to be interpreted from the intellectual plane. It is not allegory in the conventional sense at all, but philosophic myth where the action is to be explained, not by human motivation, but by the development of thought. The events of the second and third acts of *Prometheus Unbound* are a way of picturing the consequences of attaining to the conception of absolute good. Indeed, it seems to us that even the well-known, baffling cruxes of the dialogue may be explained in the same way, by reference to the philosophical meaning of the play—in particular, by reference to the Platonic content of the drama.

However this may be, in the fourth scene Asia and Panthea arrive at the cave of Demogorgon, who represents, according to Mrs. Shelley,[95] Primal Power. And well he may, for we observe that he fills the "seat of power," and is shapeless and unintelligible. There is furthermore nothing un-Platonic in the introduction of a Primal Power. Plato never limited either the elements of the world or the spirits that

94. Cf. Shelley's letter to Charles Ollier of February 22, 1821, asking, among three or four other items, for "the most copious and correct history of the discoveries of Geology. If one publication does not appear to contain what I require, send me two or three" (Julian *Works*, x, 243).

95. Cf. Mrs. Shelley's note to the 1839 reprinting of the poem.

inhabit it. He limited only the Idea of Good, that it might remain a solitary beacon, presenting a single standard, to gods and to men.

Indeed, by his own practice Plato has suggested that any concept may be mythologized for philosophical purposes. In the myth of Er not least among the personages is Necessity, beneath whose throne the souls must pass after they have selected their incarnations. Thus in *Prometheus Unbound,* by Shelley's ascription to her of the legend of Anadyomene, we perceive that Asia is meant to represent love. No doubt she includes Shelley's notion of universal sympathy. But primarily the love she represents is Platonic, in particular the great creative force that Shelley had found portrayed in the *Symposium.* In Act I of *Prometheus Unbound,* the Indian vale of Asia's exile is described as

>   rugged once
> And desolate and frozen, like this ravine;
> But now invested with fair flowers and herbs,
> And haunted by sweet airs and sounds, which flow
> Among the woods and waters, from the aether
> Of her transforming presence.

I, 827–832

At other times it is the more general Platonic notion that Asia represents, the notion of aspiration toward all things good and beautiful. In Act II Asia says,

> How glorious art thou, Earth! And if thou be
> The shadow of some spirit lovelier still,
> Though evil stain its work, and it should be
> Like its creation, weak yet beautiful,
> I could fall down and worship that and thee.

II, iii, 12–16

Though it be only in passing, we cannot forbear remarking that even in so slight a reference as the above to evil, evil is regarded as imperfection, as the result of weakness in the maker.

Yet, as in the Platonic myth, the philosophic discussion is independent of the symbolism of the characters. In the colloquy between Asia and Demogorgon the discussion is straightforward philosophic debate, unperplexed by any symbolic connotation. As to the author of good, Demogorgon finds no difficulty in replying to Asia that it is God. But when asked who made evil, he does not think its author substantial enough to merit a name. He mentions merely that he "reigns," a verb implying an end as surely as a beginning. The answer, however, hardly satisfies Asia. She still cannot understand whence comes the immedicable plague, all the more since it is quite irrational, and the evil man is the wreck of his own will. She cannot believe that

Jove is the author of it. She saw him tremble like a slave when cursed by Prometheus. "Who is his master? Is he too a slave?"

To Asia's latest queries, Demogorgon replies in almost pure Platonic phrase, "All spirits are enslaved which serve things evil," an answer suggesting the many places in Plato, especially in Book IX of the *Republic,* where evil is construed as the topsy-turvy mastery of the higher faculties by the lower, as the enslavement of the better by the worse.

Asia still seeks, however, an ultimate answer to the mystery of the universe. But when it comes to defining God, Demogorgon will commit himself no more than Plato when it comes to the Idea of Good. The deep truth is indeed imageless. Even if one could gaze upon the revolving world, what would it avail him? What would it profit to speak of Fate, Time, Occasion, Chance, and Change? The individual would still be subject to them. Only Love is exempt. Only Love is free.

Demogorgon's statement that only Love is free is perhaps the most important philosophic statement in the play. When we remember that in its essence Love to Plato is aspiration toward the good and the beautiful, we recognize how close to the thinking of Plato Shelley has come. Indeed, in the myth of Er, the grand climax of the *Republic,* the very same doctrine is presented. The souls, now finished with their thousand-year cycle in heaven or in hell, and ready again for the short hundred-year span on earth, have left the meadow of their foregathering and journeyed to the place of destiny. There presides Necessity, and her three daughters, Lachesis, Clotho, and Atropos. A herald addresses the souls: "Mortal souls, behold a new cycle of life and mortality. Your genius will not be allotted to you, but you will choose your genius; and let him who draws the first lot have the first choice, and the life which he chooses shall be his destiny. Virtue is free, and as a man honors or dishonors her he will have more or less of her; the responsibility is with the chooser—God is justified" (617 E).

The herald then casts lots upon the grass, and when each soul has picked up a lot and the order of choosing has thus been determined, the herald spreads out samples of lives—many more lives than souls, of animals as well as of men. The moment is intense, so intense that Socrates cannot forbear breaking into the narrative of Er to address Glaucon, the brother of Adeimantes and Plato: "And here, my dear Glaucon, is the supreme peril of our human state; and therefore the utmost care should be taken. Let each one of us leave every other kind of knowledge and seek and follow one thing only, if peradventure he may be able to learn and discern between good and evil, and so choose always and everywhere the better life as he has opportunity" (618 C).

The moment of choice now approaches, and for a last time the herald addresses the multitude: "Even for the last comer, if he chooses wisely and will live diligently, there is appointed a happy and not undesirable existence. Let not him who chooses first be careless, and let not the last despair" (619 B). The choosing proceeds and, as we know, the first soul, who came from heaven and in a previous existence had dwelt in a well-ordered state, and whose virtue was a matter of habit, and who was without philosophy—the first soul chooses the greatest tyranny, to beat his breast and lament his choice when it is too late. Finally, when all the choices have been made, the souls move on to have them ratified by the Fates. After that they pass beneath the throne of Necessity onto the plain of Forgetfulness, whence they enter upon their earthly existences.

The myth is the grand climax of the *Republic*, not only because it is one of the superb pieces of world literature, but because it sums up in its graphic way the thinking of the entire dialogue. The brute facts of life are clearly recognized. No one doubts that man is subject to Necessity, or, as Demogorgon puts it, to Fate, Time, Occasion, Chance, and Change. But there come moments of choice to all, moments when man's destiny is in his own hands, when the choice for good or evil is his. Such a moment came to Prometheus in the beginning of the play, and he chose wisely because his heart was filled with Love, because when he chose, the Idea of Good was before him as a beacon incapable of guiding astray. Prometheus exercised the freedom of Love, the freedom of the pursuit of good, and as we come to the third act, the consequences are enacted before our eyes.

Prometheus Unbound: ACT III

It is interesting that Shelley should have returned to the historical legend in the third act, that he should have been able to adapt it to the conclusion of his philosophic myth. The third act opens with an assembly of the gods in heaven, convoked by Jupiter to witness the incarnation of the child to be born of his union with Thetis. It has been prophesied that the child will be greater than its parents, and Jupiter expects that it will succeed where he has failed, in crushing the soul of man, where in spite of all his efforts the spark of resistance still remains alive.

Meanwhile the moment of the incarnation approaches. Jupiter in his ignorance thinks that it is Demogorgon himself who is going to leave his throne and give the dreadful might of his ever-living limbs to the new child to be born. In his pitiful lack of philosophic knowledge, comparable to that of the man who chose the dreadful tyranny in the myth of Er, Jupiter does not imagine what Asia saw, that Demogorgon is formless and without limbs. With his wisdom restricted to a knowledge of physical force, Jupiter can only suppose that the child, to be greater than he, must in some way be an incarnation of the Primal Power of the world, the only power left to be superior to his. He does not conceive that the Primal Power of the world may be the primal matrix of the world, out of whose nothingness the individualities of the world emerge.

By now the destined Hour is close at hand. Jupiter hears its chariot thundering up the slopes of Olympus. He believes that the spirit of the child to be born is even then hovering over them, awaiting the moment of its incarnation. The chariot of the destined Hour arrives, bearing Demogorgon, as Jupiter had supposed. But, far from seeking incarnation, Demogorgon proclaims himself, as he is, the child greater than its parent, Eternity. He summons Jupiter to follow him into the abyss, to dwell with him henceforth in darkness. They struggle, but the strife is useless. Together they sink, like vulture and snake outspent by mortal combat, into the void below.

Thus evil is vanquished, or rather engulfed, by eternity. Losing its spurious power because of the pity it arouses in good, evil passes (in Platonic language) from the realm of Being, through the region of Becoming, into the abyss of Not-Being. For we must remember that by the Greeks eternity and infinity as absolutes were looked upon as Not-Being. To Plato a thing did not exist until, in.the world of time and space, it had received the impress of whatever ideas were necessary to give it individuality. And even to the world of individuality, we remember, Plato would grant only the status of Becoming, not that of full Being. To Plato only the world of universals was truly real.[96]

Hence, from the point of view of Shelley's Platonic reading, there is nothing strange to Demogorgon's declaring himself to be both eternity and the child of Jupiter. In Plato's ethics, Not-Being is that into which evil finally breaks down. Thus in *Prometheus Unbound,* as soon as Prometheus has perceived evil to be the weakness that it really is, as soon as he has seen good in the perfection of the absolute Idea, eternity rises to claim evil for its own.

After an interlude between Ocean and Apollo, in which (in the manner of Ross and the Old Man in *Macbeth*) the events of Jupiter's fall are discussed, the drama turns in the third scene to the freeing of Prometheus. The philosophic myth is still working itself out, and it is not surprising that the Platonic coloring is maintained. We observe that when Hercules comes to liberate Prometheus he addresses him almost as if he were an embodiment of the Platonic philosophy. He says,

96. For the metaphysics of this paragraph, cf. *Republic* 472–520.

> Most glorious among Spirits, thus doth strength
> To wisdom, courage, and long-suffering love,
> And thee, who are the form they animate,
> Minister like a slave.
>
> III, iii, 1–4

Our chief interest, however, centers in the speech Prometheus makes upon his liberation. Hardly deigning to thank his liberator, he turns to Asia, his long-awaited bride, and in the manner of *Epipsychidion* proposes flight to an idyllic retreat. Here it is a cave rather than an island, screened in front with leaves and flowers, and illumined within by fountain and stalactite; but otherwise it is much the same. The flight to a terrestrial Elysium is, of course, purely Shelleyan, and the same might be said of the auxiliary female disciples that will accompany the lovers. Yet even in this intrusion there is a strong indication of Shelley's reigning enthusiasm for Plato. For, like the philosopher-kings in the *Republic*, Prometheus, Asia, and their companions will entertain themselves with philosophical discussion. The books and musical instruments of the usual romantic asylum are lacking. From their cave the world will be reflected upon, yet unmingled with. The group will talk of time and change, themselves unchanged, and explore their unexhausted spirits for hidden thoughts. To them will come echoes of the human world telling of love and pity (love for good and pity for evil), and bringing overtones of earthly music (one half of Plato's education) and of everything that tempers or improves man's life now free. In addition, lovely apparitions will come to them from painting, sculpture, and poetry, dim at first, but then bright, as the mind (fresh from its glimpse of beauty) casts upon the forms it has received the "gathered rays which are reality."

In the next and final scene of the act, Prometheus and his disciples arrive at the destined cave. The Spirit of the Hour returns from his trip to announce the good tidings to mankind, and with his report of the effect of his annunciation, the myth concludes.

Prometheus Unbound: ACT IV

The fourth act of *Prometheus Unbound* is not integral with the rest of the drama. In setting it is laid before the philosophic cave, but the myth has been completed, and neither Prometheus nor Asia appears again. Panthea and Ione, who are exoteric disciples and dwell outside the cave, serve as the audience of the pageant and cantata that compose the substance of the act. But their wholly appreciative and descriptive remarks do not resume the philosophic interests of the earlier part of the play. Like the last two cantos of *Queen Mab*, the fourth act of *Prometheus Unbound* is almost purely lyrical, and as such comes from a deeper stratum of the poet's nature than that of his enthusiasm for Plato, or of his composition of the first three acts. Professor White has observed that even the scientific ideas which Professor Grabo has pointed out,[97] and which serve to embellish the songs and pageantry of the act, must be the result of recollected rather than of current reading.[98] The fourth act, as Mrs. Shelley remarks in her note to the poem, is "a sort of hymn of rejoicing in the fulfill-ment of the prophecies with regard to Prometheus," and as such is expressive of mood rather than of thought.

Only in the last speech of the play, a valedictory given by Demogor-gon after his entrance very nearly at the end, does the drama return to the philosophic concerns of the first three acts. Hence as phil-osophical critics of the play our chief interest in the fourth act cen-ters in this last speech.

Demogorgon begins with a commemoration of the present occasion. It is the day which yawns for Heaven's despotism, in which Conquest will be dragged captive through the deep. From its throne of patient power in the wise heart, from the last hour of its endurance, from the very verge of its agony, Love folds its healing wings over the world. Gentleness, Virtue, Wisdom, and Endurance hasten to seal the pit over Destruction's strength.

This summary of the significance of the earlier part of the play is to us very interesting. It shows a weakening in the grasp of the Platonic ethics. Although there never was a complete carry-over of the entire scheme of the Platonic virtues, still, as late as the address of Hercules to Prometheus in the third scene of the third act, there had been a consonance between the ideology of the drama and the framework of the Platonic philosophy. As we have pointed out, Her-cules addresses Prometheus ("most glorious among Spirits") as "wisdom, courage, and long-suffering love," and assumes that he is a "form" which they animate. This is indeed no reproduction of the Platonic pyramid, but the discrepancies are those of omission rather than those of change or addition.

Yet here, in the valedictory of the play, Virtue, the category of wisdom according to Plato (as love is the desire)—Virtue is ranked with Wisdom, and the roster is completed by the inclusion of Gentle-ness and Endurance. How far this is from the Platonic tetralogy we need not observe. And the weakening grasp of the Platonic philosophy cannot be attributed to a loss of familiarity with Plato, for, as we have shown,[99] the autumn of 1819 witnessed a rereading of the *Re-public* as well as the composition of the fourth act of *Prometheus Unbound*. The weakening grasp of the Platonic philosophy can only mean what the whole fourth act means, that it comes from a deeper

97. In *A Newton among Poets* and *Prometheus Unbound*.
98. *Op. cit.*, II, 578–579.   99. *Vide supra*, p. 115.

level of Shelley's personality than the understanding of Plato, and that the essential Shelley was less affected by Plato than the first three acts of *Prometheus Unbound* might imply.

Furthermore, we have thus far considered only the opening of Demogorgon's speech. In its greatest essence, the speech is not a hymn of rejoicing like the rest of the act but a word of caution, setting forth the conditions for a second victory over evil. These, we are astonished to observe, are entirely emotional. Yet before the full significance of this fact is borne upon us we are struck by the contradiction that there should be a recrudescence of evil. Prometheus' attainment to the conception of absolute good, Jupiter's ignorance of the world of spiritual truth, his engulfment by the darkness of eternity—all this had indicated a final disappearance of evil. The significance of the philosophic myth developed by Shelley had pointed to man's acquisition, through suffering, of perfect knowledge. That Mrs. Shelley received something of the same impression is clear from her note, where she contrasts the ignorant happiness of mankind in the age of Saturn with the knowing happiness of mankind in the age introduced by Prometheus. The conception of a seesaw relationship between good and evil, while characteristic of *The Revolt of Islam,* is wholly foreign to the first three acts of *Prometheus Unbound.*

Yet here, in the final speech of the play, not only is it assumed that there may be a return of evil, but Demogorgon, forgetting the negative, terminal quality of his relationship to evil, supposes that he may lose his grasp and allow evil as a positive force to rise again in the world. It is clear that with the abandonment of the philosophic myth has come a weakening of the conception of evil as ignorance.

Let us look, though, at the remedy which Demogorgon suggests in case of a return of evil. If there is a recrudescence of evil, man is counseled

> To suffer woes which Hope thinks infinite;
> To forgive wrongs darker than death or night;
> To defy Power, which seems omnipotent;
> To love, and bear; to hope till Hope creates
> From its own wreck the thing it contemplates;
> Neither to change, nor falter, nor repent.
>
> IV, 570–575

Finally Demogorgon declares that the attainment of such a state of suffering, forgiving, defying, loving, and hoping is what it means to be,

> Good, great and joyous, beautiful and free,

and that

> This is alone Life, Joy, Empire, and Victory.
>
> IV, 577–578

CONCLUSION

Thus the Idea of Good becomes a business of the emotions rather than of the intellect. To Plato the Idea of Good had existed in a world apart, a standard for gods and for men. In its very impersonality it had offered the one sure guide to the attainment of justice and happiness. Even in its aspect as the beautiful, its apprehension had been largely a matter of the intellect, Diotima counseling the novitiate to proceed "from fair forms to fair practices, from fair practices to fair notions, until from fair notions he arrived at the notion of absolute beauty, and at last knew what the essence of beauty was" (*Symposium* 211 C). In general, in Plato, the good and the beautiful in life are good and beautiful because they are intelligible, because they take after the world of ideas. And love, though as with Shelley the highest of the emotions—love exists not in its own right, but as the impulse toward this intelligible beauty and good.[100]

Yet in Demogorgon's speech it is stated that to be good and beautiful is simply to hope, to love, to defy, to suffer, and to forgive. The good and the beautiful in human life no longer take after anything objective, but after an inner state incommensurable with the intellect. Hence, if there is any ultimate standard, it can only be an ultimate emotion. The good and the beautiful in Demogorgon's valedictory have become an emotional condition resident in the human heart.

Thus we are forced to conclude that the essential Shelley has developed but not changed. Indeed it is clear that we have returned to the prime distinction of Chapters III and IV. Though Shelley has once again fallen under the spell of an intellectualistic philosophy, and this time a more harmonious intellectualistic philosophy since it is voluntaristic rather than necessitarian, nevertheless in the end, just as at the conclusion of *Queen Mab,* Shelley's fundamental emotionalism has asserted itself. Wisdom, or knowledge informed by the Idea of Good, is now so much useless baggage. Although to Plato it had been the *sine qua non,* the quality without which the intellect could not direct the soul to justice and happiness, it is no longer necessary to anything. In the early part of the play it had been the means of Prometheus' victory over evil. But Demogorgon does not include it in his program for a second victory. Sheer motivation is now enough. In the words of the great Kant, "Nothing in the whole world, or even outside of the world, can possibly be regarded as good without limitation except a *good will.*"[101]

100. The *Symposium* distinctly states that love is only an intermediate power between the mortal and the divine (202 E–203 A).
101. The opening sentence of the *Metaphysic of Morality,* John Watson's translation.

Historically, as we need scarcely observe, the great shift in point of view came with the rise of Christianity. The classical world had held an intellectualist point of view, a belief in the supremacy of reason. As Sir Richard Winn Livingstone points out in his *Greek Ideals and Modern Life*,[102] it had united thinkers of the most opposite schools. Heraclitus, Anaxagoras, Plato, and Aristotle were all intellectualists. Even the practical Stoics and Cynics were fundamentally intellectualistic in their point of view. Christianity, however, introduced another scale of values. Feeling was set above reason. In place of the Platonic tetralogy of virtues, St. Paul offered the trilogy of faith, hope, and charity. To be sure, the revolution was not complete until 529—not until the dread decree of Justinian outlawing the teaching of heathen philosophy. But when it was complete, the revolution could not have been more utter. For parallel, one is led to think of the revolution separating the Mesozoic from the Paleozoic era in the history of the earth, or the Cenozoic from the Mesozoic. Not only had reason been deposed in favor of emotion, but life itself had been tremendously altered. As Sir Richard Winn Livingstone makes clear, Christianity now offered a *summum bonum* within the reach of all.[103] Neither intellectual powers nor education were any longer necessary for its attainment. Hence we do not wonder that, in spite of subsequent restorations of the intellectualist point of view, the world has been predominantly emotionalist ever since.

Indeed, Shelley, in his emotionalist point of view, was at one with his age and time. For the Romantic Movement was in large part a reaction to the intellectualism of the eighteenth century and, though we are prone to forget it, was in no small way a return to the position of historical Christianity. Hand in hand with the Romantic Movement in England went Wesleyanism and Evangelicalism,[104] and in Germany the Romantic Movement sent its adherents to the Roman Church by the score.[105] This is a far cry, to be sure, from our little group of Hellenic friends who in the summer of 1817 read Cobbett's *Register* as eagerly (or almost as eagerly) as their Homer. Peacock may be said even to have attained the intellectualist point of view of his beloved Greeks. But this was not the case with Shelley, who much more than Peacock was a child of his age. Indeed this is one of the conspicuous respects in which the Greek Revival did not "revive." For emotion was what sent the revivalists to Greece in the first place,

102. Sir Richard Winn Livingstone, *Greek Ideals and Modern Life* (Cambridge, Mass., 1935), pp. 149, 163.
103. *Idem*, p. 166.
104. Cf. D. C. Somervell, *English Thought in the 19th Century* (London, 1929), pp. 16–29.
105. Cf. Henry A. Beers, *A History of English Romanticism in the Nineteenth Century*, pp. 145–148.

and emotion was what they found when they arrived. Only a few perceived the intellectualism of the Greeks, and but few of these were able, in their lives, to place reason above the other faculties, to regard wisdom as chief among the virtues.

Shelley's new, Platonic intellectualism is evident only in the first three acts of *Prometheus Unbound,* which mark the high point of his Hellenism. Shelley's general enthusiasm for things Greek did not wane, and the succession of Greek poems that follow, up to and including the autumn of 1821, is striking. But any permanent conversion to the Greek point of view would have been impossible to a temperament so obviously emotional from its earliest days. After the composition of the first three acts of *Prometheus Unbound,* Shelley's mind continued to develop along lines previously in evidence. His idealism continued to advance, but it advanced within the framework of the other demands of his personality, one of which was that feeling, not thought, should be given the chief place in the world.

Yet, though Shelley relinquished the intellectualism of Plato, he remained in greater debt to Plato than to any other writer in the course of his life. Plato vindicated his belief in the fundamentally spiritual order of the universe, Plato reassured him as to man's educability and perfectibility, and Plato gave to man himself the final responsibility in the conduct of his life.

Thus, though Demogorgon fails to include wisdom as one of the "spells" by which man may reassume "empire o'er the disentangled doom," and though he finds the good and the beautiful now to be an emotional state, and evil a positive force, yet it is interesting to note that his faith in man's ability to triumph over the reappearance of evil never wavers. Demogorgon had no doubt that the human spirit could conquer its ills, even if he construed this conquest as an exercise of feeling alone. Now this faith in man's ability to overcome evil, this belief in a veritable moat separating the necessity of the outer world from the freedom of the inner world—this faith is above all what Shelley obtained from Plato. It had been denied in *Queen Mab.* It was only a hope in *The Revolt of Islam.*

It is true that Shelley could have acquired this faith from other writers (notably from Kant or his successors), or that he could have worked it out for himself. But one must remember the epistemologic paradox of the German philosophers, a paradox that is alien to the faith in the real beauty of the real world that is characteristic of poets if not of metaphysicians. As we recall, Shelley's instinctive idealism was ontologic rather than epistemologic. Furthermore, one must remember that in Drummond and Peacock, Shelley found only scorn for Kant and the Critical Philosophy.

Among those writers who could speak to Shelley it is difficult to see where, if not in Plato, Shelley could have found that vindication of the human spirit, of the human will, which he so desperately needed to find. It is doubtful also if Shelley, for all his interest in philosophy, possessed the ability to work out the problem by himself. At any rate, it was Plato who principally solved it for him, and it is Plato whom we must regard as the chief intellectual influence in Shelley's life.

4. Epipsychidion

FORTUNATELY, as we approach the last three major poems of Shelley's life, all composed in 1821 and all in the Greek Revival, our problem has been clarified by our study of *Prometheus Unbound*. We have seen that Plato gave content to Shelley's faith in the reality of the unseen world and, above all, delivered him from the incubus of determinism. What Shelley had hitherto felt simply as a mysterious presence, a "secret Strength" governing both the mind of man and the infinite dome of heaven, has now been revealed as an intelligible order capable of being understood. The secret Strength has lessened in stature. But the stature of man has increased. For, in fact, it is difficult to see how that which is of the order of mind can control the mind that apprehends it. In Plato man becomes an immortal spirit, of the same nature as, if not equal to, the gods. Though, because of the mortal nature of his steeds, it is more difficult for him than for the gods to mount to high heaven to look upon the realm of true being, nevertheless even this, Plato assumes, can with skillful driving successfully be done.

True, to Shelley the driving came to be a business of the emotions rather than of the intellect, and the strict Platonist would maintain that the white and shining horse was leading the chariot to pasture grounds of its own selection. Even so, the chariot is still a corporate unity, and the soul is still going whither one of its members chooses. This is a good deal different from being strapped to the seat of a roller coaster to endure the dizzy falls and hairpin turns until the mechanism stops. It is also different from being controlled, like a marionette, by a superior spiritual power, even if this superior spiritual power pulls the wires according to law rather than according to whim. We observe that, in spite of the loss of intellectual control, the Platonic chariot is still an independent vehicle for the soul's progress. There is still a journey to be made, with an end in view, and the chariot is still free to attain it.

Our interest accordingly shifts to the end in view, to the pasture grounds whither the white horse of the emotions is conducting the chariot of the soul. If ever a man's mind has shown a steady and to-be-expected development it is Shelley's. The idealism we perceived to be latent in *Queen Mab* has come to the fore, and the contradictory necessitarianism has been abandoned. Even in the course of *Prometheus Unbound* the mistakenly adopted intellectualism was dropped when found to be inharmonious with the rest of the poet's personality. Whither, then, will this amalgamation of Platonic voluntarism and romantic emotionalism carry Shelley? What has happened, we ask, to the Platonism and Shelleyanism of *Prometheus Unbound* in the year or more separating that poem from *Epipsychidion?* And what happened to Shelley's thought in the course of 1821? It is inevitable that our study of *Prometheus Unbound* should give to the rest of our inquiry an especial direction.

Thus as we turn to *Epipsychidion,* the first of the major Greek poems of 1821, we shall not take up the subtle question of the poem's autobiographic significance. Nor shall we study the literary debt of the poem to Dante, or to Petrarch. Our problem is by now exclusively concerned with the development of Shelley's thought, to which, as we have seen, Plato rendered a unique service.

Yet it must be that the philosophical student approaches *Epipsychidion* with diffidence. The poem is a poem of romantic love, and as such is far from Plato. Mrs. Shelley found it convenient to refer to the affair upon which the poem is based as "Shelley's Italian Platonics."[106] But the affair was not Platonic in any strict sense of the word. We must not forget that Pausanias, who in the *Symposium* is the maker of the distinction between common and spiritual love, specifically states of his Uranian Aphrodite that she was born solely of Uranus, her father. In her birth "the female had no part" (181), and the love she engenders is between males. Furthermore, in his distinction between common, or physical, love and spiritual love, Pausanias quite clearly makes it not as between black and white, but in the Greek way as between 1 and 2, where 2 includes 1. The spiritual lover does not turn his back on physical love, but only makes sure (as always with Plato) that spiritual love is uppermost in his soul. Thus we read toward the end of Pausanias' speech: "When the lover and beloved come together, . . . the one capable of communicating wisdom and virtue, the other seeking to acquire them with a view to education and wisdom, . . . then . . . may the beloved yield with honor to the lover" (184).

The idealization of passion, as a glance at the *Vita Nuova* or at the *canzonieri* of Petrarch would suggest, is medieval and romantic, not Platonic and Hellenic. In spite of popular connotations of the term to the contrary, Shelley's affair with the Contessina Viviani, in its heterosexuality and lack of fulfillment, was distinctly un-Platonic, and the corresponding elements in the poem are similarly un-Platonic.

Yet, once these elements have been recognized and disallowed, it is astonishing how closely the ideology of the first two thirds of *Epipsychidion* keeps within the framework of the Platonic philosophy. Even the first one hundred fifty lines of extravagant and al-

106. In her letter to Maria Gisborne of March 7, 1822; cf. Mrs. Julian Marshall, *The Life and Letters of Mary Wollstonecraft Shelley* (2 vols. London, 1889), I, 331.

most pure apostrophe to Shelley's latest (and at last perfect) incarnation of ideal beauty are not at all at variance with the madness the lover in the *Phaedrus* is supposed to feel at the sight of divine beauty in the flesh (254). In particular, one is struck by echoes of the *Hymn to Intellectual Beauty*, echoes now amplified by the intervening years of Platonic study.

In *Epipsychidion* Shelley speaks of the same ideal beauty to which the 1816 Hymn had been addressed—a presence felt, but not seen:

> There was a Being whom my spirit oft
> Met on its visioned wanderings, far aloft,
> In the clear golden prime of my youth's dawn,
> Upon the fairy isles of sunny lawn,
> Amid the enchanted mountains, and the caves
> Of divine sleep, and on the air-like waves
> Of wonder-level dream, whose tremulous floor
> Paved her light steps;—on an imagined shore,
> Under the gray beak of some promontory
> She met me, robed in such exceeding glory,
> That I beheld her not.
>
> 190–200

In addition to perceiving this beauty in the world of fancy, Shelley came to recognize it in the world of nature, with far greater detail and with far more universality than is described in 1816:

> In solitudes
> Her voice came to me through the whispering woods,
> And from the fountains, and the odours deep
> Of flowers, which, like lips murmuring in their sleep
> Of the sweet kisses which had lulled them there,
> Breathed but of *her* to the enamoured air;
> And from the breezes whether low or loud,
> And from the rain of every passing cloud,
> And from the singing of the summer-birds,
> And from all sounds, all silence.
>
> 200–209

But still more striking is Shelley's recognition that in the world of literature, art, and philosophy, ideal beauty is the spirit that harmonizes the whole, the essence of essences, the absolute idea. Shelley had now come to perceive that

> In the words
> Of antique verse and high romance,—in form,
> Sound, colour—in whatever checks that Storm
> Which with the shattered present chokes the past;
> And in that best philosophy, whose taste

Makes this cold common hell, our life, a doom
As glorious as a fiery martyrdom;
Her spirit was the harmony of truth.

209–216

Ideal beauty is thus the truth that informs poetry and art. It is the truth that resists materialism, that opposes "getting and spending"—which, after shattering the present, seeks to choke the past, whose legacy is largely spiritual. Finally, in that best philosophy, idealism, as Plato has shown, absolute beauty, or the Idea of Good, is the very harmony of truth. As we premised at the beginning of this section, Plato has given content to what in 1816 had been only an instinctive faith in the reality of the spiritual world.

In his youth, Shelley tells us, he had sought the embodiment of this ideal beauty, and when it evaded him he had, in the manner of the *Hymn to Intellectual Beauty,*

murmured names and spells which have control
Over the sightless tyrants of our fate.

239–240

Then followed years of falsely aroused hopes and cruel disappointments. Finally, after the greatest disappointment of all, the Vision he had dreamed about came to him through the wintry Forest of his life. As it had with Asia, the wilderness blossomed as the Vision came. Soft as an Incarnation of the Sun (Plato's analogue of the Idea of Good), she floated into the poet's cavern and summoned him up to her. He knew it was the Vision veiled so many years, "that it was Emily."

Throughout this autobiographic passage, as indeed throughout the first two thirds of the poem, it is interesting to note that Shelley does not once lose his grasp of the Platonic distinction between the beloved and the lover, between the incarnation of beauty and the emotion it gives rise to, between object and subject. Emily is object, as the idea of beauty has always been object. But as the *embodiment* of the idea of beauty she also becomes subject, a living person in her own right. Even in such a trifling detail as Shelley's use of Plato's figure of the sun, his understanding remains firm. The effluence of the sun is light, the objective radiance of an external object. But when it is transformed to its subject counterpart, an immortal spirit, the emanation becomes love. Thus, as we have mentioned already, Emily comes to the poet,

Soft as an Incarnation of the Sun,
When light is changed to love.

335–336

In view of this unexpected strictness in a poem that is essentially one of romantic love, it is interesting to go back to the passage that immediately precedes the account of Shelley's successful search for ideal beauty in a living person. In this earlier passage Shelley tells us that love increases by the multiplication of beloved objects, being in this respect like the understanding, which "grows bright gazing on many truths." The spirit, whether intellect or feeling, mounts to high heaven from the very multiplicity of the earth. Finally, Shelley states,

> Narrow
> The heart that loves, the brain that contemplates,
> The life that wears, the spirit that creates
> One object, and one form, and builds thereby
> A sepulchre for its eternity.
>
> 169–173

Now this is pure Greek thought. The very essence of Plato's and Aristotle's distinction between spirit and matter rests upon the difference that results from multiplication. To divide matter, as Shelley says, is to diminish it; to divide the bases of spirit is to increase it. Shelley correctly states that in the latter case the "part exceeds the whole." To abstract the notion of "tree," for instance, from an individual elm is to divide, yet to exceed, the elm; for the notion of "tree," although but part of the elm, embraces elms, oaks, and maples. To go on and abstract the notion of "plant" from that of "tree" is again to divide and again to exceed, the mind rising in this manner from lesser to greater wholes, until finally it comes to the greatest whole of all. So Diotima describes the mounting of love until the vision of absolute beauty is obtained. And similarly, in the more prosaic passage beginning with *Republic* 474 C, Socrates describes love as waxing upon multiplicity. "A lover," he says, "if he is worthy of the name, ought to show his love, not to some one part of that which he loves, but to the whole." Thus the lover of youthful beauty loves all who are in the flower of youth; the lover of wines loves all wines; the lover of honor, all honor; the lover of wisdom, all wisdom.

Finally, we note that Shelley again ascribes to evil an essential negativity. Division, the principle of securing pleasure (which increases), diminishes sorrow (which disappears). Shelley tells us, in fact, that this is

> the eternal law
> By which those live, to whom this world of life
> Is as a garden ravaged, and whose strife
> Tills for the promise of a later birth
> The wilderness of this Elysian earth.
>
> **185–189**

At least as regards the first two thirds of *Epipsychidion,* the persistence of the influence of Plato is amazing. The world the poem envisions is still thoroughly informed by the philosophy of Plato. The world Shelley thought about (if not the one he felt about) would seem to have received a permanent Platonic cast.

In fact, the first two thirds of *Epipsychidion* is clearly more Platonic than the fourth act of *Prometheus Unbound.* As we have seen, there has been a return to the conception of evil as negativity. Yet "return" is scarcely the word. The development of Shelley's thought has hitherto, as we have followed it, revealed no retracings of its progress, no returns to prior positions. The progress has not been uniform by any means, but it has consistently been a progress.

What has happened, evidently, has been a return not to the thinking of the first three acts of *Prometheus Unbound,* but to the psychic level of composition of those first three acts. For *Epipsychidion,* at least in its earlier portion, is clearly on the level of conscious, literary creation. The veiled autobiography, to say nothing of the philosophical passage that precedes it, implies a process of conscious creation quite different from the lyrical outburst of the fourth act of *Prometheus Unbound.*

Thus, to answer one of the questions posed at the beginning of this section, we may state that the year or more that intervened between the conclusion of *Prometheus Unbound* and the commencement of *Epipsychidion* witnessed no diminution, at least on the conscious level, of the influence of Plato.

It is a commonplace, though, that real spiritual development springs from a deeper level than that of conscious, literary composition. True, the deeper level is fed by the higher level, and the experiences that incite psychic growth are conscious to begin with. But the manufactory of spiritual development lies deep within the psyche.

Hence we turn with great interest to the last third of *Epipsychidion,* noting that it stands in the same relation to the earlier part as the fourth act of *Prometheus Unbound* stands to the first three acts. As Professor White observes,[107] the four or five lines that conclude the autobiographical portion match the four or five lines that introduce the poem, and the imaginary elopement that the last third of the poem describes is not only without reference to Mary or to Claire but is contradictory to the sentiments of the first part of the poem. The elopement, according to Professor White,[108] is "an addition imperfectly welded to a poem already artistically and logically complete." Clearly, at one point in its composition, *Epipsychidion* ended with line 387. Nor can there be any doubt that the last third of the poem represents an outflow of personal expression comparable to the

107. *Op. cit.,* II, 268.   108. *Idem,* II, 269.

fourth act of *Prometheus Unbound,* or to the concluding cantos of *Queen Mab.*

At the beginning of this portion of *Epipsychidion* the reader is struck by the sudden applicability of the quotation at the head of the poem, the quotation taken from the short essay on *Il Vero Amore* by the Contessina Viviani, which we give in the main from Medwin's translation: "The loving soul lances itself out of the created, and creates in the infinite a world for itself alone, how different from this dark and fearful den."[109] Thus at the beginning of the last third of *Epipsychidion* is sung the power of Love to transcend high walls, strong gates, and thick-set sentinels. Love is said to be more penetrating than Heaven's free breath, or than Death itself. The very elopement is a flight of Love from the "dark and fearful den" of the convent-prison to the more ideal world of the imagination.

Let us look, then, at this elopement into the world of the imagination which Shelley[110] proposes with his beloved, and at the flight into the infinite which the pair of lovers, once lodged in that world, will then make.

The dream isle, we observe, is pervaded by the essential unity of things. In the island every motion, odor, beam, and tone is in unison with the deep music that is the soul within a soul. Indeed,

> like a buried lamp, a Soul no less
> Burns in the heart of this delicious isle,
> An atom of th' Eternal, whose own smile
> Unfolds itself, and may be felt, not seen
> O'er the gray rocks, blue waves, and forests green,
> Filling their bare and void interstices.
>
> 477–482

But the chief marvel of the island is the lone tower it possesses—the property, like the island, of the lover who is proposing flight. Its builder has been long forgotten, its inscriptions have been erased, and now it is adorned with ivy, wild-vine, and parasite flowers.

In life, this tower is to be the home of the lovers. In death, they will become

> the overhanging day,
> The living soul of this Elysian isle,
> Conscious, inseparable, one.
>
> 538–540

109. *Op. cit.,* p. 283.
110. Since in his letter of June 18, 1822, to John Gisborne (Julian *Works,* x, 401), Shelley specifically says that *Epipsychidion* "is an idealized history of my life and feelings," it seems pointless to bother with the fiction of the "Writer of the following lines" who "died at Florence," etc.

In life, whether the lovers wander over the mossy mountains or by the pebble-paven shores, they will possess and be possessed by all that is, "till to love and live be one."

The longing to be one is especially evident in the passage describing the siesta the lovers will take in the hoary cavern. As they talk, the melody of their thought will become too sweet for utterance. Passing into looks, it will dart into the heart, harmonizing silence without a sound. In the cavern the breath of the lovers will intermix, their veins will beat together, and the fountains of their deepest life will be

> Confused in Passion's golden purity,
> As mountain-springs under the morning sun.

570–571

Indeed, the lovers will "become the same." They will be "one spirit within two frames."

We have noted Professor White's observation that the last third of *Epipsychidion* is contradictory to the sentiments of the first two thirds of the poem. But surely there is as great a contradiction in the thought. In the earlier portion of the poem it is stated that love increases through multiplication of the beloved objects. In the last third of the poem, not only is the excursion to the dream island contemplated with but one beloved, but the object of this pair of lovers is to get away even from their duality. As we have observed, their goal is to "become the same," to be "one spirit within two frames."

The poet goes on to describe the unity that he and his beloved will attain. The love in their twin-hearts will expand until it touches, mingles, and is transformed. Like meteors, like flames that point toward heaven and cannot pass away, the lovers in their spiritual mingling will feed upon each other, yet remain unconsumed. Their mingling will form one hope within two wills, one will beneath two minds, indeed

> one life, one death,
> One Heaven, one Hell, one immortality,
> And one annihilation.

585–587

For, of course, the merging into one premises the loss of individuality, and is annihilation just as much as it is immortality. As such, it may be the desideratum of the religious mystic, or of the philosopher. The former may never have liked life anyway; and the latter may have become so much absorbed in his thought that the dropping of individuality is just the giving up of a superfluous idea. But the poet, at least the Wordsworthian poet, has a love for the various world that is close to the very heart of him. For Shelley to give up the sifted sands and caverns hoar, the violets and jonquils peeping from the moss, the scent of lemon-flowers in the light clear air, the quick, faint kisses of the sea—for Shelley to give up the very world that *Epipsychidion* depicts so inimitably would be, perhaps, to give up the greatest love of all.

Is it any wonder, then, that as soon as the poet sees whither the flight of his loving soul is carrying him, he should recoil in horror?

> Woe is me!
> The wingèd words on which my soul would pierce
> Into the height of Love's rare Universe,
> Are chains of lead around its flight of fire—
> I pant, I sink, I tremble, I expire!
>
> 587–591

Words may be wingèd as they pour forth the feelings within us. But they also reveal whither we are journeying, and may depress the soul like chains of lead if they make clear we are proceeding in the opposite direction from what we desire. Well may the poet pant, sink, tremble, and expire if he perceives that the end of the journey is the loss of all that he holds dear.[111]

Though the charioteer is no longer the driver, and the white horse is now conducting the vehicle to a destination of its own choosing, the chariot is still a threefold unity. The charioteer is still part of the equipage, and though he has ceased to have control over the chariot's progress, he does not hesitate to tell his fellows whither the journey is tending. There is, in fact, no one else who can declare it.

For the white horse is now left with only its basic instinct to join. Its function by nature, according to Plato, is to attach itself to the intellect, and with the intellect to seek the good and the beautiful. Emotion, as Plato specifically says (*Republic* 440 A), is the natural ally of reason, cleaving instinctively to the side of intellect. We remember that Plato came to call the soldiers of his ideal state the helpers, or allies, of the rulers (*Republic* 414 B). But now alliance with the ruling partner has been put aside, and only the native tendency

111. It is doubtless unnecessary to observe that the conventional interpretation of the above passage is simply that the poet has found words incapable of expressing his meaning. Professor White (*op. cit.*, I, 581) has, furthermore, connected the last line of the cited passage with other lines of Shelley's poetry, and has derived them all from the memorable fragment of Schubart's *The Wandering Jew* that Shelley picked up in Lincoln's-Inn Fields. Though the fragment from Schubart may indeed be the source of the phrasing of the final line of the above passage, nevertheless both the dynamics of Shelley's general intellectual development, and the dynamics of the thought development of this particular poem, lead us to reject the conventional interpretation (which, after all, is a rather trite idea) in favor of the explanation we have set forth.

is left. The white horse is guided only by its instinct to join, and it seeks to unite with another chariot likewise under the guidance of its white horse and likewise seeking only to join. Yet since this is but a joining with joining, a mere intensification of the tendency already in evidence, the journey turns into a race, and the race into a leap toward annihilation—the only terminus where the joining can come to an end. Thus even the white horse feels a wave of panic come over him as the neglected charioteer cries out whither the mad course is taking them.

In other words, not only is it clear to us, but it is clear to Shelley, whither the combination of Platonic voluntarism and romantic emotionalism is conducting him. Love, having taken over the guidance of the chariot, is evidently bent on no new pasturage but simply on driving the chariot right out of existence. Like a religious of the Middle Ages, intent on renouncing as he joins his order all individuality, even his name, the romantic voluntarist seeks first to unite with another romantic voluntarist, and then with the infinite. Instead of a climb to high heaven to gaze upon the world of true being, the chariot ride has turned out to be a plunge into the abyss of Demogorgon. Well might the soul of Shelley pant, and sink, and tremble, and expire! For overwhelming as it was, Shelley's imagination was nevertheless not of the inner world, but of the glorious outer world of particularized individuality.

5. Adonais

THE composition of *Adonais*, Shelley's great elegy on the death of Keats, took place within a few months of the completion of *Epipsychidion*. *Epipsychidion* had been dispatched to London on the sixteenth of February, 1821,[112] while on the sixteenth of June, Shelley wrote John Gisborne that he was on that day sending *Adonais* to the press at Pisa.[113] Thus the composition of the poem took place while the metaphysical problems which *Epipsychidion* had brought into the open were still fresh in Shelley's mind.

It is clear that consciously or unconsciously Shelley would seek to reëxamine the metaphysical conclusions that *Epipsychidion* had seemed to indicate. We have seen that the romantic voluntarism which Shelley had adopted, far from being alien to his personality, lay in the very line of its development. Hence if the destination toward which this voluntarism was tending appeared suddenly to be a matter of alarm, it would be Shelley's instinct not to abandon the course he was following, but to look again to see if the apparent destination was really implied. To Shelley the longing to be one, the desire for unity, had seemed to premise the loss of personal individuality, of all individuality. But does it premise it? If it does, why should there be any individuality in the first place? Perhaps the One is a whole of many parts. Perhaps it is an evolving unity, made up of parts that succeed each other and yet are implicit in the dynamic whole. Clearly annihilation is not the only possibility.

Thus we turn to *Adonais* with the expectation of finding a reexamination of the metaphysical problems that had been Shelley's concern as he finished *Epipsychidion*. Unless *Adonais* is entirely on the level of the first two thirds of *Epipsychidion,* it seems hardly possible that it can be without a consideration of them.

The astonishing thing is that *Adonais* reveals the very same structural peculiarities as *Epipsychidion*. The first two thirds of the poem are again on the level of conscious, literary production; the last third is once more an outflow of relatively personal expression. In the first thirty-seven stanzas the poet seems to be composing a perfectly formal elegy. There are borrowings from Moschus, and more notably from Bion. There is a procession of contemporary poets to the death chamber of Keats, with once again a passage of veiled autobiography. Yet in the last eighteen stanzas one looks in vain for such conscious literary effort. But most remarkable is the fact that

112. Cf. letter to Charles Ollier, Julian *Works*, x, 236.
113. *Idem*, x, 277.

this time we possess an item of external evidence to support our inferences from the internal evidence. On June 8, scarcely more than a week before sending the poem to the press, Shelley wrote Ollier, "You may announce for publication a poem entitled 'Adonais.' . . . My poem is finished, and consists of about forty Spenser stanzas."[114] The conclusion is inescapable that the first thirty-seven stanzas represent the poem as Shelley originally intended it, and that in the last week Shelley wrote the remaining eighteen stanzas simply because the problems he had been mulling over since February would not be denied.

Hence our especial interest in *Adonais* begins with the thirty-eighth stanza, which, as William Michael Rossetti remarked in his memorable edition of 1891, is the turning point of the poem.[115] Hitherto, the elegy has been taken up with the particular and the concrete, with the mythological and the symbolic, with the fact of Keats's death and its attendant circumstances. Now it turns to the general and the eternal and becomes, as Rossetti says, a "paean of recantation and aspiration."[116] The echoes of Bion and Moschus, as well as of Keats and Milton, are left behind, and the poem becomes purely Shelleyan. In its treatment of immortality and the true nature of reality, this last third of the poem is, as Professor White says,[117] Shelley's own.

Let us consider, then, what is said about immortality and the true nature of reality in this last third of Shelley's great elegy.

We are told, to begin with, that the pure spirit will flow back to the burning fountain whence it came; that it is a portion of the Eternal, and hence will glow through time and change, unquenchably the same (stanza 38). Again, we are informed that Keats has been made one with Nature. His voice is now to be heard in the thunder and in the song of the nightingale. He is to be felt in darkness and in light, in herb and in stone, wherever the Power that has withdrawn him to itself moves in its never-wearied attentions of love and care (stanza 42). He is a portion of the loveliness he once made more lovely. He now bears his part in that one creative Spirit which sweeps through the sense world, supplying the forms of existence, torturing matter into that especial aspect of itself which each concrete particular wears, and ascending through trees and beasts and men to self-consciousness (stanza 43).

To all this there is an unmistakably monistic cast.

True, it is not explained whence the "unwilling dross" comes. Nor is the nature stated of what is thus tortured into an evidently un-

114. *Idem*, x, 273.
115. W. M. Rossetti, *The Adonais of Shelley* (Oxford, 1891), p. 130.
116. *Ibid.*
117. N. I. White, *The Best of Shelley* (New York, 1932), p. 498.

willing resemblance of the divine idea. The dull sense world is incontrovertibly stumbled over, and in stumbling over it, Shelley is incontrovertibly Greek. For the Greeks never succeeded in explaining matter away. The best they could do was to explain spirit away and incorporate it in the material whole. In this neglected but nevertheless unresolved dualism, Shelley is Platonic with Plato, Greek with the Greeks.

But in the coalescence of the individual spirit with the world spirit, in the monistic return of the particular soul to the matrix of all souls, Shelley is modern (or Oriental) and not Greek. In Plato's spirit world, for instance, Souls take their place with Ideas as ultimate essences. The farthest continuity Plato can trace (as readers of the *Phaedrus* or of the myth of Er will remember)[118] is from man to man, or from man to beast—never from the individual soul to the world soul, from the Many to the One, or from the One to the Many.

Furthermore we are told, in the forty-fourth stanza, that the individual soul not only will be reabsorbed into the world soul, but that in its reabsorption its destined life (if unhappily cut short) will be fulfilled. The luminous intellects[119] of this world may be eclipsed but not extinguished. Like the stars of heaven, they will complete their orbits no matter what mists obscure them from the earth. In fact Chatterton, Sidney, and Lucan, who have accordingly inherited their unfulfilled renown, rise to meet Keats coming to inherit his (stanza 45).

This, of course, is perfectly in line with monistic thinking. For, if the individual is reabsorbed into the Absolute, he inherits everything and is everything.

But the Chatterton–Sidney–Lucan passage is so interesting in itself, and so important to our ideological appraisal of the poem, that it must be looked at again, and indeed should be quoted in full:

XLV

The inheritors of unfulfilled renown
Rose from their thrones, built beyond mortal thought,
Far in the Unapparent. Chatterton
Rose pale,—his solemn agony had not
Yet faded from him; Sidney, as he fought
And as he fell and as he lived and loved
Sublimely mild, a Spirit without spot,
    Arose; and Lucan, by his death approved:
Oblivion as they rose shrank like a thing reproved.

118. *Phaedrus* 248–249; *Republic* 614–621.
119. The phrase is Rossetti's (*op. cit.*, p. 134).

XLVI

And many more, whose names on Earth are dark,
    But whose transmitted effluence cannot die
So long as fire outlives the parent spark,
    Rose, robed in dazzling immortality.
    'Thou art become as one of us,' they cry,
    'It was for thee yon kingless sphere has long
Swung blind in unascended majesty,
    Silent alone amid an Heaven of Song.
Assume thy wingèd throne, thou Vesper of our throng!'

In this passage it is especially important to distinguish figure from
thought. The statement that the thrones of the inheritors of unfulfilled renown are situated far in the Unapparent, beyond mortal
thought, tells us that the passage in whatever machinery it may employ is purely figurative. For thrones and palaces and the like para-
phernalia belong to the concrete world of visible fact. Even the
Platonic world, where their intelligible ideas, or essences, might be
said to lodge, must be placed this side of the Unapparent, since the
Unapparent is expressly stated to lie beyond human intelligence.

Hence the vestiges of mortality that cling to the three predecessors
of Keats, and the message they and the rest carry to him of the
kingless sphere long awaiting him, can only be the poet's way of expressing the inexpressible. If the One is the One, then the past is the
present and the present is the past. Chatterton's suicide is now, and
Keats's glory was then.

Clearly this is what the passage means. To assume otherwise is to
assume that Shelley was unaware of what the words "Unapparent"
and "beyond mortal thought" mean—an assumption that would be
gratuitous with any poet, and with a poet so philosophically read as
Shelley, not only gratuitous but undiscerning, to say the least.

Yet how un-Greek this is needs scarcely to be mentioned. Monism
inevitably has a tendency to lead to paradox and mysticism.[120] As
such, at least in its modern, spiritual sense, it was repugnant to the
Greek mind. We recall that the Eleatics, far from being mystical, tried
to get away from the contradictions even of ordinary speech. The
Eleatic position was that life is more logical, not less logical, than it
actually seems.[121]

120. That Shelley perceived this himself is evident from his letter to Ollier of September 25, 1821: "The *Adonais*, in spite of its mysticism, is the least imperfect of my com-
positions" (Julian *Works*, x, 328).

121. Surely this is the point of Zeno's well-known puzzles of motion, as given in
Aristotle's *Physics*. The example of the flying arrow (to take just one) seeks to prove
to the reason what the moving-picture camera now shows to the senses—that motion is

But before we attempt to say what this monism is, if it is not Greek, let us return to two or three stanzas that we have passed over.

In a passage beginning with the thirty-ninth stanza (a passage which Rossetti has already compared with a portion of the *Phaedo*),[122] we are informed that Keats is neither dead nor asleep, but one awakened from the dream of life. We are told that in the struggle of life the adversaries we strive with are but stormy visions and phantoms, that fear and grief consume us as worms the dead. In the fortieth and forty-first stanzas, we learn that the world of experience is but a shadow of night, a gloom of envy and calumny and pain and unrest, a negation of life from which Keats has awakened to life itself. It is Death that is dead, not Keats.

Now the notion that the spiritual world is the real world, that the visible world is insubstantial and unabiding, is, of course, as old as man and as universal as human thought. It occurs most frequently, perhaps, among the Orientals, but is almost as commonly met with in Christian writings. In fact, when one thinks of Plato and Berkeley and Immanuel Kant, one perceives that the doctrine is confined to no class of human beings. It is evidently a point of view quite native to the human species and, as an idea, is far more common than the doctrine of monism.

Yet, ubiquitous as the notion is, there is a distinction to be maintained. For there is a vast difference in the manner with which the thought is expressed and in the logic, or way of thought, that the manner implies.

The Greek way, which is Shelley's way and on the whole the Western way, is to take the reader, or listener, by the hand and lead him step by step from the old position to the new position. It seeks to explain and to demonstrate. Its logic might be described as linear and transitional. No better instance of it could be cited than Plato's justly celebrated figure of the cave.[123] In Plato's figure there is not a trace of the cryptic or mystical. The cave is explicitly described. The low wall along the raised way is mentioned as like a puppeteer's screen, and the passers-by carry the commodities of ordinary life. The reader is led along the homely path of everyday realities and values until suddenly he sees that he has given his entire credence to what is the opposite of reality in the ordinary sense. The very brilliance and rhetorical success of the figure depend upon the step-by-

---

imaginable only as a series of states of rest. And since motion is needed to get the object even from one state of rest to another, Zeno concluded that the whole notion is illogical and had better be given up.

122. *Op. cit.*, pp. 131–132. Note that the statement in stanza 52, "Die, if thou wouldst be that which thou dost seek!" is a precise summary of *Phaedo* 64.

123. *Republic* 514–517 A.

step solicitation of the reader's faith. It makes the final recognition of
Plato's meaning overwhelming.

The Oriental way is different. Its logic might be described not as
linear but as radial. The recurring statements do not progress, but
return to their center as the spokes of a wheel to their hub. The
Oriental monist, for example, assumes his monism as a self-evident
fact, and with one *non sequitur* after another seeks only to embellish
his central doctrine and illustrate its amazing and unexpected rami-
fications. The reader, or listener, must be in possession of the secret
to begin with, or all is lost.

To illustrate the above statement it would be natural to turn to the
Upanishads. But more is to be gained by citing Emerson's well-known
poem on Brahma, or the One:

Brahma

If the red slayer think he slays,
  Or if the slain think he is slain,
They know not well the subtle ways
  I keep, and pass, and turn again.

Far or forgot to me is near;
  Shadow and sunlight are the same;
The vanished gods to me appear;
  And one to me are shame and fame.

They reckon ill who leave me out;
  When me they fly, I am the wings;
I am the doubter and the doubt,
  And I the hymn the Brahmin sings.

The strong gods pine for my abode,
  And pine in vain the sacred Seven;
But thou, meek lover of the good!
  Find me, and turn thy back on heaven.[124]

More is to be gained by citing Emerson's poem because Emerson
is in the development not of Oriental but of Romantic monism, and in
his employment of the Oriental idiom shows how much more extreme
he is, how much farther this way of thinking has gone.[125]

124. The indebtedness of Emerson's poem to the Upanishads has been worked out
by F. I. Carpenter, *Emerson and Asia* (Cambridge, Mass., 1930), pp. 110–121.

125. In this connection it is interesting to note that Schopenhauer, for all his use of
the Upanishads, is the most Greek and Western in his idiom of all the German idealists.
In point of style, Royce (*The Spirit of Modern Philosophy*, p. 250) finds *Die Welt als
Wille und Vorstellung* comparable with the best of Plato's dialogues. Whereas Emerson's *Brahma* comes after the midcentury mark, *Die Welt als Wille und Vorstellung*

For Shelley, even in his monism, is Greek and Western in the phrasing of his thought, in the logic of his style. And with respect to the idea with which we started this discussion, the less radical idea that the world of death is more substantial than the world of life—here Shelley is extended, patient, and even mundane in his exposition. His thought advances from step to step in perfect sequence and transition. The thought of the waking of death and of the dream of life leads to a consideration of the nightmares of the dream. These suggest the pain of life, which leads to the thought of Keats's escape from life, which finally suggests in the forty-first stanza the admonition to the day and landscape to express their true happiness at Keats's liberation.

Thus Shelley seeks to convince rather than to exclaim. He would persuade rather than utter. In fact, when we link the spiritual, Oriental monism of his thinking with the un-Oriental, unmonistic way of his exposition, it is clear that we have in its essence one aspect of the whole Romantic Movement. This aspect is indeed no other than the peculiar Romantic desire to link the transcendental with the earthly.

Professor Fairchild, in his interesting and provocative analysis of the metaphysical revolt from the eighteenth century, describes it as a double reaction, up and down, from the mean plane of eighteenth-century thinking.[126] Thus, as we interpret it, the Romantic idealists sought to enter the monistic realm above the pluralistic plane of eighteenth-century thought, while at the same time they endeavored to show the palpable embodiment of this spiritual monism in the visible universe. That this characterizes the early Wordsworth is a commonplace. But does it not equally characterize the German philosophers across the Channel, across the Rhine? Does not Hegel, the exact contemporary of Wordsworth, laboriously work out the integration of his unitary thought, then laboriously trace out its manifestation in history from the earliest times to the contemporary moment? Does not Schopenhauer, the exact contemporary of Byron, hold that the mountains, the trees, and even our souls are but expressions of the same unseeing Will? And, far from being Oriental and esoteric in their way of exposition, do not they all seek to convince and prove by articulate process of thought—by linear, rather than by radial, reasoning?

Shelley similarly desires to take his readers along with him in his exposition of the true reality. In the Chatterton–Sidney–Lucan passage we observe that a key is given, and given not at the end but at the beginning. We are told at the outset that the realm of the dead lies beyond mortal thought—in other words, that all references to it are to be taken as figure and not as fact. Transcendental as the thinking

(postdated 1819) appeared toward the close of 1818. It is interesting to note that during the winter of 1818–19 Schopenhauer, like Shelley, was wandering from Venice to Naples.
126. Fairchild, *The Romantic Quest*, p. 145.

may be, the reader is yet given a cue as to its meaning. Shelley is explicitly trying to reconcile his search for unity with the various world, which in spite of personal sorrow he is unwilling, at least in idea, to give up. He is trying to think out his quest of the Absolute. Is annihilation inevitable, or is individuality included in the One? To judge from the Chatterton–Sidney–Lucan passage, Shelley is coming to think that the Many is in some way latent in the One, so that even if it fails on earth it will be fulfilled in the Absolute.

Having attained the Absolute, the elegy pauses in the next four or five stanzas. The mourner is admonished, after his sweep into the infinite, to return to earth refreshed, not cast down, by his experience. Even the evidence of the senses shows the permanence only of the not-sense. Keats adds to the glory of Rome; he does not receive glory through being buried there. He belongs to the kings of thought, who alone succeed in wresting something from the lapse of time.

Yet the thought is meager in these four or five stanzas. More attention is given to description of the ruins of Rome and the Protestant cemetery—that

> slope of green access
> Where, like an infant's smile, over the dead
> A light of laughing flowers along the grass is spread.
>
> 439–441

The elegy is evidently resting before the return of feeling brings it back to its central thought. The rhetoric is evidently gathering for the final spring, the final definition of terms.

With the question, "What Adonais is, why fear we to become?" the poem returns to its metaphysical concerns. The thinking of the entire elegy thus far is summed up in the stanza that comes next.

LII

> The One remains, the many change and pass;
> Heaven's light forever shines, Earth's shadows fly;
> Life, like a dome of many-colored glass,
> Stains the white radiance of Eternity,
> Until Death tramples it to fragments.—Die,
> If thou wouldst be with that which thou dost seek!
> Follow where all is fled!—Rome's azure sky,
> Flowers, ruins, statues, music, words, are weak
> The glory they transfuse with fitting truth to speak.

Whatever life itself may be, it brings forth the variegation of eternity. True, it does this all imperfectly. But Shelley assumes that, when life ceases, the individual will be able to join with that which he desires, with the perfect variegation which all the works of man and nature are weak to transmit with fitting truth.

The assumption that at death the individual will join with the One is in line with the monistic thinking of the poem, and has been posited from the beginning of the metaphysical portion. But the reason for the fact of individuality, for the fact of the individual's being separated from the One in the first place, is no clearer now than then. And there still remains the "unwilling dross" to be accounted for. The difficulties of the monistic position have by no means been completely explained, and undoubtedly Shelley will return to the problem.

Nevertheless one cannot but be impressed by the increasing definition which the goal of the romantic voluntarist is receiving. No longer does the end in sight seem to be mere annihilation, mere obliteration of individuality. Rather, it now seems the fulfillment of the unfulfilled on earth, the perfection of the unperfected. It now seems to be the implication of all that ever was or ever will be. In particular, one is struck by the way in which a dynamic interpretation of the One has led Shelley to ascribe to it characteristics of the subject as well as object. In the following stanza, the One is half-construed as Light and Beauty, half-construed as Benediction and Love:

LIV

That Light whose smile kindles the Universe,
That Beauty in which all things work and move,
That Benediction which the eclipsing Curse
Of birth can quench not, that sustaining Love
Which through the web of being blindly wove
By man and beast and earth and air and sea,
Burns bright or dim, as each are mirrors of
The fire for which all thirst; now beams on me,
Consuming the last clouds of cold mortality.

That Shelley would come to believe in an Absolute that is as much subject as object probably could have been predicted as early as *Queen Mab*—certainly as early as the 1816 Hymns. For if one believes in a world that is at heart of the nature or order of mind, and wishes to assert anything of that world, he cannot avoid designating it in terms of object or subject or both. It was inevitable that Plato, with his adamantine faith in the reality of the spiritual world, and with his intellectualist point of view, should have regarded the universe as composed essentially of ideas and of souls to regard those ideas. The freedom he assumed was the freedom of the subject to look upon a world not so much of the same *nature* as of the same *order* as itself. It was likewise inevitable that Shelley, with a similar idealistic faith, but with an emotionalist point of view, should have regarded the world in far other terms. Emotion, as Plato has shown, is basically a movement toward, a tendency to join. Hence, since one joins with souls rather than with ideas, the emotionalist will conceive of the spiritual world in terms of subject rather than of object. He looks upon the world as consisting not of the same *order* but of the same *nature* as himself, and the freedom he postulates is the freedom of the subject to join with subject. Whereas with Plato the individual is free to mount and view, with Shelley he is free to go and join.

But the really interesting thing is that the idealist who is also an emotionalist is led farther than this. The very fact that to him the mind seems to be subject more than it is object, that its dominant function appears to be joining rather than viewing, irresistibly leads him toward monism. Whereas the intellectualist finds no difficulty in viewing a plurality of objects, the emotionalist, to join a plurality even of souls, would have to parcel himself out. When one joins a group or organization, it is the hypostatized unity one joins far more than the separate personalities that make it up. Thus the idealist who is an emotionalist finds himself impelled toward some form of monism.[127] In fact, as we have seen, the unity toward which Shelley first felt himself impelled appeared to be simply the negation of individuality. This first, horrifying impression Shelley was able to reconstruct. But it is noticeable that he reconstructed it in terms of the subject, which is a dynamic, not a static, unity.[128] Hence the coëxistence of the past with the present, of the present with the past, in the Chatterton–Sidney–Lucan passage. And hence the stanza that we have just quoted, in which the One is conceived in terms of love and benediction as much as in terms of beauty and light.

Needless to say, the reconstruction of the end in sight has not slowed the chariot drive. It becomes increasingly apparent as *Adonais* draws to a conclusion that the longing for union so noticeable at the end of *Epipsychidion* has not weakened in the meantime. The panic that momentarily overtook the white horse and charioteer has been allayed in the intervening three or four months, and the journey presses on with renewed vigor. In fact, what has happened is that the Absolute is now adding its invitation to the individual's

127. Though we anticipate the thinking of our last chapter, we cannot forbear pointing out at this moment that the Kantian movement in philosophy was a movement informed by the emotionalist point of view. In the Preface to the second edition of the *Critique of Pure Reason* we have Kant's own word that he was led to get rid of knowledge in order to make a place for faith, and we notice in Fichte (who set the sights for the whole post-Kantian development) that the essence of spirit is activity rather than contemplation. As needs scarcely to be observed, in point of influence Kant is the Rousseau of Germany, and under his leadership the verb πράττειν came to be substituted for the verb θεωρεῖν.

128. It is interesting that Royce (*op. cit.*, pp. 202–208) should find the essence of Hegelianism to be a similar interpretation of the world in terms of the dynamic, living subject.

desire. We observe that *Adonais* concludes with the Absolute's beaconing the individual from afar:

LV

> The breath whose might I have invoked in song
> Descends on me; my spirit's bark is driven,
> Far from the shore, far from the trembling throng
> Whose sails were never to the tempest given;
> The massy earth and sphered skies are riven!
> I am borne darkly, fearfully, afar;
> Whilst, burning through the inmost veil of Heaven,
> The soul of Adonais, like a star,
> Beacons from the abode where the Eternal are.

6. Hellas

BUT in spite of the moments when the goal of the soul's journey shone clearer than at others, in spite of the moments when the spirit itself seemed to "lance out in the infinite" and approach the end in view, the very naturalism of Shelley's thought showed him that only death could bring the ultimate union that he desired. The Oriental, to be sure, seeks to attain that union while still in life. But as we have seen, there was nothing of the Oriental about Shelley's way of thinking. If, as he was coming to believe, life and death are a natural cycle, then the individual must wait until death for the consummation of his union with the One.

In the meantime, there will be opportunity for further reflection, and though it is hard to imagine that any future panic will arise inducing the white horse of the emotions to pay attention to the musings of the charioteer, yet the charioteer will continue to muse— indeed, until the moment of his union with the Absolute arrives.

In other words, it is difficult to imagine that Shelley will not again take up the unanswered problems of *Epipsychidion* and *Adonais*. The very success of his efforts thus far would seem to insure his trying to work out what remains unsolved. And besides, unless one knows the reason for there being a journey, unless one knows the reason for the equipment with which one finds himself furnished, how can one be sure that the apparent destination is the real destination? The charioteer can hardly avoid reflecting upon the problems of individuality and of the material world.

Thus we turn with much interest to *Hellas*, a poem comparable in length to *Epipsychidion* and *Adonais*. It seems scarcely possible that within the scope of this thousand-line drama Shelley will not endeavor once more to solve his metaphysical perplexities by means of the poetic medium. In this we are not disappointed. The problems that were not answered in *Epipsychidion* and *Adonais* are taken up in *Hellas*. But it is surprising, after all, that they are.

For *Hellas* is quite different from *Epipsychidion* and *Adonais*. Essentially, it is a topical poem. In the spring of 1821, when Shelley was dispirited from the suppression of the Neapolitan attempt at freedom, an attempt that had occasioned his *Ode to Naples*,[129] hostilities broke out in Greece. Needless to say, Shelley's friendship with Prince Mavrocordato and his enthusiasm for the ancient Greeks combined to give him an especial interest in this latest struggle for in-

129. Cf. White, *Shelley*, II, 221–224.

dependence. Finally, on June 26, Mavrocordato sailed for Greece,[130] and from then on Shelley had a personal interest in the Greek insurrection. Through the summer Shelley followed the fortunes of the Greek insurgents, and in the autumn he undertook to express his feelings on the struggle in the lyrical drama of *Hellas*.

Thus the poem is essentially topical. Indeed, in his Preface to the drama, Shelley states that it was "written at the suggestion of the events of the moment"; and in his letter to Ollier of November 11, he wrote, "I send you the drama of 'Hellas' . . . What little interest this poem may ever excite, depends upon its immediate publication; I entreat you, therefore, to have the goodness to send the MS. instantly to a printer, and the moment you get a proof despatch it to me by the post."[131] Hence, of the eleven hundred lines in the poem, actually some four hundred, or more than a third, are given over to report or discussion of the progress of the war between the Greeks and the Turks.

Furthermore, another four hundred lines are given over to the many lyrics that the Chorus of captive Greek women sing in the Sultan's seraglio, where the action of the play occurs. For, as Shelley also tells us in his Preface, the *Persae* of Æschylus supplied the model for his drama; and thus the Chorus, as in a Greek play, takes on a large role in the exposition of the drama, echoing the military and political struggle, and affording an interpretation of the events.

The remaining three hundred lines of the poem are accounted for by the Mahmud–Ahasuerus episode, the dramatic function of which would appear to be the evocation of the phantom of Mahomet the Second, who prophesies the fall of Islam. Even this portion, we observe, is connected with the central, topical significance of the play.

Thus *Hellas* is remote from the subjective preoccupations of *Epipsychidion* and *Adonais,* and it is surprising that the metaphysical problems of those poems should be brought into the play. As a matter of fact, they are introduced neither in the evocation of the phantom of Mahomet nor in the phantom's prophecy (the two likeliest places), but in the course of a colloquy between Mahmud and Ahasuerus that precedes the evocation of the phantom. In consequence, we can only conclude that the problems were so important to Shelley that he went out of his way to incorporate them in the poem.

In the colloquy between Mahmud and Ahasuerus it is made abundantly plain that Ahasuerus possesses no supernatural powers. Mahmud repeats to Ahasuerus, "Thou art a man, thou sayest, even as we, but raised above thy fellow-men by thought, as I by power." To this Ahasuerus assents. Yet, as though this were not enough, Shelley points out in a prose note that the subsequent evocation

---

130. Cf. *idem*, II, 299.   131. Julian *Works*, x, 335.

of Mahomet's phantom takes place purely by suggestion, that Ahasuerus simply induces Mahmud to hallucinate the phantom by himself. Meanwhile, Mahmud observes that Ahasuerus is a man who has studied "Greek and Frank philosophy" (and hence will reason like a Westerner, not like an Oriental). In addition, Mahmud perceives that Ahasuerus is a scientist, one who measures the stars and severs element from element, and that he is familiar with the geological and human history of the earth. In fact, Mahmud recognizes with disappointment that Ahasuerus is not an interpreter of dreams and cannot forecast the future.

Thus it seems reasonable to suppose that as Ahasuerus discusses the nature of reality it is Shelley himself who is speaking, and Shelley in his most Western, articulate frame of mind.

In *Adonais* the ultimate reality had been placed "far in the Unapparent." In *Hellas* the ultimate reality is likewise "the Fathomless," the predications that can be made of it being those of an all-pervasive unity. In particular, Ahasuerus regards it as "that which cannot change," as "the unborn and the undying." In *Adonais* Chatterton's suicide had been looked upon as still existent, and Keats's glory as having been present then. According to *Hellas*, we should regard Chatterton as never having died, and Keats as having been alive before he was born. There is, in fact, an unbroken continuity between the thought of *Adonais* and the thought of *Hellas*.

That this thought has developed as well as remained continuous is evident from Ahasuerus' next statement:

> Earth and ocean,
> Space, and the isles of life or light that gem
> The sapphire floods of interstellar air,
> This firmament pavilioned upon chaos,
> With all its cressets of immortal fire,
> Whose outwall, bastioned impregnably
> Against the escape of boldest thoughts, repels them
> As Calpe the Atlantic clouds—this Whole
> Of suns, and worlds, and men, and beasts, and flowers,
> With all the silent or tempestuous workings
> By which they have been, are, or cease to be,
> Is but a vision.

769–780

In *Hellas* the "unwilling dross" of *Adonais* is no longer stumbled over. Matter now takes its place in the Whole of things, "with all the silent or tempestuous workings by which they have been, are, or cease to be." Yet this Whole cannot be "the One" of which Ahasuerus was just speaking, "the unborn and the undying." Nor can it be the One which at the end of *Adonais* was beaconing the poet—beaconing him because of the very fact that it was subject rather than object. This Whole "of suns, and worlds, and men, and beasts, and flowers" is object rather than subject, and is indeed declared to be a vision. Lest there be any doubt of this, Ahasuerus goes on to say,

> All that it inherits
> Are motes of a sick eye, bubbles and dreams.
>
> 780–781

Thus the objective world, according to Ahasuerus, is wholly vision, entirely *Vorstellung*—of the same nature as the artificial flowers we can produce by rubbing our eyes. In fact, Ahasuerus declares of the world that

> Thought is its cradle and its grave, nor less
> The Future and the Past are idle shadows
> Of thought's eternal flight—they have no being:
> Nought is but that which feels itself to be.
>
> 782–785

In *Epipsychidion* and *Adonais,* more and more, Shelley had come to view the essence of the universe as subject rather than as object, as soul rather than as idea. Now he sees that things as well as ideas, ideas as well as things, are in reality but the product of subject, the function of "that which feels itself to be."

Ahasuerus makes this conception very clear. He declares that "all is contained in each"—in other words, that the whole objective world from the beginning of geologic time to the farthest ice age that man can anticipate is all comprised in the individual who thinks it. And Ahasuerus says that this is true even if it seems like putting the whole of Dodona forest in a single acorn cup. Again, Ahasuerus explains the variety of the objective world by the dynamic variety of the subject itself. He says,

> Thought
> Alone, and its quick elements, Will, Passion,
> Reason, Imagination, cannot die;
> They are, what that which they regard appears,
> The stuff whence mutability can weave
> All that it hath dominion o'er, worlds, worms,
> Empires, and superstitions.
>
> 795–801

Thus Will, Passion, Reason, Imagination, and the other faculties of the subject are the material out of which mutability weaves the world. And what is mutability if not the living, dynamic unity that is the self, or subject?

Now the thinking of Ahasuerus (and we must assume that it is the thinking of Shelley) inevitably suggests the thinking of Prospero, and we quote from *The Tempest* as undoubtedly many other students of Shelley have quoted in the past:[132]

> These our actors,
> As I foretold you, were all spirits and
> Are melted into air, into thin air:
> And, like the baseless fabric of this vision,
> The cloud-capp'd towers, the gorgeous palaces,
> The solemn temples, the great globe itself,
> Yea, all which it inherit, shall dissolve
> And, like this insubstantial pageant faded,
> Leave not a rack behind. We are such stuff
> As dreams are made on, and our little life
> Is rounded with a sleep.
>
> iv, i, 148–158

The parallel is close in thought and in words. Prospero declares the world to be as insubstantial as the visionary pageant just presented before Ferdinand and Miranda. Life itself, he says, is of the stuff of dreams, and, like a dream, is rounded with a sleep. Shelley similarly tells us that the fabric of life is woven from the stuff of thought. The world and all that it inherits, Shelley declares, is only a vision, thought being its cradle and its grave.

Yet our interest in the parallel is not in its closeness, but in the fact that it supports our theory that Shelley reached his position independently of contemporary philosophical influence. For here we have another poet saying very nearly the same thing as Shelley, and saying it before Descartes had ever uttered his famous phrase: *Cogito, ergo sum.*

Nevertheless, the idealism that Shelley is now professing is admittedly close to the psychologic idealism that in our discussion of the 1816 Hymns we rejected, not as an interest, but as an influence in Shelley's intellectual development. Shelley now, along with Berkeley and the German idealists, is coming to look upon the world as the function of subject. True, with Berkeley, the world is the function of God rather than of man, and with the German idealists it is the function of the world soul rather than of the individual soul. But one and all agree that the world is vision rather than external fact.

Yet how different has been Shelley's approach to this position! Berkeley, and even the German idealists, all stem from Locke. From Locke to Leibniz, Berkeley, and Hume; from Leibniz and Hume to Kant; from Kant to Fichte, Schelling, and Hegel, there is not one of those "trends" that scholars love to pick out, but an actual passing

132. Cf. Sir Leslie Stephen, "Godwin and Shelley," *Cornhill Magazine,* xxxix, 295 (*Hours in a Library,* No. xx).

on of the torch from hand to hand. German idealism, as well as Berkeleyanism, began with psychologic analysis and ended by regarding the world as a creation of those psychic powers which it analyzed.

How far this is from Shelley needs scarcely to be pointed out again. Shelley began not with psychologic analysis, but with faith in an outer spiritual reality. As we have seen, the idealism of the 1816 Hymns is thoroughly external and ontologic, and we recall that the ethical thinking of *The Revolt of Islam* is similarly external and devoid of psychologic explanation. In fact, Shelley's early idealism was as deterministic as it was idealistic, and it has been our contention that Plato's great service to Shelley was to explain man's freedom in an idealistic world. This freedom entailed a reconstruction of the outer spiritual reality, and we have noted that Shelley came to reconstruct it more and more in terms of the subject. Finally, he reached a position close to that of Berkeley and the German idealists, but close to that of Shakespeare also! There is only an analogical relationship between Shelley and the philosophers of his own time, not a relationship of direct influence. Shelley's solution of the problem of spirit and matter is his own, the result of forces that were set at work within him when Plato explained that man is essentially free.

But, though the problem of spirit and matter has thus been solved, the other problem that *Adonais* bequeathed to *Hellas* has not been answered. Shelley has not explained why there should be individuality. The individual is subject, the One is subject, and everything else is vision, or function of subject. But why should the individual exist in addition to the One? Why not just the One from start to finish? True, Shelley assumes that the individual proceeds from the One, and then flows "back to the burning fountain whence it came." But why the process of flowing out and flowing back, especially since the flowing out, at least on earth, is admittedly inferior to containment in the One? The problem remains unanswered, in spite of perhaps the most brilliant passage, philosophically speaking, in all Shelley's works.

We are familiar with how the German idealists, Shelley's contemporaries, solved the problem. Confronted with much the same difficulty, they gave up the notion of subject and object, so that the vision itself becomes the world. We do not see a vision; the vision includes us. The individual (legs, arms, feelings, memories) becomes part of a vast, spiritual pageant. In fact, strictly speaking, the world is no longer a vision, no longer a function of the subject, but subject itself, dynamically evolving, and as it evolves giving rise to the individual who, as Hegel made clear, is never seen anyway except in the middle of a panorama.

7. Conclusion: The Poems of 1822

WOULD Shelley in his own way have reached this novel and provocative solution?

That the philosophical matters touched upon in *Hellas* remained matters of burning consequence to Shelley, the poems of 1822 abundantly make clear. In fact, we would account for the peculiar melancholy of these poems not by biographical explanation but by philosophical explanation—by recourse to the metaphysical position reached by Shelley toward the end of 1821. For, according to this position, the world of nature is woven by mutability merely out of the stuff of the mind. It no longer has any separate reality, and the poet's faith in its independent beauty is severed at the root. We recall the panic that overtook the poet when in *Epipsychidion* he seemed to be plunging toward the outright loss of this world by annihilation. A lesser panic would now seem to have swept over him—or, rather, a settled sadness for the real beauty of the external world which thus has slipped away.

To be sure, there is no reason why one's vision should not be as beautiful as the world of nature had formerly appeared to be. Yet the beauty of the world as a standard upon which to base one's faith is lost. Even if the poet believes with Plato that the idea of beauty is more real than its embodiment, even if he believes with the youthful Shelley that the beautiful comes from a Spirit of Beauty which consecrates whatever it shines upon—even here there is something more abiding than oneself upon which to pin one's hopes. But if beauty be nothing objective at all, if it be merely the dream of the individual dreamer, then the anchor of one's aesthetic faith is gone, and there is no way out until the poet comes to see that the individual is but part of a greater individual—that it is not his own "I" but a greater "I" that is spinning the vision of the world, and spinning it beautifully as it goes along.

But this insight is not won easily. It was not until toward the end of his Jena period that Fichte advanced from the individual to the absolute ego; not until his *Bestimmung des Menschen* in 1800 that he defined this absolute ego as the "infinite moral will of the universe, God, in whom are all the individual egos, from whom they have sprung."[133] Even the precocious Schelling took a year or two to advance from the epistemological conception of the world to the notion of an absolute spirit that lies beneath it. Hence it is hardly to

133. Quoted from Robert Adamson, article on "Fichte," *Encyclopædia Britannica* (11th ed.), x, 317.

be expected that the poet Shelley would make the same progress in a matter of months. An initial reading of the completed poems and fragments of 1822 discloses no evidence of advance from the discrete position to the unitary, and this although Shelley's impulsion toward some kind of monism has already been noted in *Adonais*.

What is evident is the persistence with which Shelley dwelt upon his new conception of the world. On the one hand, it seemed to sharpen his sensitivity to the beauty around him (as if what had slipped away had become doubly precious); on the other, it made him reflect upon the relative indifference of far and near, of fact and fancy. Again, it seemed to drive him to seize the fleeting moment, as if (since the world was but the unrolling of a panorama) he should pay attention to the unrolling of the panorama lest he lose even this in the midst of its passing. Thus in the lines *To Jane: The Invitation,* we read,

> I am gone into the fields
> To take what this sweet hour yields;—
> Reflection, you may come to-morrow,
> Sit by the fireside with Sorrow.—
> You with the unpaid bill, Despair,—
> You, tiresome verse-reciter, Care,—
> I will pay you in the grave,—
> Death will listen to your stave.
> Expectation too, be off!
> To-day is for itself enough.

31–40

Similarly, in the *Lines Written in the Bay of Lerici,* we find both a heightened sense of the world's beauty and a dwelling upon the visionary character of that beauty. Thus we read,

> She left me at the silent time
> When the moon had ceased to climb
> The azure path of Heaven's steep,
> And like an albatross asleep,
> Balanced on her wings of light,
> Hovered in the purple night,
> Ere she sought her ocean nest
> In the chambers of the West.
> She left me, and I stayed alone
> Thinking over every tone
> Which, though silent to the ear,
> The enchanted heart could hear,
> Like notes which die when born, but still
> Haunt the echoes of the hill.

1–14

Even without knowledge of the specific steps in Shelley's philosophical development it would be clear from this poem that to Shelley the world has become of the nature of thought. Thus the echoes that haunt the hill are but slightly different from the notes that gave them birth, and the memory of a voice is almost as enchanting as the voice itself. Indeed the poet says,

> although she absent were,
> Memory gave me all of her
> That even Fancy dares to claim,
>
> 19–21

and he adds,

> I lived alone
> In the time which is our own;
> The past and future were forgot,
> As they had been, and would be, not.
>
> 23–26

He continues,

> I dare not speak
> My thoughts, but thus disturbed and weak
> I sat and saw the vessels glide
> Over the ocean bright and wide, . . .
> And the wind that winged their flight
> From the land came fresh and light,
> And the scent of wingèd flowers,
> And the coolness of the hours
> Of dew, and sweet warmth left by day,
> Were scattered o'er the twinkling bay.
> And the fisher with his lamp
> And spear about the low rocks damp
> Crept, and struck the fish which came
> To worship the delusive flame.
>
> 29–48

As philosophical critics of Shelley's poetry, we find our primary interest in the thought of Shelley's poetry being seriously contested by the simple, sensuous beauty of Shelley's later verse. With some poets who died young, it has often seemed that their talents were failing before they died, and that death was perhaps a merciful release rather than otherwise. But surely this is not the case with Shelley. The supreme lyrics come from the end of his life, from 1821 and 1822. As Miss Stawell has pointed out,[134] *The Triumph of Life*, upon which Shelley was at work when he died and which he left unrevised

---

134. F. Melian Stawell, "Shelley's *Triumph of Life*," *Essays and Studies by Members of the English Association* (Oxford, 1914), V, 104.

and far from complete—*The Triumph of Life,* instead of showing a diminution of Shelley's poetical talents, suggests that it might have been his greatest work. Yet *The Triumph of Life* is also a poem of vision—of a greater and of a lesser vision. Shelley's new conception of the world is as evident here as in the shorter poems, and the observation is inescapable that along with the sadness accompanying Shelley's loss of faith in the real existence of the external world went an increase in Shelley's powers as a poet.

To us there could hardly be a more interesting observation. For from the beginning we have seen that Shelley's development was in line with the development of his age. It was vigorous, constructive intellectual growth, abreast of the times and alive to the issues of the hour. As such it could only foster, not hamper, an independent artistic talent. The evidence would seem incontrovertible that the pursuit of Shelley's philosophical speculations, far from hindering, positively promoted the growth of Shelley's poetical talent.

In this respect a comparison with the poet Hölderlin is inevitable. Possessed of a supreme lyric gift, a poet who not only looked, but was, like Shelley, Hölderlin nevertheless traces in his poetical career an opposite development. He began with the epistemological philosophers, reading Kant along with his college mates Schelling and Hegel while still a student at Tübingen, and attending the lectures of Fichte at Jena. He was early proficient in that philosophy which Shelley was just approaching at the end of his life. But whether it was too abstract or whether it was simply divorced from the poetic materials of his life, it never kindled him to great poetry. Then came the influence of Susette Gontard and the Greeks. She through her own vivid personality, and the Greeks perhaps through the influence of Winckelmann, tended to pull him back into the concrete world. With their influence his poetry begins to attain the highest rank; but with their influence it also begins to be a poetry without a philosophy. And as the lack of philosophic construction grows more intense, the simple, sensuous beauty of his poetry becomes more haunting. There is much the same sadness to Hölderlin's later lyrics as to Shelley's. But it is a sadness owing to a lack of philosophical understanding rather than to the gaining of a philosophical understanding.

Thus, in a poem such as "The Middle of Life," there is a heightened sense of the world's beauty, like that of Shelley's later lyrics, and a comparable (if different) sadness. But there is not a comparable conception of the world's meaning. There is only the dread of the time when all meaning shall have flowed from the earth. There is only the dread of the poet's approaching insanity. We quote the poem from Michael Hamburger's excellent translation:[135]

135. Michael Hamburger, *Poems of Hölderlin* (London, 1943), p. 179.

The Middle of Life

With yellow pears the land,
And full of wild roses,
Hangs down into the lake,
O graceful swans,
And drunk with kisses,
You dip your heads
Into the hallowed-sober water.

Alas, where shall I find when
Winter comes, flowers, and where
Sunshine,
And the shadows of earth?
The walls stand
Speechless and cold, in the wind
Weathercocks clatter.

With such deep matters involved, it may be believed that we turn for a second time to *The Triumph of Life*. The very oppositeness of Shelley's development from Hölderlin's, his persistent clinging to the concept of the world as vision, the growth of his purely artistic powers as a poet—all these lead us to examine Shelley's latest work again for evidence as to the whither of Shelley's intellectual growth. But, as our first reading seemed to indicate, there is no evidence. Furthermore, as Professor White suggests, the poem is perhaps no more than a third completed,[136] and we observe that this third is very much on the conscious literary level. As with *Adonais*, where there were borrowings from Bion and Moschus, so here there are borrowings from Petrarch and Dante; and, as we have come to see, Shelley's philosophical thinking is not vouchsafed to such levels of poetic composition unless in a conspicuous interpolation. In *The Triumph of Life* there is a conspicuous introduction, but no conspicuous interpolation.

No, the question with which we began this section must remain unanswered. There is nothing to show whether Shelley would finally have reached the position of Fichte and Schelling and Hegel. There is nothing to show whether his philosophy would have advanced from an epistemological idealism to an epistemological monism.

Yet Professor White has pointed out that "according to his own testimony and that of most other witnesses, when Shelley wrote *The Triumph of Life* . . . he was in the best health he had felt for years and was finding his happiest enjoyment of life."[137] It is also clear that when he died Shelley was at the height of his intellectual and artistic powers. Thus we cannot believe that the intellectual progress we

136. *Shelley*, II, 631.   137. *Idem*, II, 372.

have been following with so much interest would suddenly have stopped. Rather, it is clear that Shelley was in that period of active pause through which the German philosophers passed—that period in which they were sure of their epistemological idealism, but groping for the unitary explanation that would reconcile subject and object, and bring together the Many and the One. Shelley's preoccupation with the Many and the One we have already noted in *Adonais*. That Shelley would have achieved a solution to the problem, and that his solution would have been in line with that of his contemporaries, the German idealists—all this seems certain beyond the shadow of a doubt.[138]

138. We must here pay tribute to Professor A. C. Bradley's admirable lecture on *English Poetry and German Philosophy in the Age of Wordsworth* (Manchester, 1909). If we have not referred to it before, it is only because the lecture is taken up largely with the parallel between Hegel and Wordsworth, and because in its treatment it is of necessity general rather than detailed. In pointing out the community of thought between the German philosophers and the British poets of the Romantic period, Professor Bradley has long anticipated the point of view of this study.

VII

Shelley and the Thought of His Time

IN Chapter II when we outlined the problem that lay before us, it seemed as if our last chapter would be taken up with an analogous study of Shelley's relationship with his own time. It seemed, after dissociating the Shelleyan from the Godwinian and the Revolutionary, the Shelleyan from the Platonic and the Greek, that in our last chapter we could do no less than define this Shelleyan by looking for parallels in the literatures of France and Germany. For it was our suspicion that a brief comparative glance at these foreign literatures would show that the individual element in Shelley's poetry was not unique but typical of his century.

But this comparative glance we have in a measure been forced to take already. To account for the reversal of point of view within the single scope of *Prometheus Unbound,* to account for the monism of *Adonais,* to account for the conception of the world as vision in *Hellas,* it has been necessary already to turn to the poets and thinkers of Shelley's time. Where Shelley abandoned the thinking of the French intellectualists, where he abandoned the intellectualism of Plato, it is already clear that he was at one with the spirit of his own time, that he was following the thought of his day.

Furthermore, like the problem of Shelley's Hellenism, the question of Shelley's analogous relationship with his own age is scarcely a matter that needs to be proved. Whether the comparison be between men and men, or between men and literature, or between literature and literature, one is quite overwhelmed with parallels.

There is the extraordinary parallel between the poet Hölderlin's epistolary novel *Hyperion,* and Shelley's poem *The Revolt of Islam.* Both are laid in contemporary Greece; both concern a revolt of the Greeks against the Turks (in which the revolt fails and the followers are unworthy of their leader); and, what is more extraordinary, in Hyperion, Adamas, and Diotima we find much the same conception of youthful idealist, teacher, and female disciple as in Laon, the Hermit, and Cythna. Again, when one reads Waiblinger's account of the mad Hölderlin, playing the piano years afterwards in the carpenter Zimmer's house, of whom is he reminded if not of the madman in *Julian and Maddalo?* Waiblinger writes,

Music has not quite left him. He still plays the piano correctly, but in a most extraordinary manner. When he has started playing he continues for days . . . When he has played for some time, and when his soul is moved, he suddenly shuts his eyes, raises his head, seems about to languish and pass away, and begins to sing. I could never find out in what language he sang, often as I heard him; but he did so with exuberant pathos, and it made one shudder in every nerve to see him and to hear him. Melancholy and mournfulness were the moods of his song; one could recognize what had been a good tenor voice.[1]

Then there is Goethe's youthful preoccupation with the legends of the Wandering Jew and Prometheus, and there is Fichte's expulsion from his *alma mater* on charges of atheism. And the parallel in this latter instance is not simply that two men should have been expelled from their universities a dozen years apart on similar charges, but that it would be hard in those dozen years to find two men more imbued with a sense of the divine than Shelley and Fichte. Indeed, whether it is the study of philosophy or of biography or of literature that takes the student of Shelley to the Germany of Shelley's time, he has the sense of being in a world that is very similar to that of the English poet's. Shelley's personal relations, for instance, have been a thorn in the side of many an English critic or biographer. But in Germany they would have attracted less attention. Shelley's casual shift of spouses would have found a pattern in the casual transfer of the gifted Karoline from the critic Schlegel to the philosopher Schelling. And as for the *ménage à trois* that had such a fascination for Shelley, not only do we recall the understanding that existed between Goethe's friend Johanna Fahlmer, the younger Jacobi, and the latter's wife Betty, but we remember that the problem was current enough to form the subject of one of Goethe's plays.

Again, when it comes to the bookish, unrealistic quality of Shelley's poetry (the quality that is so conspicuous in *The Revolt of Islam*), one may be unable to find a parallel among Shelley's English contemporaries. But the poet Schiller in Germany affords an example. During the last fourteen years of his life his world was almost exclusively the world of books, and Miss E. M. Butler observes that "it is entirely characteristic of Schiller that he wrote *William Tell* without ever going to Switzerland; *The Diver* although he had never seen anything more portentous than a mill-stream; and battle-scenes galore without witnessing a single military engagement."[2]

But we do not intend to write the chapter that we said we were not going to write. Even if it were appropriate in these concluding pages to offer a survey of the life and letters of the Germany or France of Shelley's time, it would reveal only what has been pointed out so

1. Quoted and translated by Michael Hamburger, *Poems of Hölderlin*, p. 86.
2. E. M. Butler, *The Tyranny of Greece over Germany* (Cambridge, England, 1935), p. 176.

many times: that the great figures of English literature are typical only of English literature, that the lesser figures are far more representative of the literatures abroad. Thus, although Wordsworth from the point of view of English literature is undoubtedly the greatest poet of his age, yet Shelley is more typical of the Romantic Movement as a whole. In Wordsworth, we recognize in the Leech-Gatherer, in Simon Lee, and in Michael the tradition of Alice of Bath and Dogberry and Parson Adams. But the very lack of such figures in Shelley's poetry brings him nearer to the literatures of the Continent. In Shelley, as well as in Wordsworth, one finds the point of view of the age. And in Shelley one also finds, because of his very abstractness and concern with philosophical ideas, a closer similarity to the writers and poets abroad.

Yet, though the problem of our final chapter, as originally planned, has been answered already, there remains a problem in connection with "Shelley and the Thought of His Time" that has not been answered, and that indeed forms a fitting conclusion to this study in the history of ideas.

We have followed Shelley's independent approach to the position of the German idealists. We began by noticing his early interest in science and Gothic romance. We observed his conversion to radicalism, largely through Godwin. We marked his espousal of the Greek Revival and viewed his subsequent conception of the world as vision. Indeed, when we left Shelley, there was only the last step to be taken, only the step to the Fichtean notion of subject-object, to the all-including *Begriff* of Hegel, for Shelley to be at one with the most advanced thinkers of his age.

Yet how different was Shelley's approach to this position from that of the German philosophers! In Germany, the prophets of the new order were Rousseau and Kant, Kant himself being a reader of Rousseau, and the person who brought Rousseau to Herder's attention. But Shelley never read Kant,[3] and although he read some Rousseau in the *Queen Mab* years, and "Julie" in the summer of 1816, in comparison with the thunderbolts of *Sturm und Drang*, the influence of Rousseau upon his life was as the force of heat lightning. On the other

3. One should remember that no edition of the *Kritik* was available in English until 1838, and that although Shelley, toward the end of his life, was able to read *Faust* in the original, he could hardly have been equal to the German of Kant. As for Born's Latin translation, we have already mentioned (p. 160) the scorn for Kant which Shelley found in his two mentors, Sir William Drummond and Peacock. Perhaps this explains why Hogg observed Shelley's Latin translation of Kant reposing "uncut and unopened" in the sitting room in Half-Moon Street (Hogg, *Life of Shelley*, II, 27). This is the translation which Shelley in *Peter Bell the Third* says he "looked on" for nine several days. But whether this nine-day observation occurred before or after the sojourn in Half-Moon Street, the modern student is inclined to agree with Hogg (*ibid.*) that Shelley never "read a single page of the transcendental philosopher."

hand, Shelley read and was profoundly influenced by Godwin, who, for all his fame in England, was relatively unknown on the Continent. There is very little, if any, community between the influences that molded Shelley's thought and those that shaped the philosophy of the German thinkers.[4] Yet Shelley traces much the same path as they, and ends with a philosophy that is close to theirs. Surely the accounting for this parallel movement is a problem worthy of our last chapter. Surely the force that led personalities so widely separate as Rousseau and Fichte and Shelley to very similar conclusions constitutes no small aspect of "Shelley and the Thought of His Time."

As for the thought of Shelley's time, probably few will object if we take this as more or less contained within the limits of Goethe's life. Goethe's birthyear of 1749 comes before the publication of Rousseau's first *Discourse,* with which we date the beginning of the emotionalist reaction. Yet Goethe's death in 1832 follows not only the deaths of Shelley and Byron, but even such events as the July Revolution and the death of Hegel. Goethe's life in no small way embraces the period of which he is perhaps the most distinguished representative.

Now it seems to us that the thought of this period is basically conditioned by a certain innate subjectivity. We have seen that the Rousseau of Chambéry long anticipated the Rousseau of the Lac de Bienne. And so it was with all the heralds of the new order—with Herder, with Goethe, with Chateaubriand, with Wordsworth. In their youths, the dreamy and internal predominated over the concrete and external. Indeed, the really remarkable thing about these men is that when they reached maturity they had the strength to stand out against the old order, which had first been vigorously attacked only by Rousseau. Hence Shelley's youthful propensity to speed

> Through many a listening chamber, cave and ruin,
> And starlight wood, with fearful steps pursuing
> Hopes of High talk with the departed dead,
> *Hymn to Intellectual Beauty,* 50–52

—Shelley's youthful subjectivity, is a trait shared by all the leading poets and philosophers of the period. With Shelley it is almost our basic datum, since we recall that even Shelley's early interest in

---

4. Perhaps it will be pointed out that the Greek Revival was a force in Germany as well as in England, and that it brought Plato to the attention of such writers as Schleiermacher and Hölderlin even as it did to Shelley. But one must remember that the Greek Revival that particularly affected Shelley was the scholarly revival of Bentley and Porson (*vide supra,* p. 95), and that in Germany, as Miss Butler has pointed out (*The Tyranny of Greece over Germany*), the Greek Revival was dominated by the misconceptions of Winckelmann. Furthermore, we must remember that with writers such as Schleiermacher and Hölderlin the influence of Plato accompanied or followed the influence of Kant, and that with no German writer did Plato have the peculiar influence that he had with Shelley.

science was largely, like Goethe's, tinged with the marvelous, and thus cannot be called scientific in the strictest sense.

A consequence of this basic subjectivity is that it led poets and thinkers alike to some form of idealism. Apparently they could interpret the world only in terms of that reality which they felt so strongly within themselves. The out-and-out, thoroughly objective thinker, whether Epicurean or D'Holbachian, has never felt constrained to explain the world in a spiritual manner. If matter in movement can produce things, why then it can produce us and our reflections of things. A tinge of subjectivity, however, whether it contemplate the mind's own "innate" ideas, or whether it be taken up with the relatively external ideas of things, produces a corresponding warp of idealism. True, the sense of subject is often no stronger than the sense of object, so that in philosophers like Plato there seems to be a true polarity, with ideas equal in rank to spirits, with the concrete taken into account as well as the abstract. But with the romantic generation there can be little doubt that the sense of subject was the strongest sense in their lives—so strong that it overran the sense of thought and became imbued with a consciousness of the mind's emotive life. Hence with the romantic generation the dominant force of the universe becomes not merely spiritual, but spirit itself.

And hence, as a second consequence of this basic subjectivity, the writers and thinkers of Shelley's time became aware of the fact that what they really cared about was feeling and not thought. Yet so great was the intellectualistic legacy of the preceding age that they were one and all nearly engulfed by it, and achieved an awareness of their true point of view long after their primary subjectivity had asserted itself. The awareness did not come to Rousseau until he was well advanced in middle age. It did not come to Fichte until the memorable summer of 1790, when he was twenty-eight, and a reader of Kant for the first time. It is doubtful if it came to Shelley until he had gone to Italy and had repudiated the intellectualism of Plato, his intellectual savior. Even the precocious Goethe had to go through all his student days at Leipzig, and the period of his sickness and recovery at Frankfurt, before he realized that "feeling is all," that the consequence of his own subjective type of mind was the emotionalist point of view. It was not until Strassburg and the days of his association with Herder that Goethe was able to shake off the shackles of the Enlightenment.

Thus to the student of the revolt from intellectualism there can hardly be a more interesting document than the First Part of Goethe's *Faust*. We know from *Dichtung und Wahrheit* that, along with *Götz*, the oldest portions of it go back to Strassburg and the *Herderzeit*. Indeed, it would be difficult to find a more succinct expression of the cleft between the intellectualists and the emotionalists, between the

Enlightenment and the Romantic Movement, than in the opening scene of Goethe's great play. The result of Faust's ten-year pursuit of philosophy, of law, of medicine, of theology, is the simple awareness that nothing can be known. Knowledge appears to him mere inanity, the empty skull whence the living spirit has fled. Wagner, Faust's *famulus*, places his faith in knowledge, but Faust desires to feel his heart glow with Nature's glow.

To Faust the highest good, the end of life, is not to be found in any benefit that knowledge can confer, but in an ecstatic moment, in a *seligen Augenblicke,* such as he glimpses when he succeeds in summoning the Earth Spirit. He wishes

> To pierce the ether's high, unknown dominions, ·
> To reach new spheres of pure activity!

So desperate is he for the intense emotion that even suicide itself seems desirable as a means of attaining

> This godlike rapture, this supreme existence.[5]

But of course the bells and singing of Easter drive the deadly cup from his lips, and he remembers that in his youth he had once found the ecstatic moment—in religion, as it happens—and had gone forth into the woods and meadows, and felt a world arise within him.

Not only is the emotionalist revolt clearly set forth in the opening scene of *Faust,* but Faust's evocation of the Earth Spirit shows us once again how primary is the union of an ontological idealism with the emotionalist point of view. The individual to whom the end of life is not the utilization of his intellect but the exercise of his emotions is unable ultimately to conceive of the world except in terms of a similar potentiality to feel. Thus the spirit that the emotionalist believes to be at the heart of the universe inevitably becomes another subject. We recall that to the Shelley of 1816 this spirit was an "unseen Power," a "secret Strength." To Goethe, the *erhabener Geist* whom he addresses again in *Wald und Höhle* teaches him "to know his brothers in air and water and the silent wood"; and when the storm breaks in the forest, this Spirit, very much like the Lord of the Psalmist, leads him to "the cave secure." It will be recalled that when we discussed the 1816 Hymns we observed that their metaphysical assumptions were those of the Greeks, of the Christian religion, and of common sense.[6] Thus it is interesting to find much the same setup when we look abroad. In truth, the belief in an Earth Spirit is almost universal among the poets and philosophers of the age. Often this

5. All quotations from *Faust* are taken from Bayard Taylor's well-known translation in the original meters.
6. *Vide supra,* p. 124.

deity is but the deity of Christian orthodoxy, paganized and naturalized. But then again, in its immanence in things, it seems to approach the pantheistic divinity of Spinoza.

In fact, an enthusiasm for Spinoza is likewise almost universal among the poets of the period (we recall that as late as November, 1821, Shelley was still translating Spinoza, this time with Williams as an ally).[7] Many of these poets were opposed to Kant, and to the "false secondary power" which was Kant's instrument, if not his end. But Spinoza—Spinoza seemed to have believed in a kind of *Erdgeist* himself. Spinoza had rejected the deity of Christian and Hebrew orthodoxy for a deity that might be called God or Nature indifferently. Indeed, this deity, when stripped of its attributes without us, might be glimpsed by the deity stripped of its attributes within us— glimpsed in that final moment of mysticism when like sees like and is one! Thus to the romantics it seemed not only as if Spinoza had been a nature worshiper along with them, but as if he too had believed in that supreme moment which Prometheus describes to Pandora in Goethe's play as the moment "which fulfills everything we have longed for, dreamed of, hoped and feared."[8]

Needless to say, however, when it came to metaphysics, the poets were on very unsure ground. They could not see that Kant, for all his use of analysis, was headed in precisely the same direction as they. They could not see (or did not see) the sweeping determinism of Spinoza, his denial of that very freedom which it was their chief role to proclaim. They did not see that Spinoza's supreme moment was not their supreme moment, but the supreme moment of the *Phaedrus*—that moment when the chariots of gods and men, having mounted to high heaven, gaze upon the realm of truth. For Spinoza's *amor intellectualis dei* is contemplative in its nature, and has nothing to do with that moment of active fulfillment described in Goethe's *Prometheus,* with that moment of active dissolution feared in *Epipsychidion,* with that moment of active union longed for in *Adonais.*

In this respect, one must pay homage to Fritz Jacobi, prince of the sentimentalists, yet enough of a thinker to perceive the gulf that in reality separated Spinoza from the emotionalists of his day. In the controversy stirred up by his *Letters on Spinoza,* Jacobi endeavored to point out the intellectualism of Spinoza and the determinism necessarily implied by its premises.

Yet it was Fichte who first possessed the technical powers necessary to perceive the gulf for what it was. To him, Spinozism was the bond-

7. Cf. White, *Shelley,* II, 336.
8. Quoted and translated by Georg Brandes, *Wolfgang Goethe* (2 vols. in one. New York, 1936), I, 156 (authorized translation from the Danish by Allen W. Porterfield).

age of the outer world, and Kantianism the truth that sets men free.
It was Kant who, in the summer of 1790, liberated him from the
determinism of Spinoza, very much as it was Plato who, a generation
later, emancipated Shelley from the determinism of the French philosophers. Similarly, it was Kant who set Fichte on the same road that
Shelley was also to follow—the road that leads to the conception of
the world as the function of subject, indeed as subject itself.

Thus we return to the thinking of Chapter I, where we observed
that, to many students of literature and philosophy, Fichte and his
disciples seem to have passed over the first and superior, to the second
and inferior, of the two *Critiques* of Kant.[9] This criticism, we see,
reveals simply the student's own *Zeitgeist,* his own returning intellectualism. For Fichte picked upon not what was old but what was
new in Kant. He had no use for the analysis and skepticism and psychology of the earlier *Critique.* He sought the construction and affirmation and universality of the second *Critique.* Indeed, as the late
Professor Adamson remarks, "only in the sphere of practical reason,
where the intelligible nature prescribed to itself its own laws, was
there the possibility of systematic deduction from a single principle."[10]
In other words, only in the *Critique of Practical Reason* could the
philosopher find the metaphysical ground for building his own world;
and Fichte, with unerring instinct, took that ground and built his own
world, as everyone knows.

It is on this point that we should like to rest this study. That the
romantic should come to regard the world as his creation seems to us
to have been implied from the start. We have already spoken of Shelley's intense subjectivity, of that powerful tendency within him which
made a goal lose its charm as soon as it was attained, which made
him bury his nose in a book even aboard the *Don Juan.*[11] We have
noted a similar tendency in Rousseau, and have indeed taken the tendency as the starting point of the thought of the age. Thus it is not surprising to find in Rousseau an expression of this starting point, an
expression which contains within it the germs of the whole development to come. It is found in the letter Julie writes to Saint-Preux on
the day before the fatal trip to Chillon, when she is imbued with a
presentiment of evil. Apropos of her own unhappy love affair, she
declares:

We enjoy less that which we obtain, than that which we hope for, and are
seldom happy but in expectation. In fact, man, made to desire every thing
and obtain little, of boundless avarice, yet narrow capacity, has received of
Heaven a consolatory aid, which brings to him in idea every thing he de-

9. *Vide supra,* p. 3.
10. Article on "Fichte," *Encyclopædia Britannica* (11th ed.), x, p. 316.
11. *Vide supra,* pp. 133–134.

sires, displays to his imagination, represents it to his view, and in one sense makes it his own; but to render such imaginary property still more flattering and agreeable, it is even modified to his passion. But this shadow vanishes the moment the real object appears; the imagination can no longer magnify that which we actually possess; the charms of illusion cease where those of enjoyment begin. The world of fancy, therefore, the land of chimeras, is the only world worthy to be inhabited; and such is the inanity of human enjoyments, that, except that Being which is self-existent, there is nothing delightful but that which has no existence at all.[12]

When we recall that the heresy of Lessing's Spinozism did not come out until after his death, we are not surprised that Rousseau should have clung to the orthodox belief of his century in a Supreme Being. For, although a representative of the new order (as Lessing was of the old), Rousseau was fifteen or twenty years the elder of the two men, and a member of the Enlightenment until he was nearly forty.

But is it not the merest of steps to return to Spinoza—to declare that that "Being which is self-existent" is the whole of existence, and that the "world of fancy" (already asserted to be the only world worth living in), far from having no existence at all, is the only world that has existence? And when we have said thus much, have we not declared that the creator of the world is none other than ourselves?

Those coming after Rousseau hastened to take the step, and in Goethe's play, after Faust has cursed the whole of the old world of orthodoxy and the Enlightenment, the Chorus of Spirits sing,

> Mightier
> For the children of men,
> Brightlier
> Build it again,
> In thine own bosom build it anew!

This thought we take to be the fundamental one of the age. Once the individual has been seen to be the builder of the world, it is a relatively secondary matter to regard the builder, along with the building, as forming part of a still vaster, unitary process. That Shelley did not live to take this step, or that few besides the philosophers took it anyway, is to us beside the issue. The main thing is that in the development of his thought Shelley, too, was led to see that the individual creates the world, that the world is in reality a function of subject. Other writers followed other paths, and many, like Goethe, never looked upon the matter philosophically, but preferred to regard it simply as a business of the will. The thought of one's age, however,

12. *Eloisa; a series of Original Letters; translated from the French of J. J. Rousseau* (3 vols. London, 1810), III, 236 (Book VI, Letter 8).

is a thing that no man may avoid, and it is a matter of high interest to us that in those very particulars in which he departed from his masters—from Plato, from Godwin, and from the French philosophers—Shelley was at one with the thought of his time.

Index of Principal Names